First World War
and Army of Occupation
War Diary

France, Belgium and Germany

1 DIVISION
Divisional Troops
Royal Army Veterinary Corps
2 Mobile Veterinary Section
4 August 1914 - 31 August 1919

WO95/1259/4

The Naval & Military Press Ltd
www.nmarchive.com
Published in association with The National Archives

Published by

The Naval & Military Press Ltd

Unit 10 Ridgewood Industrial Park,

Uckfield, East Sussex,

TN22 5QE England

Tel: +44 (0) 1825 749494

www.naval-military-press.com

www.nmarchive.com

This diary has been reprinted in facsimile from the original. Any imperfections are inevitably reproduced and the quality may fall short of modern type and cartographic standards.

Contents

Document type	Place/Title	Date From	Date To
Heading	WO95/1259/4 2 Mobile Vet Section Aug" 14-Aug" 14		
Heading	1st Division Divisional Troops No. 2 Mobile Vety Section 1914 Aug-1915 Dec		
Heading	121/742 War Diary No 2 Section A V Corps Volume I		
War Diary	Staff College.	04/08/1914	31/08/1914
Heading	War Diary. No 2 Vety Section Volume II		
War Diary	Haure	01/09/1914	30/09/1914
Heading	121/1818 No 2 Vety Section Vol III		
War Diary		01/10/1914	31/10/1914
Heading	121/2625 No 2 Veterinary Section Vol IV 1-30.11.14		
War Diary		01/11/1914	30/11/1914
Heading	1251/3872 L of d No 2. Veterinary Section Vol Vol V 1-31.12.14		
War Diary		01/12/1914	31/12/1914
Heading	1st Div No 2. Mobile Vety. Section Vol I January & February 1915		
War Diary		24/01/1915	28/02/1915
Heading	121/5022 1st Division No 2 Mobile Vety. Section Vol II 3-30.3.15		
War Diary		03/03/1915	30/03/1915
Heading	121/6206 1st Division No 2 Mobile Vety Section Vol III April May & June 1915		
War Diary	Sevelingae	01/04/1915	09/04/1915
War Diary	Locon	14/04/1915	12/05/1915
War Diary	Bethune	15/05/1915	26/05/1915
War Diary	Fouquieres	31/05/1915	25/06/1915
War Diary	Eecre	27/06/1915	29/06/1915
War Diary	Fouquieres	30/06/1915	30/06/1915
Heading	121/7437 1st Division No 2 Mob. Vet Sec. Aug 15 Vol IV		
War Diary	Fouquieres Les Bethone	04/08/1915	30/08/1915
Heading	121/7107 1st Division No 2 Mobile Vety Section Vol V Sept 15		
War Diary		02/09/1915	02/09/1915
War Diary	Lozinghem	11/09/1915	16/09/1915
War Diary	Drouvin	19/09/1915	27/09/1915
War Diary	Mazingarb	28/09/1915	29/09/1915
War Diary	Noeux Les Mines	29/09/1915	30/09/1915
Map	Area And Route Map		
Operation(al) Order(s)	Operation Order A.V.C. 1st Division		
Heading	121/7520 1st Division No 2. Mobile Vet. Sec. Oct 1915 Vol VI		
War Diary	Noeux Les Mines	02/10/1915	06/10/1915
War Diary	Mazingarb	07/10/1915	15/10/1915
War Diary	Lozinghem	17/10/1915	31/10/1915
War Diary	1st Division Divisional Troops No 2 Mobile Veterinary Section 1916 Jan-1919 Aug		
Miscellaneous	H.Q. 1st Division		
War Diary	Noeux Les Mines	01/01/1916	15/01/1916
War Diary	Lillers	18/01/1916	16/02/1916

War Diary	Drouvin	18/02/1916	04/07/1916
War Diary	Bruay	06/07/1916	06/07/1916
War Diary	Vignacourt	07/07/1916	07/07/1916
War Diary	St Gratien	08/07/1916	10/07/1916
War Diary	Dernancourt	11/07/1916	27/08/1916
Heading	A.Q. 1st Division No. 2 Mobile Veterinary Section For The Month Of September 1916		
War Diary	Dernancourt	04/09/1916	14/09/1916
War Diary	Behencourt Albert	20/09/1916	20/09/1916
War Diary	Becordel	22/09/1916	03/10/1916
War Diary	Chepy	04/10/1916	31/10/1916
War Diary	Baizeu	04/11/1916	05/11/1916
War Diary	Becordel	06/11/1916	07/02/1917
War Diary	R.Q.A. (Shul 62 D)	10/02/1917	20/05/1917
War Diary	Villers Bretonneux	26/05/1917	27/05/1917
War Diary	Berther	28/05/1917	29/05/1917
War Diary	Berthen	10/06/1917	28/06/1917
War Diary	Coxyde Bains (Sheet II)	06/07/1917	20/07/1917
War Diary	Leclipon Waggon Lines	21/07/1917	24/08/1917
War Diary	Leclipon Camp Waggon Lines	04/09/1917	22/10/1917
War Diary	Lederzeele	23/10/1917	23/10/1917
War Diary	Lederzeele Wormhout	26/10/1917	30/10/1917
War Diary	Giveny Farm 2 Miles beyond Poperinghe	02/11/1917	17/11/1917
War Diary	Poperinghe a 28. E.2.4	17/11/1917	24/11/1917
War Diary	Hamhoek	27/11/1917	27/11/1917
War Diary	Proven	28/11/1917	05/12/1917
War Diary	Ondank	05/12/1917	31/12/1917
Heading	Vol 30 War Diary of No. 2 M.V.S. 1st Div. From Jan 1st 1918 To Jan 31st 1918 (Vol I)		
War Diary	Ondank	01/01/1918	14/02/1918
War Diary	Elverdinge	15/02/1918	08/04/1918
War Diary	Vendin	09/04/1918	11/04/1918
War Diary	Lapugnoy	12/04/1918	15/04/1918
War Diary	Fouguieres	16/04/1917	16/04/1917
War Diary	Hesdigneul	17/04/1918	24/04/1918
War Diary	Barlin	24/04/1918	22/08/1918
War Diary	Dieval	23/08/1918	31/08/1918
War Diary	Capelle Fermont Arras	01/09/1918	05/09/1918
War Diary	Arras	05/09/1918	11/09/1918
War Diary	Morcourt	11/09/1918	14/09/1918
War Diary	Devise	14/09/1918	17/09/1918
War Diary	Laulencourt W 3a 7.7	17/09/1918	30/09/1918
War Diary	Caulincourt Vermand	01/10/1918	07/10/1918
War Diary	Vermand	09/10/1918	11/10/1918
War Diary	Pontru	12/10/1918	16/10/1918
War Diary	Brancourt	17/10/1918	20/10/1918
War Diary	Vaux Andigny	20/10/1918	06/11/1918
War Diary	?	07/11/1918	12/11/1918
War Diary	Cartilon	13/11/1918	15/11/1918
War Diary	Semoisies	16/11/1918	16/11/1918
War Diary	Sorle Le Chateau	17/11/1918	17/11/1918
War Diary	La Savale	18/11/1918	18/11/1918
War Diary	Boussu Lez Walcourt	19/11/1918	22/11/1918
War Diary	Vogenee	23/11/1918	23/11/1918
War Diary	St Ave	24/11/1918	30/11/1918
War Diary	Essig	30/12/1918	31/12/1918

War Diary	Munstereifel	26/12/1918	26/12/1918
War Diary	Essig	27/12/1918	30/12/1918
War Diary	Kronenburg	22/12/1918	23/12/1918
War Diary	Mulleim	23/12/1918	23/12/1918
War Diary	Munstereifel	24/12/1918	25/12/1918
War Diary	Beho	18/12/1918	19/12/1918
War Diary	Grufelingen	19/12/1918	21/12/1918
War Diary	Andler	22/12/1918	22/12/1918
War Diary	Bomal	14/12/1918	15/12/1918
War Diary	Grand Menil	16/12/1918	16/12/1918
War Diary	Fraiture	17/12/1918	18/12/1918
War Diary	Herock	08/12/1918	09/12/1918
War Diary	Briquemont	09/12/1918	09/12/1918
War Diary	Sensin	09/12/1918	10/12/1918
War Diary	Petithan	11/12/1918	13/12/1918
War Diary	Herock	04/12/1918	07/12/1918
War Diary	Anthee	01/12/1918	02/12/1918
War Diary	Blaimont	02/12/1918	03/12/1918
Heading	Vol 43 War Diary No 2 Mobile Veterinary Section For January 1919		
War Diary	Errig	01/01/1919	31/01/1919
Heading	Vol 44 War Diary of No 2 Mobile Veterinary Section For February 1919		
War Diary	Essig	01/02/1919	27/02/1919
Heading	Vol 45 War Diary For March No 2 Mobile Veterinary Section		
War Diary	Essig	01/03/1919	31/03/1919
Heading	Vol 46 War Diary No 2 M.V.S. From 1-4-19 To 30-4-19		
War Diary	Essig	02/04/1919	06/04/1919
War Diary	Dickopsh of Farm Near Sechtem	07/04/1919	21/04/1919
War Diary	Keldenich	22/04/1919	30/05/1919
Heading	War Diary No 2 M.V.S. May 1st To 31st		
War Diary	Kildinuh	01/05/1919	31/05/1919
Heading	War Diary. No 2 Mobile Veterinary Section June 1919		
War Diary	Keldenich	01/06/1919	30/06/1919
Heading	War. Diary. No 2 Mobile Veterinary Section July 1919		
War Diary	Keldenich	01/07/1919	31/07/1919
Heading	War Diary No 2 Mobile Veterinary Section August 1919		
War Diary	Keldenich	02/08/1919	22/08/1919
War Diary	Calais Kinnel Park	24/08/1919	31/08/1919
War Diary			

WO 95/1259 (4)
2 Mobile Vet Section
Aug '14 – Aug '19

1ST DIVISION
DIVISIONAL TROOPS

NO.2. MOBILE VETY SECTION

~~JAN - DEC 1915~~

1914 AUG - 1915 DEC

WAR DIARY.

121/742.

No 2 Section A V Corps

— 210

Volume I.

Aug 1914

Enc. to 121/742

Army Form C. 2118.

Confidential
War Diary
[illegible]
from 4/8/14 to 31/8/14

Instructions regarding War Diaries and Intelligence Summaries are contained in F. S. Regs., Part II. and the Staff Manual respectively. Title pages will be prepared in manuscript.

WAR DIARY
or
~~INTELLIGENCE~~ SUMMARY.

(*Erase heading not required.*)

Hour, Date, Place	Summary of Events and Information	Remarks and references to Appendices
6.30 P.M. 4th August, Staff College	Heard of order that mobilization was ordered. Left at once for Aldershot.	
5th August	Joined No 2 Section A.V.C. at 6 A.M. Had kit inspection of men then with section. No roll of men belonging to Section on mobilization received. Telephoned to O/c Records, Woolwich for names of N.C.Os & men. Received list at 4 P.M. Reported no progress to A.D.V.S., A.C.	
6th August.	Medical inspection of all ranks. Prepared mobilization area at Signalling School for occupation next day. Reported progress satisfactory.	
7th August	Reported progress satisfactory. Occupied mobilization area.	
8th "	Received & mallein'd horses. Satisfactory progress.	
9th "	Reported mobilization complete. Paid men.	
10th & 11th	Nothing important.	
12th	Received order by wire to hand in from each man one service dress jacket, one pair pantaloons, one pair boots. Also A.C. order that the one blanket possessed by each man must be handed in.	
	[signature]	

(9 26 6) W 257—976 100,000 4/12 H W V 79/3298

Instructions regarding War Diaries and Intelligence Summaries are contained in F. S. Regs., Part II. and the Staff Manual respectively. Title pages will be prepared in manuscript.

WAR DIARY
or
~~INTELLIGENCE SUMMARY~~.
(Erase heading not required.)

Army Form C. 2118.

Hour, Date, Place	Summary of Events and Information	Remarks and references to Appendices
13th August.	At 1. P.M., ~~the time~~ when the transport to take the Section to the Railway Station should have arrived, there was no sign of any wagons or motor lorries. Rode to headquarters of transport officer, & managed to get a motor bus & two wagons. Arrived at Railway Siding in good time for the train which started at 3.40 instead of 3.50. Arrived SOUTHAMPTON at 6 P.M. & finished embarkation at 9 P.M. Horses slung on board. In view of the probable length of voyage, off-saddled horses & reported same to O.C. Troops on board. Many packing cases broken when lifted by cranes. These cases are much too fragile & there is great difficulty in repairing them	
14th August.	Arrived HAVRE midday & proceeded to disembark troops at 1 P.M. Horses slung off one by one. Last horse disembarked at 7 P.M. Packing cases containing picketing gear & curry combs broken. Great difficulty in keeping them together — they are too fragile altogether. Visited by D.V.S. & D.D.V.S. who took me to see site for Base Veterinary Hospital at L'Usine Bundy. Given command of this hospital. Unable to obtain any transport but was promised a light vehicle to take rations & men's kits to L'Usine Bundy. Obtained motor lorry & sent up some kit & stores. Lorry did not return but Capt MELLARD obtained another which made several journeys to & fro & by 11 P.M. all baggage was got into camp.	

O.J.L.

(9 26 6) W 257—976 100,000 4/12 H W V 79/3298

Instructions regarding War Diaries and Intelligence Summaries are contained in F. S. Regs., Part II. and the Staff Manual respectively. Title pages will be prepared in manuscript.

WAR DIARY
or
~~INTELLIGENCE~~ SUMMARY.
(Erase heading not required.)

Army Form C. 2118.

Hour, Date, Place	Summary of Events and Information	Remarks and references to Appendices
14th August (continued)	Men & horses marched up by Capt MOSLEY at 8 P.M. Remained on the docks with fatigue party till everything was got away to camp. Weather fine all day but about midnight a terrific thunderstorm came on. Capt O'RORKE, Capt LOW & 1 man left at the docks to form a veterinary dressing station	
15th August.	Visit from D.D.V.S. A very wet day. Cleared buildings of iron fittings, & arranged for accommodation of men. Fitted up the open shed & make stabling for horses of both sections. Inspected buildings & selected places for pharmacy, barrack rooms, ~~forge~~ forge, store, forage shed, office &c. Men sleep on wood platforms on the concrete floor. 7 & 8 Sections arrived in the evening & were accommodated in No 1 building. 1 & 2 Sections provided tea for them. Baggage of 7 & 8 Sections left at the docks. Straw ordered by D.D.V.S. for all four sections, but none arrived. Two men sent to quay to assist at the dressing station.	
16th August.	Weather improved. Work in camp. Rations arrived for 7 & 8 sections. 1 & 2 sections cleared the camp of rubbish. Paddocks told off for the reception of sick horses. No straw arrived for the men who still only have their coats to sleep in. Reported to Base Commandant. Visit from D.D.V.S.	
	admitted 5 destroyed 1 total 4	O.S.D.

Army Form C. 2118.

Instructions regarding War Diaries and Intelligence Summaries are contained in F. S. Regs., Part II. and the Staff Manual respectively. Title pages will be prepared in manuscript.

WAR DIARY
or
INTELLIGENCE SUMMARY.

(Erase heading not required.)

Hour, Date, Place	Summary of Events and Information	Remarks and references to Appendices
17th August.	Visited D.D.V.S. Horse ambulance arranged for at abbatoir. Asked for interpreter. One horse died of congestion of lungs. Picketed sick horses in paddock. Inspected mineral works with a view to possible future acquisition for segregation lines. Admitted 26 – died 1 – total 29.	
18th August.	Burnt carcase of horse which died on previous day but ran short of fuel. Cut gaps in fences for gates from one paddock to another levelled banks, &c. M. Cavanagh reported his arrival as interpreter. Turned all sick horses loose in 3 paddocks to get the benefit of the grazing. Visit from D.D.V.S. R.E. officer visited camp to consider water supply. but nothing decided. Memo from D.D.V.S. re incinerator at the abbatoir. Capt O'RORKE unwell at the docks – to be relieved by Capt MOSLEY. Visit from Base Commandant who asked re in [illegible] complaints by men regarding the bread issued. Inspected & found some loaves mouldy but the majority healthy although not of a very pleasant taste. Remaining 29 – admitted 59 – total 88	

O.S.L.

(9 26 6) W 257—976 100,000 4/12 H W V 79/3298

Army Form C. [illegible]118.

Instructions regarding War Diaries and Intelligence Summaries are contained in F. S. Regs., Part II. and the Staff Manual respectively. Title pages will be prepared in manuscript.

WAR DIARY

or

~~INTELLIGENCE SUMMARY~~

(*Erase heading not required.*)

Hour, Date, Place	Summary of Events and Information	Remarks and References to Appendices
19th August.	Capt MOSLEY relieved Capt O'RORKE at the docks. Helped in work of hospital by Major EDWARDS + Capt LAKE.	
	Visited by Base Commandant who wishes his horses to stay here. Attached them.	
	One trough erected by R.E. in barn paddock.	
	Visited the Secretary + Adjutant + the Mayor of ~~[illegible]~~ GRAVILLE + asked for the Barn to be cleaned out. They, however, can only give the Barn we having to clear it ourselves.	
	Col St JOHN, R.E. (Works Dept) arrived + was shown round. Laid out lines for catarrh cases.	
	Remaining 88 – admitted 60 – total 148.	
20th August	Selected three horses fit for issue.	
	R.E. Officer visited + enquired into water supply taps &c another R.E. Officer made arrangements about the telephone. Col. St JOHN visited with local man + arranged site for taps for water. Visit from D.D.V.S.	
	Complaint from 12 men who wished to go to the front. Dealt with them.	
	4th troop of 1 section sent to docks with kits + rations at request of Capt. MOSLEY.	
	D.D.V.S. read King's speech to all men.	

O. S. J.

(9 26 6) W 257—976 100,000 4/12 H W V 79/3298

Instructions regarding War Diaries and Intelligence Summaries are contained in F. S. Regs., Part II. and the Staff Manual respectively. Title pages will be prepared in manuscript.

WAR DIARY
or
~~INTELLIGENCE SUMMARY~~
(Erase heading not required.)

Army Form C. 2118.

Hour, Date, Place	Summary of Events and Information	Remarks and References to Appendices
20th August (continued)	Arranged for yard of metal store for isolation. Occupied it at 7 P.M. – a suspicious skin case being sent there. Rode into HAVRE with D.D.V.S. who arranged for ordnance supply of brooms, buckets, pegs &c &c, unobtainable without his sanction. Asked Supply officer if hay in Barn could be removed. He informed me that A.S.C. had purchased the hay but could not remove it. He enquired if B.V. Hospital could eat the hay. Replied that this could be done in time. Sold two horses to M. A Romain, who pays us 100 francs for each live horse & takes away dead ones. Remaining 148 – admitted 46 – destroyed 2. total 192.	
21st August.	Received Standing Orders for Expeditionary Force from Base Commandant. Issued three horses to Remount. Sold 1 to M Romain (mange). Selected isolation paddock & shed for mange cases if in any numbers. Received permission to get ambulance from Hotel Bras D'Or, from Base Commandant. Visit from D.D.V.S. Telephone put in – No 18. Paid No 2 Section. No iodine in veterinary chests. Remaining 192 – admitted 56 – discharged 3 – destroyed 1 – total 244.	

O.S.I.

(9 26 6) W 257—976 100,000 4/12 H W V 79/3298

Army Form C. 2118.

Instructions regarding War Diaries and Intelligence Summaries are contained in F. S. Regs., Part II. and the Staff Manual respectively. Title pages will be prepared in manuscript.

WAR DIARY
or
~~INTELLIGENCE~~ SUMMARY
(Erase heading not required.)

Hour, Date, Place	Summary of Events and Information	Remarks and References to Appendices
22nd August	Detailed enquiries paddocks to Capt MOSLEY & ~~[illegible]~~ No 1 Section. Visited Base Commandant. Got permission for men to visit town between 6.30 & 8 PM Asked for Barn, old shed, small shed & yard of metal store to be requisitioned for hospital. R.E. officer came over to inspect them. Visit from D.D.V.S. who leaves for Hd Qrs. I.G.C tonight Wire from D.V.S. to send Capt. ORORKE to headquarters 1st Army Corps as soon as possible. Replied through Base commandant that Capt O'RORKE was ill with dysentery & would be unfit for some time. Telephone number changed to 32. Major COCHRANE & Base Depot of Veterinary Stores arrived. Detailed accommodation for them. Attached Major COCHRANE & personnel of depot to No 2 Section. Remount Dept. required office in building where our officers live Visited O.C. Supplies re hay in Barn with no result. Tested horses with mallein. Made Pte Davis police corporal & detailed 4 men as police under him. Formed a Sanitary Squad of a corporal & four men. Remaining 244 - admitted 42 - total 286	

O.S.F.

(9 26 6) W 257—976 100,000 4/12 H W V 79/3298

Instructions regarding War Diaries and Intelligence Summaries are contained in F. S. Regs., Part II. and the Staff Manual respectively. Title pages will be prepared in manuscript.

WAR DIARY

or

~~INTELLIGENCE~~ SUMMARY

(Erase heading not required.)

Army Form C. 2118.

Hour, Date, Place	Summary of Events and Information	Remarks and References to Appendices
23rd August.	Remount latrines made near house where our officers live. As our house is strictly speaking in their lines, I have arranged to clear out of it. The mess & smells round this house make living there impossible. Arranged accommodation for officers in horse dealer's (M. Lamy) ~~yard~~ house & yard at top (Harfleur) end of our domain. Opened up more fields for horses sound enough to issue to Remounts. Visit from A.S.C. officer who arranged that hay in Barn was bought by A.S.C. Handed over hay to us - gave a receipt for 20,000 bottles (approximately), the proper amount to be stated later & a receipt given by me to the owner. Barricaded Remount buildings off from A.V.C. quarters as their horses, carts & men were continually coming through our camp. Opened a canteen for the men. Asked Base Commandant that sick horses from front be detrained at ~~the~~ GRAVILLE instead of HAVRE. Remaining 286 - admitted 17 - died 1 - total 302.	

(9 26 6) W 257—976 100,000 4/12 H W V 79/3298

O.S.2.

Instructions regarding War Diaries and Intelligence Summaries are contained in F. S. Regs., Part II. and the Staff Manual respectively. Title pages will be prepared in manuscript.

WAR DIARY

or

~~INTELLIGENCE~~ SUMMARY

(Erase heading not required.)

Army Form C. 2118.

Hour, Date, Place	Summary of Events and Information	Remarks and References to Appendices
24th August	Pte. Cregan, 'Section', admitted to hospital (appendicitis).	
	One horse lost - tied up three times in the night but finally escaped. Advertised in Commandant's orders.	
	Medical Officer visited the hospital - advised as to cookhouse, night latrine, refuse pits, rubbish tins & malleined horses.	
	Remaining 302 - admitted 90 - destroyed 3 - total 389	
	Beer did not turn up as ordered.	
	Discovered drain in barrack room & decided to move men into tents.	
	Memo from D.V.S. that bi-weekly state by telegram & weekly return on A F C 399 only required by him.	
25th August.	Moved wood & iron material to Old Shed & rest hay on. Started checking hay in M. Trouflie's Barn.	
	R.E. Officer visited & was shown sites for troughs, mangers & cookhouse.	
	Capt. MELLARD arrived from the docks, his duty there being ended until arrival of next transport — to be informed by telephone.	
	More officers badly wanted in this hospital.	
	Issued 14 horses to O.C. Remounts. Supply of headropes run out, many horses having to run loose & to be fed from the ground.	

J. S. J.

(9 26 6) W 257—976 100,000 4/12 H W V 79/3298

Instructions regarding War Diaries and Intelligence Summaries are contained in F. S. Regs., Part II. and the Staff Manual respectively. Title pages will be prepared in manuscript.

WAR DIARY

or

~~INTELLIGENCE SUMMARY~~

(Erase heading not required.)

Army Form C. 2118.

Hour, Date, Place	Summary of Events and Information	Remarks and References to Appendices
25th August (continued)	no beer arrived for the men. R.E. officer inspected drain in barrack room & advised as to filling in in order to make room habitable. One set of shoeing tools for a section is totally inadequate as time is lost in taking off hind shoes. No time to shoe horses of section. Remaining 389 – admitted 120 – discharged 14 – destroyed 3. total 500	
26th August	Medical officer inspected barrack room & condemned as insanitary on account of drain in the middle. Men removed to building formerly occupied by 7+8 sections. Went to ordnance dept. & A.S.C. & arranged for harness, headropes & cart. Harness for horse ambulance, G.S. wagon for camp transport, carting forage &c. Major Martin visited us & informed us he was A.D.V.S. Base. Telegram from D.V.S. that former message re Capt. O'RORKE was cancelled. R.E. officer arranged about building incinerator. 6 officers Special Reserve A.V.C. ~~arrived 8.30 pm~~ & 114 men specially enlisted arrived 8.00 P.M. Capt O'RORKE discharged from hospital to duty. Remaining 500 – admitted 52 – destroyed 3 – died 1. total 548. O.S.D.	

(9 26 6) W 257—976 100,000 4/12 H W V 79/3298

Instructions regarding War Diaries and Intelligence Summaries are contained in F. S. Regs., Part II. and the Staff Manual respectively. Title pages will be prepared in manuscript.

WAR DIARY

or

~~INTELLIGENCE~~ SUMMARY

(*Erase heading not required.*)

Army Form C. 2118.

Hour, Date, Place	Summary of Events and Information	Remarks and References to Appendices
27th August	Six officers, Lieut WYLEY, COCKBURN, SLOCOCK, RYAN, TOWNSEND & AUCHTERLONIE, A.V.C., S.R., joined for duty. Lieut COCKBURN had no uniform & was in plain clothes. 114 specially enlisted men of A.V.C. also arrived. Four of them local sergeants. Of these 114, 16 are farriers. Divided party into four troops. Attached 1 & 2 troop to 1 Section for duty, 3 & 4 troop to 2 Section. Lieut WYLEY, SLOCOCK & RYAN attached to 1 Section " COCKBURN, TOWNSEND & AUCHTERLONIE to 2 Section. Applied to Base Commandant for horses & to ordnance for saddlery for officers. Lame, catarrh & malingering horses handed to Capt. O'RORKE. 18 horses sent to Remount. Indented for tools for farriers. Remaining 548 - admitted 23 - destroyed 2 - discharged 18 total 549.	
28th August	Telegram from O.C. 6 mobile section, informing that 24 horses & 3 men leaving PAIX. 1.40 pm for B.V.H. Arranged with railway authorities to inform us of arrival of train at HAVRE or GRAVILLE. Inspected garden re damage done to crops by horses breaking down fence. Found damage correct. Value of damage 44 francs.	

O.S.D.

Army Form C. [illegible]8.

Instructions regarding War Diaries and Intelligence Summaries are contained in F. S. Regs., Part II. and the Staff Manual respectively. Title pages will be prepared in manuscript.

WAR DIARY
or
~~INTELLIGENCE SUMMARY~~
(Erase heading not required.)

Hour, Date, Place	Summary of Events and Information	Remarks and References to Appendices
28th August (continued)	Rode in country with A.D.V.S. Base re site for hospital. Uniform for Lieut COCKBURN arrived. Sent home for horse ambulance from Hotel Bras D'Or – to be permanently left here. Sent horses for permanent transport – no result. Paid 2 Sections. Issued Standing Orders. Handed over Receiving Lines to O.C. 7 Section. Remaining 549 – admitted 28 – died 2 – discharged 20 – total 555	
29th August.	Lieut DAVIS, A.V.C., S.R., reported arrival. Troughs being erected in No 2, 3 & 4A paddock. Applied for tent for officers – received same. Chargers issued by Remounts to officers. Visit by R.E. Works officer. S.R. officers inoculated for typhoid. Received tools for 10 farriers – started them to work in forge. 24 horses arrived by train from PAIX, 6 P.M. 3 men of 7 & 8 Section with them. Telegram from O.C. 6 Mobile Section re 32 horses leaving PAIX for us 11 A.M. today. Visit by A.D.V.S. Base. Paid specially enlisted men. Remaining 555 – admitted 64 – discharged 13 – total 606.	

O. S. F.

(9 26 6) W 257—976 100,000 4/12 H W V 79/3298

Instructions regarding War Diaries and Intelligence Summaries are contained in F. S. Regs., Part II. and the Staff Manual respectively. Title pages will be prepared in manuscript.

WAR DIARY
or
INTELLIGENCE SUMMARY
(*Erase heading not required.*)

Army Form C. [illegible]8.

Hour, Date, Place	Summary of Events and Information	Remarks and References to Appendices
20th August.	Order to be ready to move at a moments notice. Packed stores etc. Memo from A.D.V.S. re move - to receive orders from A.Q.M.G. as he (A.D.V.S.) is leaving with 3rd Echelon. Went to Headquarters & made enquiries re move; also arranged with Supply Officer re supplies. Asked permission to arm cavalry reservists & A.V.C. men with rifles - permission granted. Arranged with ordnance & drew 200 rifles, bandoliers, slings & 20,000 rounds of ammunition. Total 224 men armed with rifles. Drew 647 halters from ordnance as they were being put on ship. Wire from D.V.S. to send Lieut. WYLEY & SLOCOCK (S.R.) to report to A.D.V.S. 1st Division & to travel to front with remounts. On inquiry no remounts going to front so officers are to go alone. Attached Lieut COCKBURN to 1 Section 72 horses from 6 mobile section arrived 6. P.M. 4 men of 2 & 4 sections with them. Issued orders for no one to leave camp. Remaining 576 - admitted 58 - destroyed 6 - discharged 12 - total 646	

O. S. F.

(9 26 6) W 257—976 100,000 4/12 H W V 79/3298

Instructions regarding War Diaries and Intelligence Summaries are contained in F. S. Regs., Part II. and the Staff Manual respectively. Title pages will be prepared in manuscript.

WAR DIARY
or
~~INTELLIGENCE SUMMARY~~
(Erase heading not required.)

Army Form C. [illegible]8.

Hour, Date, Place	Summary of Events and Information	Remarks and References to Appendices
31st August.	Paid 7 men belonging to 7 & 8 Sections. Col on Staff visited re move. Lieut WYLEY & FLOCOCK left by 11.39 train for the front each with a horse & servant. Packed stores &c. Issued tobacco to men. One case tested with mallein - reacted - destroyed glandered. Issued ~~rifles~~ ammunition & rifles to A.V.C. men & cavalry reservists. Put guards round camp - 18 men in all. Unable to get into communication with Headquarters as there is no one at Quai de Transatlantique. Telephone message from Base Commandant asking for strength in men & horses - urgent. Remaining 646 - admitted 17 - discharged 10 - destroyed 12 total 641 O.S.J.	O.S.J.

(9 26 6) W 257—976 100,000 4/12 H W V 79/3298

AVD

WAR DIARY.

No 2. Vety: Section.

Volume II

1st Sept 1914

Instructions regarding War Diaries and Intelligence Summaries are contained in F. S. Regs., Part II. and the Staff Manual respectively. Title pages will be prepared in manuscript.

Army Form C. 2118.

WAR DIARY
or
~~INTELLIGENCE SUMMARY.~~
(Erase heading not required.)

Hour, Date, Place	Summary of Events and Information	Remarks and references to Appendices
1st Sept. HAVRE	Visit by Base Commandant. Transport officer ordered stores to go by barge to docks. Memo from Major COCHRANE to this effect, he signing it as acting A.D.V.S. New interpreter detailed by Staff Capt No 1 Base. M. [illegible], to be attached permanently & to be mounted. Capt. WELLARD & 1 troop of 1 Section & 2 drivers (32 men) detailed for duty with Base Veterinary Stores until arrival at future destination. Orders given to him that he is under the orders of O/C B.V. Stores until arrival at new port when he is to report to A.D.V.S. Base for duty until the arrival of Base Veterinary Hospital. He is to take 5 days' rations for himself & party & to draw what veterinary stores he requires from O/C B.V. Stores.	
	Lieut COCKBURN badly shaken owing to his horse rearing up & falling back on him.	
	Remaining 641 – admitted 16 – destroyed 4 – total 653.	

(9 29 6) W 2794 100,000 8/14 H W V Forms/C. 2118/11

Instructions regarding War Diaries and Intelligence Summaries are contained in F. S. Regs., Part II. and the Staff Manual respectively. Title pages will be prepared in manuscript.

WAR DIARY
or
~~INTELLIGENCE SUMMARY.~~
(Erase heading not required.)

Army Form C. 2118.

Hour, Date, Place	Summary of Events and Information	Remarks and references to Appendices
2nd Sept.	M. Cavanagh relieved by M. Jean Léon who has been specially enlisted. We lose.	
	Visit to H^d Q^rs & received order & arranged to embark 160 men, 4 officers & 339 horses for 1 Section on the "Lestrian", with 5 days rations. This party to include the troop under Capt MELLARD detailed to go with the B. V. Stores, & former order to Capt. MELLARD cancelled, he now being directly under his own section commander. Received 2,400 francs from M. Romain for horses destroyed.	
	1 Section marched to Quai de la Plata & were embarked on the Victorian by a Staff Officer who thus upset our & all the Staff arrangements, for No 2 Section was to have embarked on this vessel. This news brought to me as I was marching to docks with the remainder of the Hospital.	
	~~Put~~ horses, men, transport &c on one side & visited	D. V. L.

(9 29 6) W 2794 100,000 8/14 H W V Forms/C. 2118/11

Army Form C. 2118.

Instructions regarding War Diaries and Intelligence Summaries are contained in F. S. Regs., Part II. and the Staff Manual respectively. Title pages will be prepared in manuscript.

WAR DIARY
or
~~INTELLIGENCE~~ SUMMARY.
(Erase heading not required.)

Hour, Date, Place	Summary of Events and Information	Remarks and references to Appendices
2nd Sept. (continued)	visited Headquarters where it was arranged to embark horses of No 2 Section, without catarrh on the "Certrian". I informed ~~Base Commandant~~ Staff Officer that if the 200 horses with catarrh & strangles were embarked with other horses of various units I would not be responsible for the condition of the latter on arrival at new Base. Consequently Capt O'RORKE & 61 men & 1 Officer remained in the Hangar du Coton with the catarrh horses, with order to follow later. Embarked on "Certrian" with 1 Officer, 118 men & 125 horses — disembarked 2 horses later — blowing badly. An unpleasant night owing to all this confusion. Remaining 657 - admitted 6 - total 6[illegible]7.	
	D. I. P.	

(9 29 6) W2794 100,000 8/14 H W V Forms/C. 2118/11

Army Form C. 2118.

Instructions regarding War Diaries and Intelligence Summaries are contained in F. S. Regs., Part II. and the Staff Manual respectively. Title pages will be prepared in manuscript.

WAR DIARY
or
~~INTELLIGENCE~~ SUMMARY.

(Erase heading not required.)

Hour, Date, Place	Summary of Events and Information	Remarks and references to Appendices
22nd Sept.	Found Capt. WELLARD & troop on board the "Caltician", so had to change his orders again. Placed him under my own orders & detached him for Base Veterinary Stores. Order from Hd Qrs (Base Commandant) to detail one officer for duty with cavalry details. Sent word to Capt O'RORKE to detail Lieut. AUCHTERLONIE for this work.	
	Finished embarking stores, forage &c. Informed Embarking Staff Officer of the stupidity of putting the horses on board first & leaving the stores &c. till next day. This appears to have been done on all ships, the horses having to stand in a foul ~~atmo~~ atmosphere for a day or two.	
	Received 900 francs from M. Romain for horses destroyed in Sept. Float sent back to owner by Capt. O'RORKE.	
	Sailed at midday. 900 horses on board. None drink the water properly – only a few mouthfuls.	
	Some of our stores, ordered to go on the barge, left.	

S. S. F.

(9 29 6) W 2794 100,000 8/14 H W V Forms/C. 2118/11

Instructions regarding War Diaries and Intelligence Summaries are contained in F. S. Regs., Part II. and the Staff Manual respectively. Title pages will be prepared in manuscript.

WAR DIARY
or
INTELLIGENCE SUMMARY.
(Erase heading not required.)

Army Form C. 2118.

Hour, Date, Place	Summary of Events and Information	Remarks and references to Appendices
3rd Sept (continued)	left behind with Base Veterinary Stores. This is a nuisance as they ought never to have been put on the barge. I did all I could to prevent it, short of becoming insubordinate. The "Custodian" is an exceedingly dirty ship.	
4th Sept.	O.C. Troops on board inspected all units. ~~[illegible]~~ Many horses developing strangles & catarrh. Major COCHRANE, O.C. A.V.C. advised O.C. Troops to disembark horses first, & this advice was agreed to by all units on board.	
	O. S. R.	

(9 29 6) W 2794 100,000 8/14 H W V Forms/C. 2118/11

Army Form C. 2118.

Instructions regarding War Diaries and Intelligence Summaries are contained in F. S. Regs., Part II. and the Staff Manual respectively. Title pages will be prepared in manuscript.

WAR DIARY
or
~~INTELLIGENCE~~ SUMMARY.
(Erase heading not required.)

Hour, Date, Place	Summary of Events and Information	Remarks and references to Appendices
5th Sept.	Arrived St NAZAIRE at 8 A.M. & disembarked our horses at midday & stores later. No transport available till evening. Was taken to site for camp by commandant. No water in the camp at all except two exceedingly filthy ponds; a large number of small fields badly fenced & with little grazing, however the land is dry & good & there is a certain amount of shade. Was informed that there was no water nearer than 1 mile, & the nearest spot to which the water supply would come was ¼ mile from camp. Explained to commandant that the last place for a Veterinary Hospital was the one without any water. No water for the men either. However there was nowhere else to go. Went back to the docks & managed to water all the horses in buckets in a back yard, as there was no water trough nearer the docks than 1 mile. No 2 Section was ordered to disembark	

(9 29 6) W 2794 100,000 8/14 H W V Forms/C. 2118/11

017

Instructions regarding War Diaries and Intelligence Summaries are contained in F. S. Regs., Part II. and the Staff Manual respectively. Title pages will be prepared in manuscript.

WAR DIARY
or
INTELLIGENCE SUMMARY.
(Erase heading not required.)

Army Form C. 2118.

Hour, Date, Place	Summary of Events and Information	Remarks and references to Appendices
5th Sept. (continued)	disembark at St NAZAIRE & to take over the horses of 1 Section on its arrival; 1 Section proceeding to NANTES. This order given by Major COCHRANE as acting A.D.V.S. D.V.S. arrived on docks in time to prevent this.	
	Refused to go to camp until I got transport sufficient for what was absolutely necessary for horses & men. Got transport later & marched to camp; picketed horses in 3 fields & put men in bivouacs.	
	Ordered not to sell horses unless an officer saw them destroyed.	

Army Form C. 2118.

WAR DIARY
or
~~INTELLIGENCE~~ SUMMARY.
(Erase heading not required.)

Instructions regarding War Diaries and Intelligence Summaries are contained in F. S. Regs., Part II. and the Staff Manual respectively. Title pages will be prepared in manuscript.

Hour, Date, Place	Summary of Events and Information	Remarks and references to Appendices
6th Sept.	Went round all fields in the neighbourhood & selected those suitable for horses. Lieut TOWNSEND made an excellent map of the surrounding country & this was of great use to me. Found a pond with tolerably fair water in the camp, & used this for watering the horses. Water for men brought up in tubs on a cart. Used the filthy ponds for catarrh & strangles cases. Applied to R E for a pump & one was promised. Got some of our stores up from the docks — many things missing & some of other peoples — everything being mixed up in the hold of the ship in the compound retirement from HAVRE. Patched up fences as well as ~~possible~~ able. 1 Section arrived, disembarked & bivouacked on the docks, no transport being available. Visited headquarters & extracted many promises. Fortunately we have plenty of forage in camp, otherwise there would be difficulty in getting any up from the supply depot.	

O.12.

Instructions regarding War Diaries and Intelligence Summaries are contained in F. S. Regs., Part II. and the Staff Manual respectively. Title pages will be prepared in manuscript.

WAR DIARY
or
~~INTELLIGENCE SUMMARY.~~

(Erase heading not required.)

Army Form C. 2118.

Hour, Date, Place	Summary of Events and Information	Remarks and references to Appendices
7th Sept.	148 horses admitted from Remount Depot, mostly with catarrh. 1 Section arrived from the docks with 337 horses. Great difficulty in keeping the horses in the fields at night they dodge the guards & break down the fences & banks. Applied for barbed wire to make up fences, also posts, ~~and~~ nails, &c.	
	Remaining 439 - admitted 176 - discharged 8 - total 607.	
8th Sept.	419 horses arrived from Remount depot. Spent the whole morning sorting them out. A large number appear to have nothing wrong with them, & were sent straight to the discharge paddock. Took 419 headropes from O.C. Remounts as ours had not arrived from the docks, except those already in use. Very great difficulty in watering all these horses nearly 1100: the ponds in camp get too muddy after a few horses have used them	

A.D.

Army Form C. 2118.

Instructions regarding War Diaries and Intelligence Summaries are contained in F. S. Regs., Part II. and the Staff Manual respectively. Title pages will be prepared in manuscript.

WAR DIARY
or
~~INTELLIGENCE SUMMARY.~~
(Erase heading not required.)

Hour, Date, Place	Summary of Events and Information	Remarks and references to Appendices
8th Sept (continued)	Some sent 1 mile away but this takes too long under the present circumstances. Put up a trough near the best pond - this was useful but many men are required to keep it full & this is just what we cannot afford. Lieut DAVIS, 1 NCO & 3 men for dock duty. Had only a certain percentage of nosebags so had to feed a great many horses from the ground, consequently great waste of oats & hay. Went to Headquarters & was promised many things. Want a pump badly, but the one promised has been sent up country. 1 Section received orders to go to advanced base at once. They packed up ready to go & sent an advance party to the station to receive orders. This increases the difficulties of watering & feeding. Wire from DVS to arrange 1 officer, 1 NCO & 3 men for dock duty & similar party ready for MARSEILLES. Replied that this was already arranged by me. Remaining 607 - admitted 419 - total 1026	

J. H.

(9 29 6) W 2794 100,000 8/14 H W V Forms/C. 2118/11

Instructions regarding War Diaries and Intelligence Summaries are contained in F. S. Regs., Part II. and the Staff Manual respectively. Title pages will be prepared in manuscript.

WAR DIARY
or
~~INTELLIGENCE~~ SUMMARY.
(Erase heading not required.)

Army Form C. 2118.

Hour, Date, Place	Summary of Events and Information	Remarks and references to Appendices
9th Sept.	A great many horses got out of the fields during the night but were caught, & the fences made up as well as possible. Watering & feeding very difficult, in fact the whole day is taken up in doing these things. No dressing, with the exception of a few of the most serious cases, is done. Capt. O'RORKE & 61 men badly wanted. Got a pump at last. Water discovered in a garden across the main road belonging to M. Picard. There is a well pipes fitted for a 3 inch hose, & a machine for pumping which requires a horse to work it. Examined the pipe & went at once to R.E. & asked them to bring a hose & explained that this would save the situation, especially if a trough be erected at once. This water supply is a great find. Saved considerable time by driving many of the horses to water, but it churns the ponds up badly & the water gets very boggy.	

(9 29 6) W2794 100,000 8/14 H W V Forms/C. 2118/11

Instructions regarding War Diaries and Intelligence Summaries are contained in F. S. Regs., Part II. and the Staff Manual respectively. Title pages will be prepared in manuscript.

WAR DIARY

or

~~INTELLIGENCE SUMMARY.~~

(Erase heading not required.)

Army Form C. 2118.

Hour, Date, Place	Summary of Events and Information	Remarks and references to Appendices
9th Sept. (continued).	Wire from D.V.S. asking whereabouts of Lieut DAVIS & attach him to B.V. Hospital. Replied DAVIS already detailed for disembarkation duty. Wire from D.V.S ordering 3 farriers & 16 specially enlisted men to go to each section – urgently required at LE MANS. Replied asking if it were possible to leave these men a little longer, & explaining difficulties of watering & feeding, arrangement of fields & shortage of men, & that if this order was complied with we would be left with 1052 horses & 132 men (61 of whom were now at NANTES) Sent letter to D.V.S. to the same effect.	
	1 Section left at 8.30 pm for Railway Station.	
	Remaining 1026 – admitted 26 – total 1052	
	G.I.L.	

(9 29 6) W 2794 100,000 8/14 H W V Forms/C. 2118/11

Instructions regarding War Diaries and Intelligence Summaries are contained in F. S. Regs., Part II. and the Staff Manual respectively. Title pages will be prepared in manuscript.

WAR DIARY
or
~~INTELLIGENCE~~ SUMMARY.
(Erase heading not required.)

Army Form C. 2118.

Hour, Date, Place	Summary of Events and Information	Remarks and references to Appendices
10th Sept.	Wire from D.V.S. to keep present staff for the present. This helps us a great deal. Capt O'RORKE expected to arrive tonight with party. Wire from A.D.V.S. Base that B.V.H. NANTES can take 200 horses. Water difficulties still very marked, ponds beginning to run low. R.E. putting up a trough ½ mile away. I think many of the horses are falling off in condition owing to bad water. A great deal of the oats & hay wasted owing to our having to feed from the ground. Regret that all this is so unlike what a veterinary hospital should be, but somewhat consoled by the fact that every other branch of the administrative services here is in a corresponding state. Mended newly made gaps in fence. Received 258 francs canteen money from Capt. MOSLEY yesterday & gave each man 1 franc today. [signature]	

(9 29 6) W2794 100,000 8/14 H W V Forms/C. 2118/11

Army Form C. 2118.

Instructions regarding War Diaries and Intelligence Summaries are contained in F. S. Regs., Part II. and the Staff Manual respectively. Title pages will be prepared in manuscript.

WAR DIARY
or
INTELLIGENCE SUMMARY.
(Erase heading not required.)

Hour, Date, Place	Summary of Events and Information	Remarks and references to Appendices
10th Sept. (continued)	Applied for authority to send 200 horses to Veterinary Hospital NANTES – not granted on account of landing of 6th Division. O.C., Base Horse Transport asked if we could issue him with fit horses. Replied that permission must be obtained from D.V.S. Several horses admitted from 6th Division.	
11th Sept.	Wire from D.V.S. not to take hind shoes off horses in hospital owing to difficulty in shoeing up again. Visited R.E. (works) & asked for troughs, barbed wire, mangers, &c. Inquired how interpreters were to be paid – French authorities say that the English pay them, the British assert that the French pay them – no decision arrived at. New water trough working ¼ mile from camp.	

(9 29 6) W 2794 100,000 8/14 H W V Forms/C. 2118/11

O.S.P.

Instructions regarding War Diaries and Intelligence Summaries are contained in F. S. Regs., Part II. and the Staff Manual respectively. Title pages will be prepared in manuscript.

WAR DIARY

or

~~INTELLIGENCE SUMMARY~~.

(Erase heading not required.)

Army Form C. 2118.

Hour, Date, Place	Summary of Events and Information	Remarks and references to Appendices
11th Sept (continued)	- this saves time. Key of it given to us to keep. Lieut MARSHALL reported his arrival & was sent to NANTES to report to A.D.V.S. Base. Asked Base Commandant if horses could be taken to NANTES by road by cavalry details but this was not allowed. Base Commandant informed me that horses could not be sent to NANTES by train until 6th Division had completed disembarkation. Many horses continue to get out of the fields during the night. Wrote to D.V.S.	
12th Sept.	R.A. Officer arrived with order from Staff Captain to get 14 horses from us. Issued fourteen. Also issued three to North Staffords under a like order. Put up wire round weak places in the fences. Detailed Lieut COCKBURN for MARSEILLES & put him under orders for that place.	

O.B.

(9 29 6) W2794 100,000 8/14 H W V Forms/C. 2118/11

Instructions regarding War Diaries and Intelligence Summaries are contained in F. S. Regs., Part II. and the Staff Manual respectively. Title pages will be prepared in manuscript.

WAR DIARY
or
~~INTELLIGENCE~~ SUMMARY.
(Erase heading not required.)

Army Form C. 2118.

Hour, Date, Place	Summary of Events and Information	Remarks and references to Appendices
12th Sept (continued)	Very wet & windy day. Got another pump from R.E. & worked the small pond of filthy water - a great saving of labour. Difficulty in keeping horses in the fields at night. Wire from D.V.S. asking for Lieut DAVIS & if he was on duty at the hospital; also order for Lieut COCKBURN to go to NANTES. Replied that Lieut DAVIS was attached to hospital but was doing dock duty; also that Lieut. COCKBURN was detailed for MARSEILLES with one man A.V.C. for duty; also that Lieut DAVIS would be available to go to NANTES in a day or two as soon as 6th Division had completed disembarkation. Put hay down in bales in the fields in order to prevent waste - seems successful. Memo to D.V.S. re issue of horses &c. Wire from Base Commandant re Lieut COCKBURN going to NANTES. Replied as to D.V.S. Wire from D.V.S. that Lieut COCKBURN could go to MARSEILLES.	

(9 29 6) W2794 100,000 8/14 H W V Forms/C. 2118/11

Instructions regarding War Diaries and Intelligence Summaries are contained in F. S. Regs., Part II. and the Staff Manual respectively. Title pages will be prepared in manuscript.

WAR DIARY
or
~~INTELLIGENCE SUMMARY.~~
(Erase heading not required.)

Army Form C. 2118.

Hour, Date, Place	Summary of Events and Information	Remarks and references to Appendices
12th Sept. (continued).	Wire from Headquarters D.G.C. that horse ships should be carefully disinfected. Forwarded by Base Commandant with order to purchase disinfectants locally.	
13th Sept.	RE Officer arrived & brought a hose & um on M. Picard's tap, to enable us to fill a trough in a field near his house. This will be a tremendous help. The Officer also brought canvas for mangers. Made arrangements with Supply Officer for Lieut DAVIS to draw saponified cresol for disinfecting horse ships, as required. Worked out the estimate at 8 oz per horse, as a working basis. This should enable seamen to thoroughly disinfect the ship & its fittings, &c; Lieut DAVIS arranging this with the captain of each ship.	

D.V.J.

Instructions regarding War Diaries and Intelligence Summaries are contained in F. S. Regs., Part II. and the Staff Manual respectively. Title pages will be prepared in manuscript.

Army Form C. 2118.

WAR DIARY
or
~~INTELLIGENCE~~ SUMMARY.
(Erase heading not required.)

Hour, Date, Place	Summary of Events and Information	Remarks and references to Appendices
13th Sept (continued).	Asked DADRT to arrange for 200 horses to go by train to NANTES tomorrow, to the Base Veterinary Hospital. Unable to send them today as 800 remounts have arrived here & are being sent to NANTES. Made further enquiries re interpreter's pay but learned nothing new. Lieut COCKBURN left for MARSEILLES with Colonel MONEY & party.	
14th Sept.	Put up more wire fences & strengthened the others. Promoted Ptes. Cox & Page unpaid Lance corporals. Order from Base Commandant to issue 40 ~~horses to~~ heavy draught horses to O.C. Horse Transport. Issued 40. The Filthy Pond dried up. Ground here very good – even in wet weather. Parties of loose horses trot or gallop past the camp from the docks – newly disembarked remounts.	[illegible]

(9.29 6) W 2794 100,000 8/14 H W V Forms/C. 2118/11

Army Form C. 2118.

Instructions regarding War Diaries and Intelligence Summaries are contained in F. S. Regs., Part II. and the Staff Manual respectively. Title pages will be prepared in manuscript.

WAR DIARY
or
~~INTELLIGENCE SUMMARY.~~

(*Erase heading not required.*)

Hour, Date, Place	Summary of Events and Information	Remarks and references to Appendices
14th Sept (continued)	We caught 17 of them & informed Hd Qrs. These horses come during the night & early hours of the morning & disturb our sentries & our horses.	
	Put up new water trough - filled by hose from M. Ricaud's house - a great assistance.	
	RE put up 2 marquees for us. Sent 200 slighter cases by train to NANTES - to OC, Base Veterinary Hospital there. Wired to OC, B.V.H. of their departure.	
	The water supply on the hill & at the casino cut off for some reason, causing much inconvenience.	
	Acquired a new field for debility cases.	
	Wire from A.D.V.S. saying he would visit on Tuesday afternoon.	
	Advised AA & QMG of 17 horses strayed in here.	
	Remaining 1089 - discharged 240 - total 849.	
	[illegible initials]	

(9 29 6) W 2794 100,000 8/14 H W V Forms/C. 2118/11

Instructions regarding War Diaries and Intelligence Summaries are contained in F. S. Regs., Part II. and the Staff Manual respectively. Title pages will be prepared in manuscript.

WAR DIARY
or
INTELLIGENCE SUMMARY.
(Erase heading not required.)

Army Form C. 2118.

Hour, Date, Place	Summary of Events and Information	Remarks and references to Appendices
15th Sept.	Parties of remounts continue to stroll through our camp, some with headcollars, some without, some with collars, others with nosebags. Put up more wire fences. O.C. Remounts sent for the horses which strayed into our camp. Memo to O.C. Remounts asking if he could take 100 fit horses – reply that he is choked up with horses but is getting some away to NANTES & will receive ours later. Congestion relieved somewhat by the departure of 200 horses yesterday, but the 25 men who went with them are badly needed. Flying visit by D.D.V.S. Base, to see Hospital. Showed him as much as was possible in the time. A very wet day, but in spite of this the ground is in good order although rather slippery. The catarrh cases seem to be recovering & fewer horses are coughing.	

O.S.B.

(9 29 6) W2794 100,000 8/14 H W V Forms/C. 2118/11

Instructions regarding War Diaries and Intelligence Summaries are contained in F. S. Regs., Part II. and the Staff Manual respectively. Title pages will be prepared in manuscript.

WAR DIARY
or
~~INTELLIGENCE~~ SUMMARY.
(*Erase heading not required.*)

Army Form C. 2118.

Hour, Date, Place	Summary of Events and Information	Remarks and references to Appendices
15th Sept. (continued)	Telephone message from Base Commandant to say that all outstanding accounts must be settled in case of a sudden change of base.	
	Received 700 francs from Capt O'RORKE for horses sold by him to Romain at HAVRE, during the time he was detached from the Hospital.	
	Remaining 849 - admitted 23 - discharged 6 - total 866	
16th Sept.	Put up more wire fences. Remounts still stroll quietly through our camp.	
	Two men (specially enlisted) awarded 14 days No 2 FP for breaking out of camp & being drunk. Have to carry out punishment ourselves as there is no PM or APM.	
	Party returned from NANTES bringing our medicine with them. Three men left behind stragglers.	
	Rumours of a change of base - rather a nuisance just as it looks like our soon becoming settled.	
	J.S.J.	

(9 29 6) W2794 100,000 8/14 H W V Forms/C. 2118/11

Instructions regarding War Diaries and Intelligence Summaries are contained in F. S. Regs., Part II. and the Staff Manual respectively. Title pages will be prepared in manuscript.

WAR DIARY

or

~~INTELLIGENCE~~ SUMMARY.

(Erase heading not required.)

Army Form C. 2118.

Hour, Date, Place	Summary of Events and Information	Remarks and references to Appendices
16th Sept (continued).	Watering & feeding going on fairly well now, in spite of the pump breaking.	
	Handed in 700 francs to paymaster - money fr Capt O'RORKE for horses sold at HAVRE.	
	Visit to Headquarters re new interpreter, & to see about sending fit horses away. No interpreter to be had yet, M. Lion having been sent elsewhere, thank Heaven.	
	Capt O'RORKE & Lieut TOWNSEND malleined about 100 horses. Arranged with OC Remounts to hand over 100 or more fit horses tomorrow.	
	Wire from DVS to send him daily numbers remaining, discharged & admitted. Sent yesterday's list.	
	Repaired pump.	
	Remaining 866 - admitted 7 - destroyed 5 - died 3	
	~~Total~~ 867	
	857	

Instructions regarding War Diaries and Intelligence Summaries are contained in F. S. Regs., Part II. and the Staff Manual respectively. Title pages will be prepared in manuscript.

WAR DIARY
or
~~INTELLIGENCE~~ SUMMARY.
(Erase heading not required.)

Army Form C. 2118.

Hour, Date, Place	Summary of Events and Information	Remarks and references to Appendices
17th Sept.	Repaired fences. Horses of one field stampeded in the night & broke through the wire fence into the next field & out into the road. All returned by the morning. Issued 134 horses to OC Remounts. This helps considerably to relieve the congestion. Lieut YOUNG reported his arrival & was directed to report to A.D.V.S., Base, at NANTES. The ground is excellent in spite of the wet weather. Put aside a well shaded field with good grazing (such as it is) for debility horses. Remaining 867 - admitted 8 - discharged 134 - destroyed 1 total 740.	
	B.S.d.	

Army Form C. 2118.

Instructions regarding War Diaries and Intelligence Summaries are contained in F. S. Regs., Part II. and the Staff Manual respectively. Title pages will be prepared in manuscript.

WAR DIARY
or
~~INTELLIGENCE~~ SUMMARY.

(Erase heading not required.)

Hour, Date, Place	Summary of Events and Information	Remarks and references to Appendices
18th Sept.	18 horses got out in the night but were recaptured. Work going on more easily. Asked O.C. Remounts if he could take any horses but he is leaving for NANTES so horses must be sent there by train. Arranged to send 100 tomorrow & borrowed men from A.S.C. Base Depot to take them on the train. Note from Staff Captain re wire from A.G. saying that farriers & shoeing smiths required by mounted units, & asking how many farriers at bases, & stating one farrier required at once for each Field Ambulance. Replied that 18 farriers A.V.C. here, three being ordered to each veterinary section by D.V.S. Remaining 740 – admitted 3 – discharged 3 – died 1 – destroyed 1 – total 738. J.S.J.	

(9 29 6) W 2794 100,000 8/14 H W V Forms/C. 2118/11

Army Form C. 2118.

Instructions regarding War Diaries and Intelligence Summaries are contained in F. S. Regs., Part II. and the Staff Manual respectively. Title pages will be prepared in manuscript.

WAR DIARY
or
INTELLIGENCE SUMMARY
(*Erase heading not required.*)

Hour, Date, Place	Summary of Events and Information	Remarks and References to Appendices
19th Sept	Message from Staff Capt requiring detailed return of all ranks for C in C. Complied	
	99 horses ready to go to NANTES but train not available yet.	
	Sent 4 troops under Capt O'RORKE to bathe in the sea.	
	Staff Capt & a major of RA arrived & asked for loan of farriers to shoe horses at docks. Sent Capt. Surridge & 8 farriers to help.	
	Memo from D.V.S. re my issue of horses to Horse Transport, & ordering me to clear hospital here gradually & as soon as possible owing to possible change of base; also to keep him informed by wire how I stand.	
	Wired D.V.S. that 100 horses ready for NANTES but awaiting train. also that I could send him farriers & subordinates for three sections & asking where he required them most; informed him I was borrowing labour.	
	Arranged with Staff Captain to borrow labour for routine & stable duties when necessary & for embarkation also when required.	
	Am trying to send men to D.V.S. as I can manage here as long as we do not move, but if we move then there are transport, fatigue & other duties which call for more men.	
	Remaining 726 – died 1 – destroyed 1 – total 724	

(9 26 6) W 257—976 100,000 4/12 H W V 79/3298

0 18

Instructions regarding War Diaries and Intelligence Summaries are contained in F. S. Regs., Part II. and the Staff Manual respectively. Title pages will be prepared in manuscript.

WAR DIARY
or
INTELLIGENCE SUMMARY
(Erase heading not required.)

Army Form C. 2118.

Hour, Date, Place	Summary of Events and Information	Remarks and References to Appendices
20th Left	Wired state to D.V.S. explaining mistake of 12 horses in excess shown in state. These horses strayed in & we thought they were remounts but they were our own, & we handed them to remounts with other horses as theirs. Issued 5 horses to a heavy battery. 4 troops went bathing under Lieut. TOWNSEND. Wire from D.V.S. in reply to mine of yesterday, to send 3 farriers & 16 [illegible] to Section [illegible] at Nantes [illegible] ? Cannot [illegible] of LE MANS. Another from D.V.S. to make arrangements for disembarkation duties for Indian troops, & asking if Lieut COCKBURN left for MARSEILLES. Replied making arrangements & that Lt COCKBURN had left on 13th. Made enquiries & am told no Indian troops disembark here but supply column for them comes here from England. Sent 3 farriers & 15 men to 5th 6 Section at NANTES with [illegible] horses for Remounts there. Wired to C.Os. [illegible] break through barbed wire fences in the night & get into other fields. Sent nominal roll of men sent to O.C. Veterinary Hospital NANTES. Sent recommendations for promotion to O i/c A.V.C. Records, A.G.'s [illegible] Remaining 724 — admitted 7 — discharged 118 — died 2 — total 611	

O.S.D.

(9 26 6) W 257—976 100,000 4/12 H W V 79/3298

Instructions regarding War Diaries and Intelligence Summaries are contained in F. S. Regs., Part II. and the Staff Manual respectively. Title pages will be prepared in manuscript.

WAR DIARY
or
~~INTELLIGENCE~~ SUMMARY

(*Erase heading not required.*)

Army Form C. 2118.

Hour, Date, Place	Summary of Events and Information	Remarks and References to Appendices
21st Sept.	No bran obtainable today. The debility cases of which there are a fair number, suffer in consequence. Most of these are recovering or have recovered from Strangles & are very poor. Capt. Ormonde arrived from NANTES where he had been drawing ordnance stores. He brought everything except cap badges which have not come from England yet. Men without badges who have been checked for losing them, swear that these are stolen from them either on the docks or whenever they put their caps or coats down to work. I think there is much truth in this as all the French women & children take them whenever they can lay their hands on them. They take shoulder badges from the coats when the men stand in the streets. Memo to O.C. Remounts NANTES re horse issued. Visited Lieut. Davis at the docks. Visited supply officer re bran &c. Sent 3 farriers & 15 specially enlisted men to O.C. 7 Section at LE MANS. When party moved off two men were drunk & were sent under arrest. O.C. 7 Section informed by wire of this. Received a private pony from Rev. Fleming who is not allowed to take his horse with him to the front. Remaining 611 – admitted 3 – died 1 – destroyed 2 – total 611. O.S.D.	

Army Form C. 2118.

Instructions regarding War Diaries and Intelligence Summaries are contained in F. S. Regs., Part II. and the Staff Manual respectively. Title pages will be prepared in manuscript.

WAR DIARY
or
INTELLIGENCE SUMMARY
(Erase heading not required.)

Hour, Date, Place	Summary of Events and Information	Remarks and References to Appendices
22nd Left	Selected horses to go away to NANTES. Asked for train to take 60. Duty in camp. Visited HdQrs. Remaining 611 - destroyed 1 - died 1 - total 608.	
23rd Left	Issued 22 horses to O.C. Base Horse Transport, & 1 to Comdt Infantry Base Depot. - by order of Staff Capt. Visited hospitals to see our men, but two of them could not be traced. Capt. JENNINGS, 5th Lancers, sent here for duty at the hospital but as he has no men I have nothing for him to do. Got coal from docks which enables the shoeing of horses to be carried out. This has been much delayed owing to lack of coal. There are strong rumours that we do not move, but nothing definite can be ascertained. Wire from A.D.V.S. Base ~~that~~ saying that he will visit about midday Thursday. Memo from O.C. Remounts NANTES asking for a return of horses issued. Remaining 608 - discharged 23 - died 1 - destroyed 1 - total 583.	

[illegible initials]

(9 26 6) W 257—976 100,000 4/12 H W V 79/3298

Instructions regarding War Diaries and Intelligence Summaries are contained in F. S. Regs., Part II. and the Staff Manual respectively. Title pages will be prepared in manuscript.

WAR DIARY
or
INTELLIGENCE SUMMARY
(Erase heading not required.)

Army Form C. 2118.

Hour, Date, Place	Summary of Events and Information	Remarks and References to Appendices
~~25th~~ Sept 24th.	One man charged with striking Sergt. Major Mason last night. Remanded for Court Martial, but no evidence forthcoming. Visited Headquarters. Notice for horses to go to NANTES. Sent 60. Visit from A.D.V.S. Base who inspected hospital & urged the shoeing of horses to be pushed on. Base Commandant gave order for men from Cavalry ~~Details~~ Reinforcements to help us in stable duties. Applied for 100 of these from Camp Adjt, Grand Marais Camp. Wire from D.V.S. to send 3 farriers & 16 men to one section at ~~Villen~~ VILLENEUVE St GEORGES as soon as possible. Note from O.C. Australian Hospital asking for a V.O. to see one of King's horses which had colic. Sent Lieut TOWNSEND. Horses seem to be picking up well. Another interpreter reported his arrival. Remaining 583 - admitted 1 - discharged 60 - died 1 - total 523.	

Instructions regarding War Diaries and Intelligence Summaries are contained in F. S. Regs., Part II. and the Staff Manual respectively. Title pages will be prepared in manuscript.

WAR DIARY
or
INTELLIGENCE SUMMARY.
(Erase heading not required.)

Army Form C. 2118.

Hour, Date, Place	Summary of Events and Information	Remarks and references to Appendices
25th Sept.	Capt. JENNINGS 5th Lancers + 100 men from Cavalry Reinforcement arrived for stable duties in camp. Put them on watering, grooming horses & cleaning up lines after which they are dismissed till afternoon. This helps us considerably. New interpreter arrived M. M. Barot. Inspected growing maize near camp & asked permission to buy some for convalescent horses. This will be excellent, as the maize is in good, succulent condition. The thin horses should pick up rapidly on it. Three farriers + 12 men (specially enlisted) left 7.15 A.M. by train for 1 Section at VILLENEUVE TRIAGE. Wired departure to D.V.S. & O.C. 1 Section. Men from neighbouring rest camps continually breaking into the garden of M. Picard & stealing fruit. M. Picard is very kind to our men, who are annoyed about this fruit stealing. Am laying a trap hoping to catch one or two thieves. Mare of owning farm next our camp (north side) suffering from catarrh – caught from our horses. Owner claims compensation & asks for mare to be valued. Am taking action. Remaining 523 – admitted 4 – died 3 – total 525. O.S.J	

(9 26 6) W 257—976 100,000 4/12 H W V 79/3298

Instructions regarding War Diaries and Intelligence Summaries are contained in F. S. Regs., Part II. and the Staff Manual respectively. Title pages will be prepared in manuscript.

WAR DIARY
or
INTELLIGENCE SUMMARY.
(Erase heading not required.)

Army Form C. 2118.

Hour, Date, Place	Summary of Events and Information	Remarks and references to Appendices
26th Sept.	Visit from Adjutant. VILLE ET MARTIN camp re damage done by men from Rest Camp. He instructed our police to shoot any man who refused to halt when told to.	
	Large numbers of horses of Indian Transport passed through the camp during last night & this morning, some with head collars, some with collars & nosebags. Caught several & handed them over.	
	The debility horses seem to pick up well. Applied for train to take 32 horses to NANTES.	
	Lieut. GREEN. AVC. (T) reported arrival with Indian Transport. He motored to NANTES for veterinary stores.	
	Visit from Comte Jean de Sales who wished to buy cast horses & get them well & then return them to us. Explained the situation to him, with thanks &c.	
	Visited Headquarters. Recd 80 francs for horse destroyed by M. Dumandet.	
	Visited Indian transport & saw V.Os in charge.	
	Remaining 525 - admitted 8 - died 1 - total 532.	
	O. S. J.	

(9 26 6) W 257—976 100,000 4/12 H W V 79/3298

Instructions regarding War Diaries and Intelligence Summaries are contained in F. S. Regs., Part II. and the Staff Manual respectively. Title pages will be prepared in manuscript.

WAR DIARY
or
INTELLIGENCE SUMMARY.
(Erase heading not required.)

Army Form C. 2118.

Hour, Date, Place	Summary of Events and Information	Remarks and references to Appendices
27th Sept.	O.C. 12th Lancers wished to have a truck load of horses to take with him to front: but no order forthcoming from Base Commandant. Visited Indian Transport. Many horses standing loose in their camp. They are reported to have 100 horses missing owing to the stampede. Some horses (3) down at docks unable to be moved here - treated there by the Veterinary dressing station. Received veterinary & other stores from NANTES - also 500 doses of mallein. Remaining 532 - admitted 15 - died 1 - total 546. O.S.	

(9 26 6) W 257—976 100,000 4/12 H W V 79/3298

Instructions regarding War Diaries and Intelligence Summaries are contained in F. S. Regs., Part II. and the Staff Manual respectively. Title pages will be prepared in manuscript.

WAR DIARY
or
INTELLIGENCE SUMMARY.

(Erase heading not required.)

Army Form C. 2118.

Hour, Date, Place	Summary of Events and Information	Remarks and references to Appendices
28th Lett.	Am delighted with the rapid progress of the debility cases toward condition. They are picking up in an extraordinary quick manner - one which was very thin 7 days ago ~~[illegible]~~ is now fat. Arranged to get 20 metres x 9 metres of green maize for 20 francs - very cheap. This is to be used for the treatment of the strangles cases. It was originally intended for the debility cases but they have done so well on oats & bran that the green stuff cannot be spared for them. I think the fine weather has helped the horses a great deal. Also the grooming given by the cavalry reinforcements (100 men daily) has made a very great difference to the appearance & condition of the horses. The shoeing is progressing well. No decrease in the number of cases of strangles - so many cases of ~~[illegible]~~ catarrh develop there at the docks; also Indian transport ~~Visited dressing station~~ camp (Grand Marais) which is still in more or less confusion. Wire from D.V.S. asking when I could clear St NAZAIRE & NANTES. Remaining 546 - admitted 13 - destroyed 1 - total 558. [signature]	

(9 26 6) W 257—976 100,000 4/12 H W V 79/3298

Army Form C. 2118.

WAR DIARY
or
INTELLIGENCE SUMMARY.
(Erase heading not required.)

Instructions regarding War Diaries and Intelligence Summaries are contained in F. S. Regs., Part II. and the Staff Manual respectively. Title pages will be prepared in manuscript.

Hour, Date, Place	Summary of Events and Information	Remarks and references to Appendices
27th Left	Cut some green maize for strangles cases – much appreciated. Replied to D.V.S.'s wire of yesterday that I could leave here two days after train for horses for NANTES was available. Visited headquarters & asked Commandant if he could lend men to take horses to NANTES in case we were to move – answer in affirmative. Asked transport officer if he could supply the necessary transport at once in case we move – same answer. Told Commandant I would leave dressing station here. Visit from A.D.V.S. Base re move & he orders Lieut DAVIS & 10 men to be left at dressing station to send any sick horses by train to NANTES & keep those unable to move ~~for treatment~~ until able to go by rail. Memo. that all headcollars are to be sent to C.O.O. – replied that no headcollars in ~~stock~~ use. Sent 32 horses to Remounts NANTES. Received 80 francs for one horse destroyed on 27th M. Touandet. Remaining 558 – admitted 3 – discharged 32 – died 1 – destroyed 1 Total 527	

O. L.

Instructions regarding War Diaries and Intelligence Summaries are contained in F. S. Regs., Part II. and the Staff Manual respectively. Title pages will be prepared in manuscript.

WAR DIARY
or
INTELLIGENCE SUMMARY.
(Erase heading not required.)

Army Form C. 2118.

Hour, Date, Place	Summary of Events and Information	Remarks and references to Appendices
30th Sept.	Obtained [illegible] from M. Bichon to supply green maize 20 x 9 metres. Collected posts & barbed wire & packed up ready to go away. Visit from Staff Capt. who said that Base Commandant wanted to know if we could evacuate sick to NANTES now, pending the order to move. Wired A.D.V.S. Base to find out if the horses could be taken now. Gave instructions to Lieut. Davis re duties on our departure. Am leaving Sergt. Rogers & 9 men with him. Visited Paymaster who wished us to close our imprest account. He informs me that a certificate is required stating the number of horses destroyed, that the price obtained was the best possible & that the best means of destruction was carried out. Sent 40 horses to O.C. Remounts NANTES. Remaining 527 – admitted 9 – discharged 41 – died 1 – total 494.	

[illegible]

121/1818

No 2 Vety: Section

Vol III

Oct 1914

Army Form C. 2118.

WAR DIARY
or
INTELLIGENCE SUMMARY.
(Erase heading not required.)

Instructions regarding War Diaries and Intelligence Summaries are contained in F. S. Regs., Part II. and the Staff Manual respectively. Title pages will be prepared in manuscript.

Hour, Date, Place	Summary of Events and Information	Remarks and references to Appendices
1st October.	Wire from ADVS Base saying hospital at NANTES very congested – could not take our horses – & to await orders. RE officer visited re compensation to local landowner. Wire from D.V.S. to clear horses to NANTES & prepare section for movement forward & to leave Lieut. Davis & party behind at docks having strengthened them. Sent wire on to ADVS.; shortly afterwards received wire from A.D.V.S. to clear horses to NANTES as soon as possible & hold section ready to move. Consulted DADRT re trains & 3rd Echelon re cavalry reinforcements to take horses to NANTES. Memo from O.C. Cavalry Record to approve of promotion of Pts Cox & Page to Lce Cpl. Packed up wire fences & timber which could be spared. Memo from D.V.S. re appointment of 4 lce corporals from A.V.C. men or cavalry reservists. Remaining 494 – admitted 2 – died 4 – destroyed 1 – total 491. O.B.	

Instructions regarding War Diaries and Intelligence Summaries are contained in F. S. Regs., Part II. and the Staff Manual respectively. Title pages will be prepared in manuscript.

WAR DIARY

or

~~INTELLIGENCE SUMMARY.~~

(Erase heading not required.)

Army Form C. 2118.

Hour, Date, Place	Summary of Events and Information	Remarks and references to Appendices
2nd October.	Notice came at 8.30 AM that trains would be available for all the horses – 300 at 11 AM & 200 at 1 P.M. Sent orderly on bicycle to O.C. Reinforcements asking for men to take horses, but orderly smashed bicycle & had to walk, thus causing delay. Sent 305 horses by 1st train, 141 by second – both posts for Veterinary Hospital, NANTES. Sent 40 horses to O.C. Remount NANTES. Wired to O.C. both units. Wired to D.V.S. that horses were cleared out & readiness to move. Heard rumour that 7th Division was not to land here, so went to H.Q.rs to find out, but only heard that arrangements were being made to take away the horse boxes from the docks. Wired to A.D.V.S. reporting rumour & asking him to find out so that I could withdraw some of the men detailed to be left at the docks with Lieut. DAVIS. Sent 3 farriers & 15 men to O.C. 8 Section at LEMANS. Rumours that we go to HAVRE. Remaining 491 – admitted 8 – destroyed 10 – died 1 – discharged 488. Total nil	
3rd October	Cleared up camp & packed up equipment & stores.	
4th Oct.	Wire from D.V.S. advising Capt O'RORKE & proceed to 3rd Army for duty.	

O. S. J.

(9 26 6) W 257—976 100,000 4/12 H W V 79/3298

Instructions regarding War Diaries and Intelligence Summaries are contained in F. S. Regs., Part II. and the Staff Manual respectively. Title pages will be prepared in manuscript.

WAR DIARY
or
~~INTELLIGENCE SUMMARY~~
(*Erase heading not required.*)

Army Form C. 2118.

Hour, Date, Place	Summary of Events and Information	Remarks and References to Appendices
5th October.	Capt O'RORKE left by 6.15 AM. train for 3rd Army Railhead. Visited headquarters & see if there was any news regarding the disembarkation of horses. Was told that Base Commandant & 2 officers had left for new base & the remainder expected to follow. Wired this to D.V.S. & A.D.V.S. also stating that more horses were not expected to disembark at ST NAZAIRE & that I was keeping Lieut DAVIS & party with me until I received further instructions. I learn that 7th Division is not to disembark here. Wire from D.V.S. saying [illegible] 1st Echelon has been asked to move to HAVRE as soon as possible.	
6th Oct.	The order to move to HAVRE came suddenly in the morning but we could not get the transport in time to catch the midday train. Left by the 9.30 PM train.	
7th Oct.	7th October. Journey by train.	
8th Oct.	Arrived HAVRE. Visit D.V.S. & went with him to visit camps & see [illegible] about Remount Camp. In afternoon visit D. [illegible] Base Commandant & other RE officers & inspected site for veterinary hospital &c &c.	

O. R. J.

(9 26 6) W 257—976 100,000 4/12 H W V 79/3298

Army Form C. 2118.

Instructions regarding War Diaries and Intelligence Summaries are contained in F. S. Regs., Part II. and the Staff Manual respectively. Title pages will be prepared in manuscript.

WAR DIARY
or
~~INTELLIGENCE SUMMARY~~

(Erase heading not required.)

Hour, Date, Place	Summary of Events and Information	Remarks and References to Appendices
9th October.	Sent Section & site choosen & went personally with D.V.S. for a tour of neighbouring country. [illegible] horses did not arrive till late in day having gone the wrong road. Put up tents, arranged accommodation for horses, forge, stores &c. Got rooms for self & Lieut TOWNSEND in Chateau de Montgeon, with a dining room in the farm for a mess. Influenza amongst horses of Remounts & also at docks..	
10th October.	Made up fences where necessary. Put up mangers. Put up troughs in farmyard to be filled from tap in yard. Arranged place for pharmacy. Put picket lines on the rides in the wood. Admitted 223 horses from Remounts, mostly catarrh with some few cases of influenza which were put in the wood. The wood is most excellent for bad cases of this kind. The slope field is very sheltered also & is a capital place for catarrh cases. Visit from ~~CRE~~ D.D. of works & M.O. re sites for buildings, forges, pharmacy, office, dining room, &c.	

O.S.Z.

(9 26 6) W 257—976 100,000 4/12 H W V 79/3298

Army Form C. 2118.

Instructions regarding War Diaries and Intelligence Summaries are contained in F. S. Regs., Part II. and the Staff Manual respectively. Title pages will be prepared in manuscript.

WAR DIARY

or

~~INTELLIGENCE SUMMARY~~

(Erase heading not required.)

Hour, Date, Place	Summary of Events and Information	Remarks and References to Appendices
11th October	Memo from Base Commandant quoting wire from D.V.S. directing me to personally inspect horses of 2nd Signal Squadron & report to him. 3 Truck loads of horses arrived from the front but no station mentioned in the telegram announcing their arrival. The Slope Field very difficult to manage in the way of feeding & watering as the men have the greatest trouble to catch the horses if they are up the hill. Hence the delay in watering. The influenza cases are doing very well in the woods owing to the quiet & shade. Visited Base Commandant who asked my advice re the influenza. Heard a rumour that remounts arriving by sea were to be left on board for the night so I went at once & advised Commandant & advised him to have them disembarked at once in order to avoid the spread of catarrh & other like affections which [illegible] develop so quickly on a stationary ship. He asked where the horses could be sent & [illegible] L'Usine Buildg. Horses disembarked & came up to Remount Camp in the night. O.C. Remounts not having seen the right place at L'Usine Buildg where the water was. Visit from R.E. (works) officer re water supply, requirements &c. Remaining 223 – admitted 215 – destroyed 1 – total 437. O.S.D.	

(9 26 6) W 257—976 100,000 4/12 H W V 79/3298

Instructions regarding War Diaries and Intelligence Summaries are contained in F. S. Regs., Part II. and the Staff Manual respectively. Title pages will be prepared in manuscript.

WAR DIARY
or
INTELLIGENCE SUMMARY

(Erase heading not required.)

Army Form C. 2118.

Hour, Date, Place	Summary of Events and Information	Remarks and References to Appendices
12th October	Inspected 2nd Signal Squadron & found a few cases of catarrh – wired result to D.V.S. & informed Base Commandant. Went in car lent by R.E. (works) officer – a great convenience otherwise the whole morning would have been taken up by this inspection. R.E. officer went round camp noting requirements. Visited Hd Qrs. Memo from Base Commandant to personally inspect horses of Heavy Brigade R.G.A. in No 2 Camp which have influenza amongst horses, & also to inspect with O.C. Remounts the horses issued by him to these batteries. Also to send a senior farrier by train with them when they left for the front – to return afterwards. A farrier attached to Remounts was detailed for this. Visited batteries & advised as to management & disposal of sick – to send all cases to Hospital, prevent healthy horses from sweating at exercise & getting cold, disinfection of nosebags, &c. Their camp is very exposed & the horses are soft in condition. Reported result of inspection &c to Hd Qrs but missed Commandant who came to hospital to see me. Applied for a motor car as so much time is taken up running about that I have no time to see to the hospital. No motor available. Remaining 437 – admitted 41 – total 478. O. S. L.	

(9 26 6) W 257—976 100,000 4/12 H W V 79/3298

Army Form C. 2118.

Instructions regarding War Diaries and Intelligence Summaries are contained in F. S. Regs., Part II. and the Staff Manual respectively. Title pages will be prepared in manuscript.

WAR DIARY
or
~~INTELLIGENCE SUMMARY~~

(*Erase heading not required.*)

Hour, Date, Place	Summary of Events and Information	Remarks and References to Appendices
13th October.	82 horses arrived from heavy batteries – all catarrh. Slope Field very slippery in wet weather – horses & men slide down the hill. in fact the horses can only get down by doing this. It is dangerous for the men leading the horses up the hill to water them, so arranged to bring iron tank to the top to be filled by water cart so that the horses can water themselves. This also saves the congestion at the water troughs – as two hours are taken up in watering. Influenza cases improving rapidly in the wood. The Slope Field is also excellent owing to it being so sheltered by trees & by the slope away from wind. Visited shed at Quai de Pondichéry with M.L.O. & arranged to disinfect it tomorrow. Also arranged place in telephone shed there for a dressing station. Visited Hangar du Croton & arranged disinfection of part occupied by horses. Went to Conference of Base Commandant & asked for more water troughs & an office for A.D.V.S.; pointed out the exposed condition of No 2 Camp for mounted units but am told they will only be there one night. Arranged building for Base Veterinary Stores. Remaining 478 – admitted 105 – discharged 37 – died 3 – destroyed 1 – total 542 O.S.L.	

(9 26 6) W 257—976 100,000 4/12 H W V 79/3298

Instructions regarding War Diaries and Intelligence Summaries are contained in F. S. Regs., Part II. and the Staff Manual respectively. Title pages will be prepared in manuscript.

WAR DIARY
or
~~INTELLIGENCE SUMMARY~~
(Erase heading not required.)

Army Form C. 2118.

Hour, Date, Place	Summary of Events and Information	Remarks and References to Appendices
14th October	Wire from A.D.V.S. 33rd Division notifying 37 sick + 18 sick horses sent from Abbeville at 20.40 yesterday; also indenting for medicines - forwarded latter to O/c B.V. Stores. Horses sent to Rouen but diverted to HAVRE. Visited Hangar du Coton which has not yet been disinfected, also Quai de Pondicherie which is done. Dressing station put there today - 1 N.C.O. + 2 men - no officer available. Visited H.Q. L. of C. where it is desired to keep horses arriving by boat on board till morning. I pointed out the folly of this + advised that they be disembarked at once, explaining the rapid development of respiratory diseases on a stationary ship, then then left leaving them to decide. Visit from R.E. officer re troughs &c. Remaining 542 - admitted 1 - died 1 - destroyed 1 - total 541	

O.S.R.

(9 26 6) W 257—976 100,000 4/12 H W V 79/3298

Army Form C. 2118.

Instructions regarding War Diaries and Intelligence Summaries are contained in F. S. Regs., Part II. and the Staff Manual respectively. Title pages will be prepared in manuscript.

WAR DIARY
or
~~INTELLIGENCE SUMMARY.~~
(Erase heading not required.)

Hour, Date, Place	Summary of Events and Information	Remarks and references to Appendices
15th October.	Visited by D.D. of Works who arranged plans for buildings &c. New site for stables chosen – outside the farm in the warm sheltered corner south of the large paddock & east of the slope field. This is a much better arrangement as it allows the large paddock to be kept as a paddock. Surprise visit by Lt Col. Larnder D.D. Remounts War Office, who is on his way to see D.V.S. Showed him round & gave information of requirement of a Section on mobilization such as a motor ambulance, a pump & one or two canvas troughs & remarked that each officer (R.O.T.) sent out should be accompanied by a servant, because if he joined a hospital temporarily that hospital gave him a servant & when he left for another unit & took his servant the hospital lost a man, & consequently when many officers passed through it was a great drain on the establishment of a section. It is also necessary for the officer to have a servant. 27 horses arrived by train from ABBEVILLE. Remaining 541 – admitted 69 – discharged 8 – died 2 – total 600 O. S. R.	

(9 26 6) W 257—976 100,000 4/12 H W V 79/3298

Army Form C. 2118.

Instructions regarding War Diaries and Intelligence Summaries are contained in F. S. Regs., Part II. and the Staff Manual respectively. Title pages will be prepared in manuscript.

WAR DIARY
or
INTELLIGENCE SUMMARY.
(Erase heading not required.)

Hour, Date, Place	Summary of Events and Information	Remarks and references to Appendices
16th Oct	Visited Hd Qrs & inquired when telephone would be put in. Went to Remount Shed at Hangar du Coton. Visit by Sanitary Officer who says our camp will give him [illegible]. Another visit to Hd Qrs re horse rugs. Ordnance will not supply without authority. Missed seeing C.O. Met Col. Larder. Remaining 600 – admitted 68 – discharged 11 – died 2 Total 655 O.L.J.	

Instructions regarding War Diaries and Intelligence Summaries are contained in F. S. Regs., Part II. and the Staff Manual respectively. Title pages will be prepared in manuscript.

WAR DIARY

or

~~INTELLIGENCE~~ SUMMARY

(Erase heading not required.)

Army Form C. 2118.

Hour, Date, Place	Summary of Events and Information	Remarks and References to Appendices
17th October.	Went to Ordnance Depot to try to get horse rugs as we are very short of them. None obtainable. Asked for 1500. Reported to Commandant that there was no more influenza. Lieuts Little & Lowe (SR) reported for duty. About 8 P.M. the horses in the large paddock stampeded ~~[illegible]~~ & They galloped into the farmyard & orchard having crashed through the gate into the orchard, the guard being knocked out. They galloped towards the main gate but the guard turned out very quickly & fortunately had Sergt. Peacock's hurricane lamp, so having closed the gate they held up the lamp & stopped the horses there. The horses turned back & galloped round the orchard as hard as they could go, & it being pitch dark it was very dangerous to get in their way. Nothing but a lamp would stop them. One horse came over the bank out of the paddock & another broke its leg - probably against a tree - ~~the~~ he was destroyed by an intravenous injection of strychnine it being too risky to shoot him. Eventually quieted them down & got them back to the paddock. At 4 o'clock they started again, but we had barricaded the gate with the float. About 9.35 a drunken civilian was arrested outside the gate - he may have caused the stampede but difficult to say. The horses were very restless all night. Remaining 655 - admitted 38 - died 4 - total 689.	

O. S. F.

(9 26 6) W 257—976 100,000 1/12 H W V 79/3298

WAR DIARY
or
~~INTELLIGENCE SUMMARY~~
(Erase heading not required.)

Instructions regarding War Diaries and Intelligence Summaries are contained in F. S. Regs., Part II. and the Staff Manual respectively. Title pages will be prepared in manuscript.

Army Form C. 2118.

Hour, Date, Place	Summary of Events and Information	Remarks and References to Appendices
18th October.	Visited DC. Remounts & advised as to disembarking horses at once. Sent arrested man to Commissaire de Police under escort. The whole of the picket lines in the large paddock flattened out by the stampeded horses also the fence between the two paddocks. Repaired fences & put up white rags on the wire so that the horses see it at night. Repaired the gates. Although the stampeding horses went through the surgical paddock the horses on the lines there were still tied up & did not get loose. There were very few injuries & these were very slight. The numerous [?] cats in the wood stampeded the horses, as every time the cats made a noise the horses became excited again. It is very fortunate having the farmyard between the horses & the outside country otherwise we should not have seen them again. Posted Lieut LITTLE to the Dressing Station at the docks. The horseboxes are too small for Shire horses especially after wet weather. Telephone put in but on a switch at Remount Depot – however it is a start.	
	13 horses arrived by train from the front.	
	Remaining ~~[illegible]~~ 689 – admitted 13 – discharged 12 – died 1 – destroyed 1	
	~~Total 690~~	
	total 690	
	O.V.F.	

(9 26 6) W 257—976 100,000 4/12 H W V 79/3298

Instructions regarding War Diaries and Intelligence Summaries are contained in F. S. Regs., Part II. and the Staff Manual respectively. Title pages will be prepared in manuscript.

WAR DIARY

or

~~INTELLIGENCE SUMMARY~~

(Erase heading not required.)

Army Form C. 2118.

Hour, Date, Place	Summary of Events and Information	Remarks and References to Appendices
19th October.	Went to C.O.O. & asked for permission to buy rope for picket lines wanted. Ordered 2000 metres. Also 6 hurricane lamps very necessary for the guards at night. Getting rather too many horses in now, & have very few men. Asked for reinforcements to be sent - but they are 4 miles away. Asked H.Q.R.E. if water supply could be hurried up as one 1 inch pipe has to water 800 horses. The water cart is going all day filling the troughs in the Slope field & Surgical paddock. The horses in the large paddock having to be led to water which takes a long time. Put some horses on a picket line south of large paddock. The feeding is becoming very difficult on account of the time taken in watering & the small number of men here. Put up some canvas troughs. Wire from D.V.S. to warn Lieut LITTLE to be ready to proceed to front. Wire from D.A.G. Base asking for name, number & unit of all regimental farriers & shoeing smiths - Complied. One consignment of sick horses unable to be got up from station as the railway authorities had shunted the train away from siding - also they had no headstall on. 181 horses arrived by train from the front. Remaining 690 - admitted 167 - discharged 8 - died 3. destroyed 2 - total 844 O.S.P.	

(9 26 6) W 257—976 100,000 4/12 H W V 79/3298

Instructions regarding War Diaries and Intelligence Summaries are contained in F. S. Regs., Part II, and the Staff Manual respectively. Title pages will be prepared in manuscript.

WAR DIARY

or

~~INTELLIGENCE SUMMARY~~

(*Erase heading not required.*)

Army Form C. 2118.

Hour, Date, Place	Summary of Events and Information	Remarks and References to Appendices
20th ~~Sept~~ October	Put 42 troughs in large paddock – a great help – lots of hose put together by saddler brings water from the tap. Lost 13 horses during the night but got them back later. Received wooden picketing posts from R.E. Watering & feeding exceedingly difficult to manage properly. Made detailed list of establishment showing number of men working with the horses – only 70 to [illegible] horses. Asked Base Commandant for reinforcements. He promised them & also 30 convalescent men to do light duty. He also communicated with R.E. Wire from D.V.S. posting Lieut Smith to this hospital. Wired D.V.S. for permission to buy operating aprons – reply yes. Saw Col. LARADER & asked him about Sergt Vane transferring to A.V.C. Saw Capt WADLEY, and D.D.V.S. Visit from Commandant – showed him how all our horses were watered from one tap. He said he did not know how we managed it at all, & promised 50 men from Remount Depot to help. Asked for 50 iron ~~troughs~~ mangers & 10 tanks as canvas troughs & mangers got broken by the loose horses. 71 horses arrived in the night from Hazebrouck, none having been watered or fed since Sunday – 7 dead – 3 were destroyed. 114 horses arrived by train from the front. Remaining 844 – admitted 170 – destroyed 2 – dead 5 total 1007.	

O. V. L.

Instructions regarding War Diaries and Intelligence Summaries are contained in F. S. Regs., Part II. and the Staff Manual respectively. Title pages will be prepared in manuscript.

WAR DIARY
or
~~INTELLIGENCE SUMMARY~~
(*Erase heading not required.*)

Army Form C. 2118.

Hour, Date, Place	Summary of Events and Information	Remarks and References to Appendices
21st October	50 men arrived from Remounts – a great assistance. Division Officer R.E. came re water supply & arranged water to be laid on in Slope Field at once. Went to water works with him & showed manager where to lay it on. D.D. of Works came & enquired into things. Wire from D.V.S. re weekly return of horses discharged to be wired him. Wire from Commandant that B.V. Store had left NANTES night of 19th. Another R.E. Officer came re fences, water &c. Telephoned to Ordnance re tent boards, ropes, &c. Rope we bought arrived from the shop. Wired detail of strength to D.V.S. & pointed out that 70 men looked after 1006 horses. Also wired ~~him~~ asking ~~of~~ him to give orders that no horses unfit to travel by rail were sent us as several were dead on arrival. Message that 196 horses being sent from YPRES. Wired D.V.S. not to stop sending horses on account of former wire. Commandant came & took me round country & we got more fields down in the valley. 4 tanks, 8 mangers arrived – also 100 yards of hose. 16 cavalry reinforcements, 30 convalescent men & 7 more for police arrived bringing tent. 14 horses arrived by train from the front.	
	Remaining 1007 – admitted 51 – discharged 19 – died 8 – total 1031	
	O. S[?].	

(9 26 6) W 257—976 100,000 4/12 H W V 79/3298

Instructions regarding War Diaries and Intelligence Summaries are contained in F. S. Regs., Part II. and the Staff Manual respectively. Title pages will be prepared in manuscript.

WAR DIARY
or
~~INTELLIGENCE SUMMARY~~
(Erase heading not required.)

Army Form C. 2118.

Hour, Date, Place	Summary of Events and Information	Remarks and References to Appendices
22nd October.	100 men & some officers arrived for Cavalry details. Officers are rather a nuisance unless I am there myself as my N.C.Os cannot very well give them an order. Asked Commandant that no officers be sent. Feeding goes on well now — watering much better — there is still only the 1 tap, but up mangers in Slope Field & tanks in Large Paddock. Water laid on this day by R.E. in Slope Field — a tremendous help. The 100 yards of hose is doing good work in Large Paddock. Divisional Officer R.E. promised 300 yards more for use in surgical paddock & woods. Great difficulty in getting messages through on the telephone as we still go through Remount. Wired D.V.S. asking for instructions re 3 year old gelding — with a view to casting or sending this horse. Arranged with D.A.D.R.T. that horses arriving for us by train ~~are~~ to be detrained by N.C.O. i/c Dressing Station & fetched, watered & left by him till we fetch them. This will save our men many journeys to & from HAVRE — a party went down at 6 this morning & the horses were unable to be detrained till evening — great waste of time & men — especially as we are ~~[illegible]~~ so short. Watered & fed in good time all today. A.A. & Q.M.G. telephoned asking opinion on outbreak of influenza which occurred on 8th. 197 horses arrived from the front by train: of these 11 were dead. Remaining 1031 — admitted 197 — dead 13 — destroyed 1 — total 1214	

O.R.D.

(9 26 6) W 257—976 100,000 4/12 H W V 79/3298

Instructions regarding War Diaries and Intelligence Summaries are contained in F. S. Regs., Part II. and the Staff Manual respectively. Title pages will be prepared in manuscript.

WAR DIARY
or
~~INTELLIGENCE SUMMARY~~
(Erase heading not required.)

Army Form C. 2118.

Hour, Date, Place	Summary of Events and Information	Remarks and References to Appendices
23rd October	Troughs put up in Slope Field - a great saving of time. An enormous tank brought there also. This field can now be easily managed by a few men. Another large tank came for [illegible] paddock. Of 196 horses sent from Boulogne on 20th 11 died in the train & others fell down exhausted when brought up here. Wired to D.V.S. that insufficient rations for men & horses were put on these trains. Men report that they sometimes get 1½ days' rations & at others no rations on departure from railhead. Wired D.V.S. to ask when extra personnel might be expected from England. Men from Remounts did not turn up after breakfast so we did not finish watering till 2 P.M. They came in afternoon after 4 P.M. Officer in command of them very angry because he saw our men having tea when he fell out at 5.45. These were men working in other paddocks & who had been working hard all day. Visit by Base Commandant to see progress. Details of mounted units ordered to join Base Details tonight so we lose 40 men. Some of these are men from the front who came with sick horses.	
	111 horses arrived by train from the front - 1 dead in train.	
	Remaining 1214 - admitted 110 - discharged 7 - destroyed 1	
	died 1 - total 1315.	
	O. S. T.	

(9 26 6) W 257—976 100,000 4/12 H W V 79/3298

Army Form C. 2118.

Instructions regarding War Diaries and Intelligence Summaries are contained in F. S. Regs., Part II. and the Staff Manual respectively. Title pages will be prepared in manuscript.

WAR DIARY
or
INTELLIGENCE SUMMARY
(Erase heading not required.)

Hour, Date, Place	Summary of Events and Information	Remarks and References to Appendices
24th October.	~~Rode~~ Went round new field which has good grazing. Put up some mangers in large paddock. Water being laid on with proper pipes. Water difficulties still much in evidence & one tap continues to supply water for the whole of the horses. Visit by D of Works, I.G.C. & other R.E. officers. Broken brick brought in to put down round water troughs. Wire from D.V.S. asking if I could spare Lieut. TOWNSEND for 5th D.G. as he could not be recommended for a commission till after serving with a field unit. Replied would do anything for his advantage but must have one permanent, reliable & able officer here; asked for Lieut. DAVIS, S.R. Reply that latter ~~he~~ had been ordered to join & would relieve Lieut TOWNSEND. Difficulty in getting dead horses removed quick enough - am going to have a large pit dug. Wire from D.V.S. to send 3 year olds to Remount for shipment to England.	
Visited Hd Qrs & B.V. Stores at Folies Bergeres. →	9 horses arrived by train from the front.	
	Remaining 1315 - admitted 7 - discharged 11 - died 4 - destroyed 2 - total 1307.	
	O.S.J.	

(9 26 6) W 257—976 100,000 4/12 H W V 79/3298

Instructions regarding War Diaries and Intelligence Summaries are contained in F. S. Regs., Part II. and the Staff Manual respectively. Title pages will be prepared in manuscript.

WAR DIARY

or

~~INTELLIGENCE SUMMARY~~

(Erase heading not required.)

Army Form C. 2118.

Hour, Date, Place	Summary of Events and Information	Remarks and References to Appendices
25th October.	Rode round newly acquired fields: cattle still in them but expect to put horses in tomorrow. Lines in wood looking well in fact things are just beginning & show little improvement in general. There are still water difficulties but with the men for cavalry details the horses do get watered & fed properly. More mangers put up in large paddock. Some officers who have come out of Some Rest camps for horses on L of C, arrived & asked for "tips about horses". They wanted to know how they were watered & how one could tell whether a horse was dead or not. This looks promising for the Rest Camps. Still a lot of sorting out among the horses. Made up another troop & put them under Sergt. Rogers. 45 horses by train from the front. Remaining 1307 – admitted 45 – discharged 37 – destroyed 6 died, 9 – total <u>1298</u>. O.S.D.	

Instructions regarding War Diaries and Intelligence Summaries are contained in F. S. Regs., Part II. and the Staff Manual respectively. Title pages will be prepared in manuscript.

WAR DIARY
or
~~INTELLIGENCE SUMMARY.~~
(Erase heading not required.)

Army Form C. 2118.

Hour, Date, Place	Summary of Events and Information	Remarks and references to Appendices
26th. October	Sent 35 horses out to No 1 Farm. Rode round there fence with R.E. Officer to arrange fencing &c, made passage to river in No 2 Farm. Went to Dressing Station to see horses there. These were a very poor lot, all from the front. Some arrived (50) with no men to look after them. Reported by wire to D.V.S. Inspected a field with a view to putting horses in it from the train. Met Base Commandant & informed him about horses being left at Dressing Station till well enough to come up to hospital & explained that our people were not always informed when horses arrived by train. Later visited headquarters & asked for L'Hoiny [?] Bundy for grazing purposes. Granted & applied for. Wire from D.V.S. asking if I could send any horses to Convalescent Depot at GOURNAY, & to get grazing locally if possible. Wire from D.V.S. to indent for 1000 horse rugs — replied that I had already asked for 1700 & would later require 2000.	
	142 horses from the front by train.	
	Remaining 1298 — admitted 142 — discharged 3 — died 4 — destroyed 2 — total 1431.	
	B. S. J.	

(9 26 6) W 257—976 100,000 4/12 H W V 79/3298

Instructions regarding War Diaries and Intelligence Summaries are contained in F. S. Regs., Part II. and the Staff Manual respectively. Title pages will be prepared in manuscript.

WAR DIARY
or
~~INTELLIGENCE~~ SUMMARY
(*Erase heading not required.*)

Army Form C. 2118.

Hour, Date, Place	Summary of Events and Information	Remarks and References to Appendices
27th October.	Rode out to No 1 Farm where horses appear to be doing well. Lieut. DAVIS & 3 men arrived for St NAZAIRE. Rode to No 2 Camp at request of Commandant, & saw horses of Cavalry reinforcements. Advised them removed to more sheltered site, their being given rugs, & their being given long slow work to get them fit & to avoid overeating. Did not advise them to form any sick lines as slight cases would be just as easily treated in their own lines. Sent 5 cases to hospital. Reported all these things to Commandant. Water laid on in large paddock, & more mangers put in. Lieut TOWNSEND left for 5th Dragoon Guards. Lieut. DAVIS took over his duties. Truck of horses found in station by Sergt. Bean with no one in charge. He unloaded them & took them away. Had some prisoners up to dig a pit to bury dead horses in but it will be a long job. Visit by Commandant who wants a field to be taken near station to put horses in which are to come to come to camp. Showed me a site on the map. Went to C.O.O. ~~for~~ to ask for horse rugs which have arrived from England. Wired D.V.S. that no horses fit for GOURNAY as they would not stand the journey, & that I had grazing here including Lazaret Brandy. D.V.S. ~~[illegible]~~ wires to mallein all horses sent to Remounts & those cast for sale. 14 horses by train from the front. Remaining 1431 – admitted 19 – died 5 – destroyed 2 total 1443:	
	A.J.D.	

(9 26 6) W 257—976 100,000 4/12 H W V 79/3298

Instructions regarding War Diaries and Intelligence Summaries are contained in F. S. Regs., Part II. and the Staff Manual respectively. Title pages will be prepared in manuscript.

WAR DIARY
or
INTELLIGENCE SUMMARY.
(Erase heading not required.)

Army Form C. 2118.

Hour, Date, Place	Summary of Events and Information	Remarks and references to Appendices
28th October.	Rode round Farm ~~[illegible]~~ Horses appear to be doing well. Did some sorting out – some debility horses others for discharge – to be mallined. Cast 1 horse as unfit for further service. Sent 50 debility cases to No 2 & 19 to No 1 Farm. Later on Station where there are 13 cases too bad to be brought up here. Visited field mentioned by Commandant – not a good one but the one south of it is good & could be used for horses from the trains. Informed Commandant of this but also told him that HARFLEUR was a better place to detain horses for this hospital if it could be managed. This will probably be arranged. Complaint by M.O. about dead horses lying in road at bottom of the hill. This is unfortunately the case as the knacker cannot get enough carts to remove them. Arranged for him to get some from T.O. Our pit is not yet finished & will probably be some time. New order that horses from V. Hospitals are not to be sold when inefficient. This makes things twice as difficult in disposing of carcases. Officer from Horse Rest Camp here again today asking stupid questions. Home rugs arrived. more mangers also. Remaining 1443 – admitted 29 – died 4 – destroyed 1 Total 1467. [signature]	

(9 26 6) W 257—976 100,000 4/12 H W V 79/3298

Instructions regarding War Diaries and Intelligence Summaries are contained in F. S. Regs., Part II. and the Staff Manual respectively. Title pages will be prepared in manuscript.

WAR DIARY
or
~~INTELLIGENCE SUMMARY.~~
(Erase heading not required.)

Army Form C. 2118.

Hour, Date, Place	Summary of Events and Information	Remarks and references to Appendices
29th October	Rode round farms. Horses appear to be doing well. Shortly afterwards the horses of No 2 Farm stampeded & broke out through the wire fence, but were caught by some infantry & put in the Lost Chaud Farm where we recovered them. A detachment of French cavalry sounded a trumpet & this is ~~supposed~~ said by the men to have excited the horses & made them break loose. Horses also got out of the Slope Field. They are mostly cart horses, & they can walk through barbed wire as if it were a silken thread. R.E. men working near this field made gaps in the fence when crossing the field. Reported it to O.C. detachment. Horse rugs arrived at last (1750), issued them out. [illegible] paddock is foot deep in mud so removed all the 300 horses from it to new lines in the wood. Large paddock is also in a filthy state — one's boots being nearly sucked off on walking through it. Dead horses not yet removed as contractor says he can get no carts. Pit not yet finished. Lieut. WOODS (S.R.) & 44 farriers arrived from England. Memo from D.V.S. that 16 men would join us shortly for 1 Section, as they were due to us from the last draft, & no others would be obtainable except reinforcements & Class B [illegible]. Rode into HARFLEUR to look for field for horses arriving by train. Remaining 1467 — admitted 2 — died 4 — discharged 21 total 1444. O.S.[illegible]	

Instructions regarding War Diaries and Intelligence Summaries are contained in F. S. Regs., Part II. and the Staff Manual respectively. Title pages will be prepared in manuscript.

WAR DIARY

or

~~INTELLIGENCE SUMMARY.~~

(Erase heading not required.)

Army Form C. 2118.

Hour, Date, Place	Summary of Events and Information	Remarks and references to Appendices
30th October.	Rode round farms 1 & 2 where horses are doing well. Fields ~~[illegible]~~ will in future be known as follows ~~[illegible]~~ – The Slope Field No 1, Large field No 2. Surgical Paddock No 3, Wood No 4. New paddock by bottom gate of Chateau No 5, No 2 Farm 6. No 1 Farm 7. Two more mangers & water troughs arrived. Put up water troughs in Wood. Large number of dead horses removed, hope to get the remaining 6 away tomorrow. Wire from DVS to send roll of horses cast for veterinary reasons to him by wire & confirm by despatch, & that instructions re cast horses were being issued. Visit by I.G.C., Base Commandant, D of Works & staff. Showed them round & asked for boots for men – boots like those worn by gunners at practice camp – as the going is so wet & muddy that the men's feet are never dry. I.G.C considers this camp too exposed for horses in winter. Remaining 1444 discharged 35 – died 9 – destroyed 2 – total 1398. O.K.L.	

(9 26 6) W 257—976 100,000 4/12 H W V 79/3298

Army Form C. 2118.

Instructions regarding War Diaries and Intelligence Summaries are contained in F. S. Regs., Part II. and the Staff Manual respectively. Title pages will be prepared in manuscript.

WAR DIARY
or
~~INTELLIGENCE SUMMARY.~~

(Erase heading not required.)

Hour, Date, Place	Summary of Events and Information	Remarks and references to Appendices
31st October	Visited 6 & 7 paddocks where horses seem to be doing very well & some rapidly getting fat, so I shall be able to change them for others which require grazing. Picked out large number of poor horses for grazing & am badly in need of L'Usine Bunel to put them out to graze. Hope to send some to Convalescent Depot at GOURNAY as soon as they are fit enough for the train journey. Remounts wish to send us another 500 horses - mostly catarrh - but have no room at present, but hope to take some tomorrow. Wire from D.V.S. posting Lieut. WOODS to this hospital. Sent some parties of the 44 shoeing smiths to ROUEN, LE MANS, NANTES & VILLENEUVE. Five remain here. Great scarcity of tents, the Commandant wanting some of them. Put No 1 Troop in Barn. Put section horses in a shed as weather is so cold, they grow long coats very quickly. Want more horses for sections as there is so much riding work, orderlies, transport &c. Wire from D.V.S. asking no. of reinforcements employed & if I could get more & to send list of establishment & grades. Complied saying that I might get reinforcements when available. What we want now is to be properly equipped with fittings, buildings, water, more fields, &c. We are rather handicapped for room clearly. Visited Headquarters but unable to complete business owing to absence of Commandant. Remaining 1398 - discharged 73 - died 7 - total 1318	

O. J.

(9 26 6) W 257—976 100,000 4/12 H W V 79/3298

L. of C. 121/2625

No 2. Veterinary Section.

Vol IV 1–30.11.14

Army Form C. 2118.

Instructions regarding War Diaries and Intelligence Summaries are contained in F. S. Regs., Part II. and the Staff Manual respectively. Title pages will be prepared in manuscript.

WAR DIARY
or
INTELLIGENCE SUMMARY.
(Erase heading not required.)

Hour, Date, Place	Summary of Events and Information	Remarks and references to Appendices
1st November.	Did some sorting out. Gave Lieut. WOODS charge of lame horses & debility cases. Visit by Transport Officer who is sending our forage by motor lorrie instead of by carts. He promised carts for dead horses, but they did not arrive, so we are still behindhand in this way. Building of stables has started. It is said that they will be up by 1st December. These finished & forging in full swing, things will be less difficult. At present we are handicapped for room. Remaining 1318 - admitted 132 - discharged 27 - died 7 - destroyed 1 total 1415.	
2nd November	Visit by A.D.V.S. Base, who informs me that an Indian Veterinary Hospital is being sent here as an annex to this one. Discussed this iniquitous threat of sending a warrant officer over our own senior N.C.O. He agrees with me that it will be a great blow to the A.V.C. & also to the personnel of hospitals. A quartermaster will be a nuisance also & will most likely carry out the duties less efficiently than the N.C.O. already doing the work. I am glad that both he & Col. Butler are much against the proposed measure. Remaining 1415 - admitted 51 - died 13 - total 1453.	

O.S.F.

(9 26 6) W 257—976 100,000 4/12 H W V 79 3298

Instructions regarding War Diaries and Intelligence Summaries are contained in F. S. Regs., Part II. and the Staff Manual respectively. Title pages will be prepared in manuscript.

WAR DIARY
or
~~INTELLIGENCE SUMMARY.~~
(Erase heading not required.)

Army Form C. 2118.

Hour, Date, Place	Summary of Events and Information	Remarks and references to Appendices
3rd November.	Rode round near ROUELLES to look for site for Indian Section. Land in continuation of [illegible] No 5 paddock is suitable although it has a northerly aspect. Am told the prevailing wind in winter & north west, but find the east & south east winds are the coldest. Our camp is most exposed to S & S.E. Commandant wishes them to go on to No 7 field, but it is a pity to waste the grazing there. Visit by A.D.V.S. Base. Arranged to give Capt LITTLE charge of No 1 & 2 Camps as well as the Dressing Station. Visited Headquarters of Leicestershire & [illegible] Yeomanry & arranged with Base Commandant to inspect horses with him at 10 & 11 tomorrow. Wire from D.V.S. to speak to him on telephone. Spoke to D.V.S. on telephone re establishment, & other matters.	
	Remaining 1453 – discharged 33 – died 7 – destroyed 4 – total 1409.	

[illegible]

(9 26 6) W 257—976 100,000 4/12 H W V 79/3298

Army Form C. 2118.

Instructions regarding War Diaries and Intelligence Summaries are contained in F. S. Regs., Part II. and the Staff Manual respectively. Title pages will be prepared in manuscript.

WAR DIARY
or
INTELLIGENCE SUMMARY.
(Erase heading not required.)

Hour, Date, Place	Summary of Events and Information	Remarks and references to Appendices
4th November	Inspected Leicestershire & Lancashire Yeomanry with Base Commandant. Horses in good condition & seemed well cared for. Arranged to provide farrier with 25th chest & wallets. at V.O. with each regt. Lieut RICHARDSON, A.V.C. (T) with former regt. No cavalry reinforcements came as they have all been ordered up to the front, so had to manage by ourselves which is very difficult, especially as 44 men who came with horses for the front have been ordered to join their regiments at once. Arranged to get some gunners (100) as soon as possible. I hear that Horse Rest Camp has 20 men so I shall try to get them. Visited Headquarters. Still a difficulty in getting away dead horses. Remaining 1409 - admitted 62 - discharged 46 - died 4 - destroyed 2 - total 1419. O.S.F.	

Army Form C. 2118.

Instructions regarding War Diaries and Intelligence Summaries are contained in F. S. Regs., Part II. and the Staff Manual respectively. Title pages will be prepared in manuscript.

WAR DIARY
or
INTELLIGENCE SUMMARY.

(Erase heading not required.)

Hour, Date, Place	Summary of Events and Information	Remarks and references to Appendices
5th November	Sent away 43 men who came with horses from the front. Conversed with D.A.D.V.S. on telephone. He informs me the 16 men who belong to us will be here in a day or two. No reinforcement arrived, so all dressing & shoeing stopped in order that horses may be watered & fed properly. Went to L'Usine Baudy where the grazing is most excellent. Arranged to take it over tomorrow. It should take 200 horses easily. Met Lieut. LESSEUR of the French A.V.S., visited Base Commandant & attended a conference.	
	Remaining 1419 – admitted 3 – discharged 30 – destroyed 4 – died 7 – total 1381	
6th November	Inspected horses of 8th Division. No 5 paddock now fitted up with water & mangers. Put 25 horses in it – debility with wounds. Sent 30 horses down to L'Usine Baudy. Grazing there very good & horses enjoyed it. They worked even with the journey down – 2 miles – they are so weak. Corporal [illegible] & 2 men, [illegible] & [illegible] Sergts FORREST & PARRIT reported for duty from England.	
	Remaining 1381 – admitted 30 – died 8 – destroyed 2 total 1401.	

[illegible initials]

(9 26 6) W 257—976 100,000 4/12 H W V 79/3298

Instructions regarding War Diaries and Intelligence Summaries are contained in F. S. Regs., Part II. and the Staff Manual respectively. Title pages will be prepared in manuscript.

WAR DIARY
or
INTELLIGENCE SUMMARY.

(Erase heading not required.)

Army Form C. 2118.

Hour, Date, Place	Summary of Events and Information	Remarks and references to Appendices
7th November	Instructions by telephone last night from D.V.S. re posting of 2 officers & 100 men. Lieut FORREST to FORGES LES EAUX & Lieut PORRIT to ABBEVILLE, each to report to O.C. Veterinary Hospital at their respective places. Men to be divided up amongst 14 mobile sections. I am to get 4 horses per section for them. Arranged this with O.C. Remounts. Each man to have 2 blankets, 1 ground sheet & 1 canvas or other bucket. Officers leave by 10 PM train. Inspected Herts Regt & 4 R. Welch Fus (T) at request of Commdt. Most infantry transport horses very bad in condition but these regts had good horses. Inspected transport horses of Infantry Bde, 8th Division. Many horses sent to hospital. There looks like some chaos when these 100 men [illegible] however no more are available. Major HARRIS here as A.D.V.S. 8th Division. Remaining 1401 — admitted 152 — discharged 36 — destroyed 2 — died 4 — total 1511. [illegible]	

Instructions regarding War Diaries and Intelligence Summaries are contained in F. S. Regs., Part II. and the Staff Manual respectively. Title pages will be prepared in manuscript.

WAR DIARY
or
~~INTELLIGENCE SUMMARY.~~
(Erase heading not required.)

Army Form C. 2118.

Hour, Date, Place	Summary of Events and Information	Remarks and references to Appendices
8th November	Sent 70 horses to L'Usine Bund(?). Capt. WALKER A.V.C. commanding No 15 Mobile Section came to the hospital. Also Lieut GILLARD A.V.C. (T.) who is with R.F.A. Some dead horses removed by contract at 10 francs ~~per~~ horse. Went to No 2 Camp to see Territorial infantry transport but the regiment had gone. Met Commandant who advised me to keep the 100 A.V.C. men but told him of D.V.S. instructions that I should send them up country as soon as equipped. So he is going to send 200 Class B infantry, who will have to receive a certain amount of instruction. Visit by Gen. LANDON who was shown round stables & [illegible] paddock. He had no time to see the wood.	
	Remaining 1511 – admitted 182 – discharged 88 – died 9 – total 1596.	
9th November	9th November. Horses at present doing very well indeed. They pick up rapidly. The grazing at L'Usine Bund(?) is excellent & the horses prefer it to their oats. D of Works & D.O. of Works visited camp. Equipment of men of mobile sections is slow owing to difficulty of getting saddles. Too much competition here now.	
	Remaining 1596 – admitted 102 – died 3 – destroyed 2 – total 1693	
	[illegible initials]	

(9 26 6) W 257—976 100,000 4/12 H W V 79/3298

Instructions regarding War Diaries and Intelligence Summaries are contained in F. S. Regs., Part II. and the Staff Manual respectively. Title pages will be prepared in manuscript.

Army Form C. 2118.

WAR DIARY
or
~~INTELLIGENCE~~ SUMMARY.
(*Erase heading not required.*)

Hour, Date, Place	Summary of Events and Information	Remarks and references to Appendices
10th November	2 officers & 200 men RHA & RFA reinforcements arrived. 16 men AVC arrived from Convalescent Horse Depot & taken on strength of establishment. Talked to DVS on telephone re [illegible] boots for men at Convt Depot, promotions, men, clipping horses, &c. Visit of Base Commandant.	
	Remaining 1693 - admitted 61 - died 6 - total 1748.	
11th November	Lieut C T BRAY reported his arrival for duty. 120 men of RHA sent away early to embark for front. Put up line of wagons under the trees for standing cover. Called up on telephone by DVS who wants an officer for 1st Life Guards, none available here.	
	Remaining 1748 - admitted 2 - died 3 - destroyed 1 - discharged 94 = total 1652.	
12th November	Telephoned to DADVS re officers (8) arriving & other matters. 1 officer & 101 men RFA arrived reinforcements. Found collars & harness left by 6th Division Train very useful. Moved [illegible] to Rendezvous de Chasse chalet in wood. Complaint re dead horses by ADMS - dealt with it. Started [illegible] well - one for 100 horses [illegible] in 5 days time. Capt PORTEOUS & Lieut TRACEY & 70 men arrived by ship at [illegible]. Talked to DVS re telephone re posting of officers.	
	Remaining 1652 - admitted 50 - died 11 - destroyed 2 - total 1689.	
	[illegible signature]	

(9 26 6) W 257—976 100,000 4/12 H W V 79/3298

WAR DIARY
or
~~INTELLIGENCE~~ SUMMARY
(Erase heading not required.)

Instructions regarding War Diaries and Intelligence Summaries are contained in F. S. Regs., Part II. and the Staff Manual respectively. Title pages will be prepared in manuscript.

Army Form C. 2118.

Hour, Date, Place	Summary of Events and Information	Remarks and References to Appendices
17th October.	Communicated with D.V.S. & informed him of arrival of Lieut T. DAVIS A.V.C. & asked for instructions concerning him. Lieut DAVIS now being fit for duty, is ready to go to front. Lieut F. G. M. S. LANE, 4th Hussars, who arrived with party last night to ROUEN, asked Commandant 206 Camp for fatigue party of 100 men daily to dig holes in which to bury dead horses. The price paid by us for removal of dead horses is 10 francs per horse - very expensive but very necessary. Contractor has begun to build a incinerator. Large pit already finished & can be used. Very wet & windy weather. Numerous [illegible] brought for stragglers cases in wood. Advised Base Commandant to have a machine clipper in each Rest Camp for the use of mounted troops on their way to the front. Reported to D.A.Q.M.G. that tent boards had not been received although asked for ever since we came here. Several men [illegible] owing to cold & wet. Unable to get ground sheets for men of mobile section, but blankets, buckets & saddles are ready. Wired D.V.S. that Remounts had no authority yet to issue 56 horses for these men & asked him to arrange with D.R.	
	Remaining 1689 - admitted 51 - died 5 - destroyed 4 - discharged 44 - Total 1687.	
	D. R.	

(9 26 6) W 257—976 100,000 4/12 H W V 79/3298

Instructions regarding War Diaries and Intelligence Summaries are contained in F. S. Regs., Part II. and the Staff Manual respectively. Title pages will be prepared in manuscript.

WAR DIARY
or
~~INTELLIGENCE~~ SUMMARY.
(Erase heading not required.)

Army Form C. 2118.

Hour, Date, Place	Summary of Events and Information	Remarks and references to Appendices
14th November	wire from D.V.S. to send 39 of the draft of 70 men, to Veterinary Hospital ROUEN, & remainder to stay here. Sent 39 to ROUEN. Instructions from D.V.S. to Base Commandant to try & obtain STABLEFORTH of J.G.C.N. for [illegible]. Lieut. GREEN, YOUNG, HUGHES & BOSWE reported arrival here – have been detailed by D.V.S. to ABBEVILLE, 1st Divisional Train, & ABBEVILLE (2) respectively. Telephone message from Remounts that 60 horses have been ready for men of mobile sections. Men ready to go now except that there are no ground sheets to be had for them. They must go without. Contractor who removes dead horses objects to our burying them, so must keep some for him, in case we get behindhand again – he refuses to take them. Hear unofficially that there are 100 men on their way out, so applied for tents for them but none available	
	Remaining 1687 – admitted 18 – died 3 – destroyed 6 – total 1696	
	O. S. L.	

Instructions regarding War Diaries and Intelligence Summaries are contained in F. S. Regs., Part II. and the Staff Manual respectively. Title pages will be prepared in manuscript.

Army Form C. 2118.

WAR DIARY
or
~~INTELLIGENCE SUMMARY~~.
(Erase heading not required.)

Hour, Date, Place	Summary of Events and Information	Remarks and references to Appendices
15th November	Gave D.D.S. list of horses sent in from 5th Division over the telephone – the number was 431 – mostly catarrh & debility. Fitted Lieut YOUNG out with a horse & equipment. Got 100 pairs Canada boots for the men as the ground here is very boggy & wet underfoot – the paddocks being mud a foot deep in mud. Appalling weather. Medical authorities ordered the evacuation of 401 paddock on the slope, & Commandant gave me the order to clear out, before to go into the wood or lines where more water is laid on. Sent return of ages of all cases of catarrh & strangles to DDVS for information of War Office. <u>Strangles</u> 3 years 1, 4 years [illegible], 5 years 93, 6 years 65, 7 years 24, aged 27 – total 225. <u>Catarrh</u> 3 years 2, 4 years 9, 5 years 21, 6 years 47, 7 years 101, aged 300 – total 480.	
	Remaining 1696 – admitted 19 – died 3 – destroyed 1 – total 1711.	
	O. S. F.	

(9 26 6) W 257--976 100,000 4/12 H W V 79/3298

Army Form C. 2118.

Instructions regarding War Diaries and Intelligence Summaries are contained in F. S. Regs., Part II. and the Staff Manual respectively. Title pages will be prepared in manuscript.

WAR DIARY
or
INTELLIGENCE SUMMARY.

(Erase heading not required.)

Hour, Date, Place	Summary of Events and Information	Remarks and references to Appendices
16th November	Drew 95 horses from Remounts, fitted saddles & sent parties off to Railway Station. Lieut Tracey in command of party. He had instructions in writing to take charge of them up to Pailham. O.C. party for each section had orders in writing as to the formations they were to join. Here there was much confusion at the station in spite of all being carefully detailed to their various sections. Put up more lines in the wood to accommodate horses from the paddocks, but it only got to have owing to stiffening state of ground & the consequent difficulty in collecting the horses. Issued Canada boots to some of the men. Weather very cold & wet. The horses at L'Oeuvre Bridge are doing very well [illegible] a large number of them would never have got right had it not been for the grazing at this place. Visited headquarters to see about room for the men. Remaining 1711 – admitted 45 – died 6 – destroyed 2 – discharged 68 total 1680.	

(9 26 6) W 257--976 100,000 4/12 H W V 79/3298

Instructions regarding War Diaries and Intelligence Summaries are contained in F. S. Regs., Part II. and the Staff Manual respectively. Title pages will be prepared in manuscript.

WAR DIARY
or
~~INTELLIGENCE~~ SUMMARY.
(Erase heading not required.)

Army Form C. 2118.

Hour, Date, Place	Summary of Events and Information	Remarks and references to Appendices
17th November	Lieut. Stableforth arrived for temporary duty till the promulgation of his court-martial. Went over 7 & 8 paddocks & selected some horses for [illegible], [illegible] old & not worth it. A report to DADRT [illegible] that party sent off yesterday had no orders & the officer [illegible] nothing. Replied in detail, contradicting the statements & commenting upon attitude of the young officer. Each party and its own orders clearly laid down & officer had a nominal roll with him as well as written orders. Remaining 1680 – died 5 – destroyed 3 – total 1672.	
18th November	6 Hand carts arrived for forage to various paddocks. Moved horses from 2 paddocks into 3 paddocks owing to boggy state of the ground, before I put them in the wood tomorrow as soon as more space is available. 50 RFA details left for 103 Camp [illegible]. Lieuts. BARR & MAYNARD & [illegible] LOANE, COOKE, ARMSTRONG, ALDERSON, WOOD, FLOOD, IVES, WILLIAMS, HILDYARD & BORAN, 4 farriers & 150 men arrived. Sent all officers to town for the night as there is no room here, pending instructions from DVS. 1 man of 9th [illegible] returned [illegible] instructions from DVS on telephone [illegible] Remaining 1672 – admitted 35 – died 2 – destroyed 1 – discharged 78 – total 1634	

O. I. J.

Instructions regarding War Diaries and Intelligence Summaries are contained in F. S. Regs., Part II. and the Staff Manual respectively. Title pages will be prepared in manuscript.

WAR DIARY
or
~~INTELLIGENCE SUMMARY~~.
(Erase heading not required.)

Army Form C. 2118.

Hour, Date, Place	Summary of Events and Information	Remarks and references to Appendices
19th November.	[illegible] parties of the [illegible] mobile sections [illegible] 5 to each section. [illegible] reported here for duty [illegible] from DVS [illegible] convalescent [illegible] hospital [illegible] reinforcements [illegible] about 230 for the [illegible] horses [illegible] the ground in a good order [illegible] the wood except [illegible] which is still on the [illegible] from ADVS [illegible] that he would visit tomorrow.	
	Remaining 1634 – destroyed 2 – discharged 21 – total 1611.	
20th Nov.	[illegible] DVS [illegible] to Remove [illegible] at G.H.Q. [illegible] report to DDVS. [illegible] left at [illegible] ADVS [illegible] hospital. [illegible] manager of YMCA who is setting up a [illegible] of that institution here.	
	Remaining 1611 – admitted 99 – died 7 – destroyed 4 – discharged 45 – total 1658.	
		O. S. L.

Instructions regarding War Diaries and Intelligence Summaries are contained in F. S. Regs., Part II. and the Staff Manual respectively. Title pages will be prepared in manuscript.

WAR DIARY
or
INTELLIGENCE SUMMARY.

(*Erase heading not required.*)

Army Form C. 2118.

Hour, Date, Place	Summary of Events and Information	Remarks and references to Appendices
21st November.	[illegible]	
	Remaining 1658 - admitted 21 - died 5 - destroyed 2 - discharged 2 - total 1660.	
22nd November.	22nd November	
	[illegible]	
	Remaining 1660 - admitted 97 - died 5 - destroyed 1 - discharged 21 total 1730	

(9 26 6) W 257—976 100,000 4/12 H W V 79/3298

Instructions regarding War Diaries and Intelligence Summaries are contained in F. S. Regs., Part II. and the Staff Manual respectively. Title pages will be prepared in manuscript.

WAR DIARY
or
~~INTELLIGENCE SUMMARY.~~

(Erase heading not required.)

Army Form C. 2118.

Hour, Date, Place	Summary of Events and Information	Remarks and references to Appendices
23rd November.	Canteen [illegible] good profits. List of promotions received from D.V.S. [illegible] not in accordance with my 2nd list [illegible] will be dealt with later. Table of new establishment received from D.V.S. [illegible]	
	Remaining 1730 - admitted 5 - died 5 - destroyed 1 - total 1729.	
24th November.	A.D.V.S. visited Remount Depot. 153 R.F.A. details arrived.	
	Remaining 1729 - admitted 43 - died 9 - destroyed 3 discharged 94 - total 1666.	
25th November.	Occupied 2 of the new stables - 30 horses. Notice of 200 men [illegible] MULLANE embarking today. Arranged to put them up in No 6 camp [illegible] which have been notified [illegible] D.V.S. 400 [illegible]	
	Remaining 1666 - admitted 80 - died 5 - destroyed 5 - total 1736	
26th November.	[illegible] MULLANE & draft of 200 men arrived - put up in No 6 camp [illegible] tents [illegible]	
	Remaining 1736 - admitted 25 - died 4 - destroyed 1 - total 1756.	

[illegible initials]

Army Form C. 2118.

Instructions regarding War Diaries and Intelligence Summaries are contained in F. S. Regs., Part II. and the Staff Manual respectively. Title pages will be prepared in manuscript.

WAR DIARY
or
INTELLIGENCE SUMMARY.
(*Erase heading not required.*)

Hour, Date, Place	Summary of Events and Information	Remarks and references to Appendices
27th November.	Remaining 1756 – admitted 45 – died 5 – discharged 21 – total 1775.	
28th November	Wire from DVS to send 500 horses to Convalescent Horse Depot & take over sick from Remount Depot. Informed Base Commandant & repeated wire. There are not 500 horses suitable for Convalescent Depot here as all ours have stomach or wounds. [illegible] left the 200 at No 4 & 7 paddocks [illegible] Road. Visited Base Commandant about fresh ground for more horses. Remaining 1775 – admitted 35 – died 5 – discharged 37 – total 1772.	
29th November	Visit of DVS & ADVS. He stayed for the day & went round the whole place. DVS arranged for me to send 200 to Convalescent Horse Depot, 250 to the [illegible] at FORGES LES EAUX & 200 [illegible] to ROUEN. This will relieve the congestion. Saw Base Commandant & arranged to take over brick shed & stables near [illegible] for about 250 horses. Asked A.P.M. for 30 men for [illegible] work. Remaining 1772 – admitted 66 – died 5 – discharged 45 – total 1788 [illegible]	

(9 26 6) W 257—976 100,000 4/12 H W V 79/3298

Instructions regarding War Diaries and Intelligence Summaries are contained in F. S. Regs., Part II. and the Staff Manual respectively. Title pages will be prepared in manuscript.

WAR DIARY

or

~~INTELLIGENCE SUMMARY.~~

(Erase heading not required.)

Army Form C. 2118.

Hour, Date, Place	Summary of Events and Information	Remarks and references to Appendices
30th November	Went with Requisition Officer to MONTEVILLIER to look for place for horses, as the brickworks chosen by D.V.S. has already been taken for Base Horse Transport. The corn exchange & a stable near it look like holding 500 or more horses. Arranged to send 248 horses, 1 officer & 77 other ranks to Veterinary Hospital at FORGES LES EAUX tomorrow at 10.15 A.M. Asked for 100 more reinforcements to replace our own men sent with these horses, as reinforcements are not allowed to go with horses by train.	
	Remaining 1788 - died 4 - discharged 1 - total 1783.	
	[initials]	

L. of C. 121/3872

No 2. Veterinary Section.

Vol V. 1–31. 12. 14.

Army Form C. 2118.

Instructions regarding War Diaries and Intelligence Summaries are contained in F. S. Regs., Part II. and the Staff Manual respectively. Title pages will be prepared in manuscript.

WAR DIARY
or
~~INTELLIGENCE~~ SUMMARY.

(Erase heading not required.)

Hour, Date, Place	Summary of Events and Information	Remarks and references to Appendices
1st December	Sent off 257 horses by 10.15 a.m. train to FORGES LES EAUX & 148 by 1 P.M. train to Convalescent Horse Depot, & 510 by 4 P.M. train to ROUEN. Much confusion & disorganization occurred in camp owing to the shortage of men as the 100 reinforcements promised did not turn up. One horse of the last party was abandoned on the road, having fallen down though all looked fit enough when they left here.	
	This unit is temporarily short of 2 officers, Lieut [illegible] & WOODS, 3 senior N.C.O.s & men all A.V.C. The care of the remaining horses is now carried out chiefly by R.F.A. Great difficulty in watering & feeding horses as the men who took the horses to the station did not return till late in the afternoon except the 1st party which returned at midday.	
	Took Lieut STABLEFORD down to Headquarters to hear sentence of his C.M. – "dismissed from His Majesty's Service". I afterwards took him down to the Southampton boat & put him on board. 10 P.M.	
	Remaining 1783 – admitted 25 – died 9 – transferred 717 – total 1082	
	[initials]	

(9 26 6) W 257—976 100,000 4/12 H W V 79/3298

Instructions regarding War Diaries and Intelligence Summaries are contained in F. S. Regs., Part II. and the Staff Manual respectively. Title pages will be prepared in manuscript.

WAR DIARY
or
~~INTELLIGENCE SUMMARY~~.
(Erase heading not required.)

Army Form C. 2118.

Hour, Date, Place	Summary of Events and Information	Remarks and references to Appendices
2nd December.	All the lines are in a filthy & boggy condition, men & horses stand in mud all day. It is no use keeping horses on lines in the winter as ~~they~~ ground always becomes impossible. Told this to Base Commandant who agrees with me. Looked at a brick ~~[illegible]~~ yard but sheds too low. nothing to be had in the way of buildings at all in HAVRE. Inspected horses of Essex Yeomanry some of which are rather herring-gutted. Lieut HOSKINS & 102 men arrived suddenly without any notice of their ever having left England. Wired D.V.S. for instructions. As expected, none are for this hospital. A lot of inconvenience is caused by these drafts arriving as we have no tents for them & have to make out nominal rolls, orders, arrangements for them as well as fit them out with blankets & ground sheets. Also getting them away by train is a trying business as they lose themselves or their transport on the way to the station. We supply guides for them & draw rations at the station for them. Visit by Base Commandant who informed me of men selling their kits & asked me to warn mine. Lieuts. HARDING, ELLISON & BARRY arrived without warning. 1 officer & 100 men, reinforcements arrived at 6 P.M. having been promised yesterday morning - not wanted now, so handed over to Remounts. Remaining 1082 - admitted 47 - died 9 - destroyed 3 - total 1117.	

(9 26 6) W 257—976 100,000 4/12 H W V 79/3298

Instructions regarding War Diaries and Intelligence Summaries are contained in F. S. Regs., Part II. and the Staff Manual respectively. Title pages will be prepared in manuscript.

WAR DIARY
or
~~INTELLIGENCE SUMMARY.~~

(Erase heading not required.)

Army Form C. 2118.

Hour, Date, Place	Summary of Events and Information	Remarks and references to Appendices
3rd December	Inspected horses of Essex Yeomanry again & rejected 9 horses with catarrh. Ordered to inspect them by Base Commandant as the regiment was under orders to entrain at midday. ~~Both~~ parties of men returned from taking horses to SOURNAY EN BRAY & FORGES LES EAUX. Got 300 horses into the stables. Weather drier today. Memo from Major WALKER R.E. to send list of Officers & N.C.Os who were at L'Usine Bundy in August as a heavy bill for damages has been claimed by the late owners ~~who~~ were bankrupt. This is their chance of getting straight apparently. Gave a list of No 2 Section, & mentioned 1 Section, B.V. Stores & Remount Depot as also being in L'Usine Bundy. Four horses died on the rail journey to ROUEN. This was expected as I am certain that catarrh cases when sent by train or turned out to grass ~~[illegible]~~ often develop pneumonia. One horse jumped out of the train on the way to SOURNAY EN BRAY & one broke its leg on the journey to FORGES LES EAUX. Remaining 1117 – admitted 37 – died 5 – destroyed 5 – total 1144. O.S.J.	

Army Form C. 2118.

WAR DIARY

or

~~INTELLIGENCE SUMMARY.~~

(Erase heading not required.)

Instructions regarding War Diaries and Intelligence Summaries are contained in F. S. Regs., Part II. and the Staff Manual respectively. Title pages will be prepared in manuscript.

Hour, Date, Place	Summary of Events and Information	Remarks and references to Appendices
4th December	Memo from Base Commandant forwarding a report from R.T.O. on the sorry condition of the ~~to~~ 250 horses sent to FORGES LES EAUX & stating that their wounds were undressed, they had no head collars but only head ropes, & that they had not been watered &c. &c. There would have been no complaint if it had not been for the train for Sonnay having been put in between the one for FORGES LES EAUX at 10.15 & the train for ROUEN at 4 P.M. This caused a complete disorganisation of the parties arranged for & consequent hurry & confusion. Four cases of influenza reported in Remount Depot. Saw them & arranged for no horses to be sent up country for a week. This caused me to be told off by D.V.S. on the telephone; I replied that I was acting in a similar manner to himself during the last outbreak when he ordered no horses to move for 14 days. I am told not to create a fuss, but it had nothing to do with me as the matter was reported to D of R before I was told about it. I also informed D.V.S. that A.D.V.S. when here last gave the impression here that HAVRE was responsible for the influenza up country, hence the precautions of safety taken by O.C. Remounts. Capt. SCOTT-NIMMO arrived at Remount Depot. Another telling off from D.V.S. for not taking over the 800 sick from Remounts. Replied that I had no room except in the wood (which he says is not to be used for horses) as new ground was not ready. Much wordy warfare. Several other minor disturbances making altogether an unsatisfactory but interesting day.	
	Remaining 1144 - admitted 7 - died [illegible] - destroyed 2 - total 1145.	

O.S.P.

(9 26 6) W 257—976 100,000 4/12 H W V 79/3298

Army Form C. 2118.

Instructions regarding War Diaries and Intelligence Summaries are contained in F. S. Regs., Part II. and the Staff Manual respectively. Title pages will be prepared in manuscript.

WAR DIARY
or
INTELLIGENCE SUMMARY.
(Erase heading not required.)

Hour, Date, Place	Summary of Events and Information	Remarks and references to Appendices
	Wire from A.D.V.S. that case of psoroptic mange had been found out of the horses sent from here. Am not surprised as they all had long coats, but there was no trace of it here in the lot sent to FORGES LES EAUX. Am not sure yet whether this wire is sent for information or as a threat.	
5th December.	Lieut HARDING went off by 11.39 train to 2nd Cavalry Brigade. Sick horses from Remount Depot arrived. Sent lame cases except the foot cases, out grazing. The new land near ROVELLES is being got ready for our lines. Half another stable occupied today making 350 horses in stables. 100 more reinforcements arrived.	
	Remaining 1145 – admitted 421 – died 5 – discharged 74 – total 1487.	
6th December	A very wet & windy day. The lines get worse & worse. We seem to have made no improvement at all since we came here. Visit by V.D. of French Army. Showed him round. He was much struck by the veterinary equipment that we have. They appear to have nothing at all in this way. Got another 50 horses into the stables. Only 50 out of the 100 extra reinforcements arrived. Made enquiries.	
	Remaining 1488 – admitted 87 – died 5 – destroyed 3 – discharged 58 total 1509	
	O.S.R.	

(9 26 6) W 257—976 100,000 4/12 H W V 79/3298

Army Form C. 2118.

Instructions regarding War Diaries and Intelligence Summaries are contained in F. S. Regs., Part II. and the Staff Manual respectively. Title pages will be prepared in manuscript.

WAR DIARY
or
INTELLIGENCE SUMMARY.
(*Erase heading not required.*)

Hour, Date, Place	Summary of Events and Information	Remarks and references to Appendices
7th December	Incessant rain all day, making the whole place into a bog. The wood is quite impossible, so am putting up lines outside on the top of the hill, south of the stables. This is very exposed but with any luck will be less boggy than the wood - for a day or two at least. Wire from D.V.S. asking if I can send 42 of class 4 & 93 of class 6 & class 10 to Convalescent Depot. At present I cannot manage to sort them out; also they have to be shod up which will take time. Visit by Base Commandant who saw state of stables & lines. Col. SPROT is collecting evidence of the damage done at L'Usine Bandy & want a statement from each N.C.O. who was there in August last. Of the 100 extra reinforcements, only 56 are available as 25 are sick & the remainder required in camp. Talked with D.V.S. on telephone & informed him about sheds in brickfields. He jumped at the idea. I told him they were low but would do for small horses. He has applied for stables for 500 more horses. These stables to be put up in the valley near ROUELLES.	
	Remaining 1509 - admitted 195 - died 7 - destroyed 2 - total 1695.	
	O. K. J.	

(9 26 6) W 257—976 100,000 4/12 H W V 79/3298

Instructions regarding War Diaries and Intelligence Summaries are contained in F. S. Regs., Part II. and the Staff Manual respectively. Title pages will be prepared in manuscript.

WAR DIARY
or
INTELLIGENCE SUMMARY.
(Erase heading not required.)

Army Form C. 2118.

Hour, Date, Place	Summary of Events and Information	Remarks and references to Appendices
8th December	Went to try horse in brick sheds. A 15.2 horse will go under most of them allright. Water can be pumped up from pond into a trough. Letter from Base Commandant notifying a shed for 100 horses between Graville Station & Harfleur. Went to see it. It is just near the grazing we have taken & would do but 100 horses in a small detachment & means 20 men to look after them. Wire from D.V.S. to Commandant re brick sheds & extra stabling being asked for & asking him to expedite work of building stables. Stables not getting on very fast now. Put some (150) horses out of wood on to picket lines but ground will not hold heel pegs. Asked for camping ground & have got the use of it. This ground is more or less dry & hard. Arranged to draw 500 buckets for stables, 1 for each horse. Am putting in for 1500. Message from Major WALKER that brick sheds may be tried & hired at [illegible] month. Message that a stray horse is at St MARTINS 16 kilometres from here. Most likely ours, so am sending for it. Visit by Base Commandant. Asked for 100 more reinforcements as I only got 50 of the last lot owing to sickness. Difficulty in getting any owing to the Canadian Division coming in in a few days. No rain today.	
	Remaining 1695 – admitted 37 – died 7 – destroyed 4 – total 1721.	
	O. S. J.	

(9 26 6) W 257--976 100,000 4/12 H W V 79/3298

Instructions regarding War Diaries and Intelligence Summaries are contained in F. S. Regs., Part II. and the Staff Manual respectively. Title pages will be prepared in manuscript.

WAR DIARY
or
~~INTELLIGENCE~~ SUMMARY.

(*Erase heading not required.*)

Army Form C. 2118.

Hour, Date, Place	Summary of Events and Information	Remarks and references to Appendices
9th December	Very wet weather. Everything is in a horrible mess. Got some more horses on picket lines, out of the wood. Wire from D.V.S. to Commandant asking for number of cases of catarrhal influenza for each shipment sent to Veterinary Hospital, also names of transport & number of cases for same transport falling sick during the first week. Memo from D.V.S. re treatment of mange. Got 500 buckets from ordnance to put in the mangers. Visit by Capt. CAMPBELL & Dr. McCALL who are selecting hunter mares to send back to England for Breeding purposes. Told them to come to me later on as I was in rather a disorganized condition & could not show them round properly. Visit by Base Commandant, [illegible] asked for sleepers for stables to be put into stalls under the hind legs of the horses, as the ground gets into such a muddy state. Wire from D.V.S. [illegible] Lieut. WOODS to 11th Hussars, Capt. T. JACKSON being sent here.	
	Remaining 1721 - admitted 92 - died 8 - destroyed 2 - total 1803	
	O. S. F.	

(9 26 6) W 257—976 100,000 4/12 H W V 79/3298

Instructions regarding War Diaries and Intelligence Summaries are contained in F. S. Regs., Part II. and the Staff Manual respectively. Title pages will be prepared in manuscript.

WAR DIARY
or
~~INTELLIGENCE SUMMARY.~~
(Erase heading not required.)

Army Form C. 2118.

Hour, Date, Place	Summary of Events and Information	Remarks and references to Appendices
10th December	Went to see brickshed, put two horses in & picketed them down. They fitted in very well. This would have been an excellent place for horses but I fear ~~[illegible]~~ the sheds are too fragile, because the wind blew about 30 yards of them down in the night. If there had been any horses under them they would have all been killed. So am not going to risk taking them on. Told Ch. & D.O. Lands. Put 300 horses on lines on the camping ground which is so far quite clean & dry. Terrific wind in the night. Tobacco, cigarettes & matches sent to O.C. 2 Section from Daily Despatch. Acknowledged. Visited V.O. i/c Remounts who was unable to take any horses. Fortunately had none to send. He appears to have 120 sick. Visited 6 & 7 forms & selected horses to go to Convalescent Depot. Remaining 1803 - admitted 21 - died 7 - destroyed 1 - total 1816. O.S.J.	

Instructions regarding War Diaries and Intelligence Summaries are contained in F. S. Regs., Part II. and the Staff Manual respectively. Title pages will be prepared in manuscript.

WAR DIARY
or
INTELLIGENCE SUMMARY.
(Erase heading not required.)

Army Form C. 2118.

Hour, Date, Place	Summary of Events and Information	Remarks and references to Appendices
11th December	Last night unable to telephone to D.V.S., same this morning, so sent telegram to him to that effect. This is a great nuisance as I could arrange things with him without going into a long correspondence. Applied to Base Commandant for permission. A soaking wet day. The horses in the stables get exhausted walking through the mud & water. Have got some [illegible] in the mangers this saves a mess being made of the standings. The horses on picket lines on the camping ground are on excellent standings in spite of the wet. Hope to get more lying down there tomorrow. Rivers of water run over the whole place. Wire from D.V.S. to send number of strangles & catarrh cases. Sent number shown in return & stated that most of others had a discharge as well as other affections. Got spades from Ordnance. Sent horses from E paddock to [illegible] [illegible] to be near station for transfer to Convalescent Horse Depot. Remaining 1816 admitted 5 - died 7 - destroyed 3 - discharged 53 total 1756. O.S.B.	

(9 26 6) W 257—976 100,000 4/12 H W V 79/3298

Army Form C. 2118.

Instructions regarding War Diaries and Intelligence Summaries are contained in F. S. Regs., Part II. and the Staff Manual respectively. Title pages will be prepared in manuscript.

WAR DIARY
or
~~INTELLIGENCE~~ SUMMARY.

(Erase heading not required.)

Hour, Date, Place	Summary of Events and Information	Remarks and references to Appendices
12th December	Inspected horses & mules of Rock Artillery Brigade in No 2 Camp. Mules all very fit. Rejected 11 horses (8 h.d. 1 l.d. 2 r.). Very cold afternoon. Did not get Sergt. Beer's [?] troop watered & fed till 6 pm & the reinforcements working with him having changed camp or been ordered to do so & then the order countermanded. 60 horses at 2nd Marine Buildings [?] ready to go to C.H.D. [?] as soon as we can manage to get the men. Every man taken from the lines to take horses to the station means that the horses cannot be watered & fed properly. This is not understood by anyone who is not actually running a hospital under very adverse circumstances. Order for A.A. & Q.M.G. to send away any men from the front now with L of C units as servants, clerks &c. none here. Order for Base Commandant to draw [?] gum boots & Southwesters for men who are exposed to weather. Put in for 100 of each as we already have 100 Canada boots & 100 mackintoshes. Advised O.C. No 2 General Base Depot to do same as his men are working in the hospital. Sent list of 12 men of cavalry 56 remounts to O/c A.V.C. Records to be transferred & made corporals.	
	Remaining 1756 – admitted 61 – died 8 – destroyed 1 – discharged 31. Total 1777	
	O.S.L. [?]	

(9 26 6) W 257—976 100,000 4/12 H W V 79/3298

Instructions regarding War Diaries and Intelligence Summaries are contained in F. S. Regs., Part II. and the Staff Manual respectively. Title pages will be prepared in manuscript.

WAR DIARY

or

~~INTELLIGENCE~~ SUMMARY.

(Erase heading not required.)

Army Form C. 2118.

Hour, Date, Place	Summary of Events and Information	Remarks and references to Appendices
13th December	New A.D.V.S. Lt Col. DUNLOP-SMITH & Major MARTIN arrived fr ROUEN. Showed them all round the [illegible] & explained that I could only send 150 horses away - without catarrh, as the others all had catarrh. Informed them that the horses at grass did not bother me as so few men were necessary to look after them. Protested against the order fr DVS of some time ago to turn catarrh horses out to grass & explained that I would take no responsibility in the matter as I knew that they would die. Informed Base Commandant & DDRMG that I was sending horses without rugs as they were from grass. As a matter of fact A.D.V.S. orders no rugs to go with them. Order fr Col. ~~[illegible]~~ SPROT to send NCOs down at 10 AM on Tuesday to give evidence re L'Usine Remy - also to attend [illegible]. Arranged with him to send at 10 AM & 2 PM. This is very inconvenient as it takes these senior NCOs fr their work. Sergts Todd & Cox have been transferred to DVC. & promoted to Sergt but posted to other sections. This is iniquitous as I particularly chose these NCOs & transferred them because they were good men. Asked to have them back! Remaining 1777 admitted 37 - died 9 - destroyed 2 - total 1803. [signature]	

(9 26 6) W 257—976 100,000 4/12 H W V 79/3298

Instructions regarding War Diaries and Intelligence Summaries are contained in F. S. Regs., Part II. and the Staff Manual respectively. Title pages will be prepared in manuscript.

WAR DIARY
or
INTELLIGENCE SUMMARY
(Erase heading not required.)

Army Form C. 2118.

Hour, Date, Place	Summary of Events and Information	Remarks and References to Appendices
14th. December	Took 150 horses down to the station but had to send back 29 with discharge from the nose. 121 horses & 25 other ranks went by train to SAUMONT LA POTERIE at 10.15 A.M. 185 horses sent from Remounts - chiefly from docks. 19 of them had nothing the matter with them at all. Sent 50 light horses with catarrh to L'Usine Bundy. Asked for more men - 200 as out of 400 reinforcements supposed to be here with us only 269 are available. & of ours own 183 total strength 64 only are available to work with the horses. 100 men sent provisionally by Commandant No 6 Camp. News from Base Commandant that no extra accommodation will be put up at HAVRE for horses, therefore unless I can keep my numbers down to 1000 & do this quickly he will take the matter up with I.G.C. Wired this to D.V.S. also informed him by wire that I had no more cases without catarrh except 90 surgical cases. Visited headquarters & saw Base Commandant re his minute. He recommends a motor to be supplied for my use. Inspected S.S. SIPTAH with 250 horses on board. No fault to be found with ventilation. Remaining 1803 - admitted 185 - died 9 - destroyed 1 - transferred 121 - discharged 34 - total 1823.	

O. S. S.

(9 26 6) W 257—976 100,000 4/12 H W V 79/3298

Army Form C. 2118.

Instructions regarding War Diaries and Intelligence Summaries are contained in F. S. Regs., Part II. and the Staff Manual respectively. Title pages will be prepared in manuscript.

WAR DIARY
or
INTELLIGENCE SUMMARY
(Erase heading not required.)

Hour, Date, Place	Summary of Events and Information	Remarks and References to Appendices
15th December	Attended Court of Enquiry at 131. Rue de Strasbourg, & gave evidence. Rows with Capt. NIMMO re horses discharged from hospital & admitted to hospital. He accused me of not acting straightly in reporting to him that 19 horses of those admitted yesterday were fit. Informed him that I went twice personally to the Remount Depot but could not find him & I informed him that evening when I saw him. I previously accused him of being the cause of friction between us & Remounts which did not exist before his arrival. I consented to withdraw this statement, & he his statement. We agreed to work without any trouble by seeing each other should occasion arise. In spite of this I receive a report at midday from O.C. Remounts stating that S.V.O. Remounts reports that on the last three occasions very large numbers of unfit horses were sent to the Depot from the Veterinary Hospital. E.R. I informed Capt. NIMMO by telephone that I would now take up the matter officially, as that I have been forced to do so. This is a pity but I see no other course. Capt. G.T.T. JACKSON reported arrival & was appointed adjutant. Wire from D.V.S. notifying his arrival tomorrow. S.G.C. also due to arrive tomorrow. Remaining 1823 - admitted 63 - died 12 - destroyed 1 - total 1873. O.S.J.	

(9 26 6) W 257—976 100,000 4/12 H W V 79/3298

Instructions regarding War Diaries and Intelligence Summaries are contained in F. S. Regs., Part II. and the Staff Manual respectively. Title pages will be prepared in manuscript.

WAR DIARY
or
INTELLIGENCE SUMMARY
(Erase heading not required.)

Army Form C. 2118.

Hour, Date, Place	Summary of Events and Information	Remarks and References to Appendices
16th December	D.V.S. & A.D.V.S. arrived & were horrified at the condition of the hospital. I don't wonder. 3 officers & 200 men A.V.C. arrived & were posted as follows. Lieut. BLACKBURN & 30 men to this hospital. 70 men to FORGES LES EAUX. – these to remain here & take 700 horses there from this hospital. Lieut & Qr Mr FISHER & 30 men to ROUEN. also Lieut POWERS to ROUEN. 30 men to 5 Hospital ABBEVILLE. 50 men to 10 Vety Hospital PORTE LE BRIQUES, BOULOGNE. I.G.C. & Base Commandant came up to camp but not to hospital. I.G.C. arranged for transport to bring up material for spaces between stables. D.V.S. saw brick sheds & in spite of my previous experience, large horses were put into brick sheds. All horses ordered out of woods, & D.V.S. is seeing them tomorrow pending 200 going to Convalescent Depot & 700 to FORGES LES EAUX. Stopped for trains tomorrow or next day. D.V.S. recommended motor car as mentioned by Base Commandant. I.G.C. gave permission for reinforcements to take horses by train; this should prevent the disorganization which happens when our own N.C.Os are taken for this duty.	
	Remaining 1873 – admitted 32 – died 12 – destroyed 4 – transferred 1 – total 1888.	

(9 26 6) W 257—976 100,000 4/12 H W V 79/3298

Army Form C. 2118.

Instructions regarding War Diaries and Intelligence Summaries are contained in F. S. Regs., Part II. and the Staff Manual respectively. Title pages will be prepared in manuscript.

WAR DIARY
or
~~INTELLIGENCE SUMMARY~~

(*Erase heading not required.*)

Hour, Date, Place	Summary of Events and Information	Remarks and References to Appendices
17th December	D.V.S. came up at 9 A.M. & inspected all the horses – had them all out & sorted them into different parties for ~~hospital~~ Convalescent Horse Depot & Remounts. A very stormy day. Accused of every kind of incompetence, as well as all other officers & N.C.Os. In fact nothing & no one was right. 167 horses went by train to GOURNAY EN BRAY. Went to Lichfields with D.O. Billets & took them. Water laid on already. Men did not get dinner till 4 P.M. Much confusion owing to all men being scattered about. Veterinary Receiving Station is to be done away with, as we are supposed to be doing nothing. I don't know how to manage properly without them down at the docks, as so many horses have to be left there unable to get to camp & the float cannot bring them up this hill. Remaining 1888 – admitted 36 – died 12 – transferred 167 discharged 94 – total <u>1651.</u> O. S. L.	

(9 26 6) W 257—976 100,000 4/12 H W V 79/3298

Army Form C. 2118.

Instructions regarding War Diaries and Intelligence Summaries are contained in F. S. Regs., Part II. and the Staff Manual respectively. Title pages will be prepared in manuscript.

WAR DIARY
or
INTELLIGENCE SUMMARY.
(Erase heading not required.)

Hour, Date, Place	Summary of Events and Information	Remarks and references to Appendices
18th December.	Sent 350 horses by 10.15 A.M. train to Forges les Eaux under Lieut DAVIS. & 356 to same place by 2.15 P.M. train under Lieut BLACKBURN. Capt. JACKSON saw them off. Got 50 horses into brick sheds. All horses taken off lines put up on new ground near RONDELLES yesterday. A.D.V.S. up in camp most of the day & picked out 14 horses for Remount.	
	Remaining 1651 - admitted 91 - died 8 - destroyed 2 - transferred 706 - discharged 14 - total 1012.	
19th December	Put down more lines round brick sheds & arranged water supply with R.O. Camps. Wire from D.V.S. to Base Commandant to post me to command of No 9 Mobile Veterinary Section on relief by Capt. McKENZIE, & Capt. JACKSON to No 5 Veterinary Hospital ABBEVILLE on relief of Capt HODGINS. This is no more than I expected & I am glad to go to the front.	
	Remaining 1012 - admitted 59 - died 4 - destroyed 4 - total 1063.	
20th December	Lieuts DAVIS & BLACKBURN & party returned from journey to FORGES LES EAUX. Got 300 horses into brick sheds. They do not look like holding these sheds. One fell down onto a horse. The water supply looks like running out.	
	Remaining 1073* - admitted 43 - died 13 - destroyed 5 - Total 1098	
	*10 were not sent away yesterday as shown & are added in today's state.	

O.S.P.

Army Form C. 2118.

Instructions regarding War Diaries and Intelligence Summaries are contained in F. S. Regs., Part II. and the Staff Manual respectively. Title pages will be prepared in manuscript.

WAR DIARY
or
~~INTELLIGENCE SUMMARY.~~

(Erase heading not required.)

Hour, Date, Place	Summary of Events and Information	Remarks and references to Appendices
21st December	Sent more horses to brickfields. One shed fell down this morning but it was held up until the horses were got out. Sgt. [illegible] doing good work in paving the spaces between the stable with bricks. Water supply is rather meagre. The horses are watered out of buckets. Wired to D.V.S. asking for an order to move 300 horses as we are getting full up & train traffic is congested owing to 27th Division passing through. One case ~~[illegible]~~ [illegible] mange in [illegible] horses – reported to D.V.S. Asked D.V.S. by wire if mange cases could be sent to L'Usine Bundy – that place to be used only for mange cases. Terrific thunderstorm this morning. The ground gets more & more muddy on the lines ~~[illegible]~~ on the crowding camping ground are getting bad. [illegible] Farmer refuses to let us have the [illegible] for 50 francs per day as he formerly arranged to do & in spite of the fact that he signed a statement to that ~~[illegible]~~ effect.	
	Remaining 1098 – admitted 105 – destroyed 6 – died 9 – remaining 1188.	
	[illegible signature]	

(9 26 6) W 257—976 100,000 4/12 H W V 79/3298

Instructions regarding War Diaries and Intelligence Summaries are contained in F. S. Regs., Part II. and the Staff Manual respectively. Title pages will be prepared in manuscript.

WAR DIARY
or
~~INTELLIGENCE SUMMARY.~~
(Erase heading not required.)

Army Form C. 2118.

Hour, Date, Place	Summary of Events and Information	Remarks and references to Appendices
22nd December	Wire from D.V.S. that a move had been ~~made~~ arranged – horses to go to LA CHAPPELL EAUX POTS. possibly today. D.V.S. has no objection to ~~[illegible]~~ mange cases going to L'Union Party provided they are kept under cover. Brickbeds looking well – the spaces between sheds paved with brick. This place is the 1st that has looked like a veterinary hospital since I have been out here. Hope the sheds will not fall down. Train arranged for 700 horses to LA CHAPPELL EAUX POTS at 6.59 – a rush to get them away in time – notice only arriving at 1.45 PM. & it is 3 miles to the station. Sent 11 horses to Base Horse Transport Depot for 4 double harness carts + 3 single carts. Lieut DAVIS going with the 700 horses. Remaining 488 – admitted 57 – died + destroyed 5 – transferred 279 – discharged 3 – total 400. O.S.J.	

(9 26 6) W 257—976 100,000 4/12 H W V 79/3298

Instructions regarding War Diaries and Intelligence Summaries are contained in F. S. Regs., Part II. and the Staff Manual respectively. Title pages will be prepared in manuscript.

WAR DIARY

or

~~INTELLIGENCE SUMMARY.~~

(Erase heading not required.)

Army Form C. 2118.

Hour, Date, Place	Summary of Events and Information	Remarks and references to Appendices
23rd December	Began clearing away manure in new cart. Horses not very fit. Bruchfields looking well, but one shed nearly down owing to kick of a horse. Brought up 50 horses from L'Orme Bench & brought them up here – all had a slight discharge & had not improved since being turned out. At 8.45 P.M. was informed that 1 officer & 250 men were at docks & being sent up here. Arranged for tents in No 6 Camp as we have no tents for the party, but tents for our own reinforcements have been applied for. Lieuts. WARD, REID & WHITMORE are the officers. Wired D.V.S. as to [illegible] & received information of the matter. 20 men for this hospital. Sergt. Cox & [illegible] to No 10 Section. This is not quite fair as one goes to much trouble to select good N.C.Os for the work ~~[illegible]~~ transferred to A.V.C. & then they are sent to other sections. It is impossible to carry on in the future if this is going to be done. Remain 308 – admitted 113 – died 6 – destroyed 5 – sick 18 Total 442	

O. S. L.

Instructions regarding War Diaries and Intelligence Summaries are contained in F. S. Regs., Part II. and the Staff Manual respectively. Title pages will be prepared in manuscript.

WAR DIARY
or
INTELLIGENCE SUMMARY.
(Erase heading not required.)

Army Form C. 2118.

Hour, Date, Place	Summary of Events and Information	Remarks and references to Appendices
24th December.	Capt J. R. HODGKINS reported his arrival. Capt G. T. T. JACKSON having been granted 48 hours leave left for ABBEVILLE. Received Princess MARY'S Xmas gifts & applied to D.V.S. for travel [illegible] money & am to send them to FORGES LES EAUX on 26th. Sent 24 mange cases & [illegible] to be kept in the barns there.	
	Remaining 992 – admitted 100 – died 7 – destroyed 4 – discharged 27	1054
25th December	Arranged for 300 horses [illegible] FORGES LES EAUX at 11.57 am [illegible] distributed [illegible] [illegible] LA CHAPELLE AUX POTS.	
	Remaining 1054 admitted 47 – died 8 – destroyed 4 – discharged 17 Total 1072	

[illegible signature]

Instructions regarding War Diaries and Intelligence Summaries are contained in F. S. Regs., Part II. and the Staff Manual respectively. Title pages will be prepared in manuscript.

WAR DIARY
or
INTELLIGENCE SUMMARY.
(Erase heading not required.)

Army Form C. 2118.

Hour, Date, Place	Summary of Events and Information	Remarks and references to Appendices
26th December	Capt McKENZIE arrived. 301 horses left for 7 & 9 Veterinary Hospitals at FORGES LES EAUX. Report from Major OSBORNE re the unsuitability of [illegible] for horses [illegible] to [illegible] me. He also mentions that trucks are used to [illegible]. This absolutely [illegible] that it was mentioned [illegible] in my report. The disinfector arrived. Spoke with DDVS on telephone re [illegible] being taken away [illegible] list of drivers [illegible] were being taken.	
	Remaining 1074 - admitted 55 - died 7 - destroyed 4 - Transferred 301 - Total 8[illegible]	
27th December	Brick [illegible] falling down in parts. Got [illegible] for R.E. to [illegible] them up & strengthened others. Wire from DVS directing Lieut LOWE to proceed to 2nd Division for duty with 44th Bde R.F.A. Memo from ADRS Remount Dept asking for receipts for horses sent on certain dates which seemed to be short as follows:- 6.12.14 - 4 short, 9.12.14 - 12 short, 12.12.14 - 29 short, 13.12.14 - 6 short, 16.12.14 - 4 short, 19.12.14 - 17 short, 20.12.14 - 1 short, 21.12.14 - 12 short. As all horses coming in are counted by an officer I do not see how we can have made any mistake. Replied to this effect. The remount [illegible] they having given receipts for horses handed to them by us.	
	Remaining 1121 - admitted 66 - died 4 - destroyed 1 - Total 1182	

[illegible signature]

(73989) W4141—463. 400,000. 9/14. H.&J.Ltd. Forms/C. 2118/10.

Instructions regarding War Diaries and Intelligence Summaries are contained in F. S. Regs., Part II. and the Staff Manual respectively. Title pages will be prepared in manuscript.

WAR DIARY
or
INTELLIGENCE SUMMARY.
(Erase heading not required.)

Army Form C. 2118.

Hour, Date, Place	Summary of Events and Information	Remarks and references to Appendices
28th December	Prisoners did not turn up so could not get much manure removed. Incessant rain preventing any burning of manure. Only two horses removed from [illegible] field of M. Thomas leaving 9 still there. Reported to Staff Capt. who arranged for a [illegible] to come & remove them. At 4 P.M. this had not turned up. Went to see Base Commandant re [illegible] belonging to [illegible]. If we could get these I think there would be less difficulty in dealing with the mange cases, as [illegible] only hold 20 at the most & we have more than that now. Mange cases could go in [illegible] stables & the new [illegible] could hold all surgical cases & the remaining horses on the picket line. Unable to see Commandant or [illegible].	
	Remaining 1152 – admitted 57 – died 3 – destroyed 1 – transferred 301. Total 936	
29th December	Many of the carts break when pulling loads of manure & cause delay in the removal of it. If loaded too much the horses cannot move the cart out of the mud. The whole thing seems waste of time but I have been ordered to do it. The carts would be better employed carrying broken brick for the stable floors – however no work can be done in this direction until the manure is removed which will take a month at the present rate. 190 men taken away – applied to DAAG to have the matter put right. Another shed blew down – the gale last night.	
	Remaining 936 – admitted 65 – died 10 – destroyed [illegible] – discharged [illegible]. 976	
	[illegible signature]	

(73989) W4141—463. 400,000. 9/14. H.&J.Ltd. Forms/C. 2118/10.

Army Form C. 2118.

Instructions regarding War Diaries and Intelligence Summaries are contained in F. S. Regs., Part II. and the Staff Manual respectively. Title pages will be prepared in manuscript.

WAR DIARY
or
INTELLIGENCE SUMMARY.
(Erase heading not required.)

Hour, Date, Place	Summary of Events and Information	Remarks and references to Appendices
30th December	Shifted more manure but very little progress made. It is great waste of time. It would be better to wait & move the manure heaps until dry weather comes when it could be moved more easily. Besides this the repairing of the stable floors in brickfields is more important as there are 800 horses out in [illegible]. These could be got under cover in about 2 weeks [illegible] allowed to do as one thing [illegible]. M. [illegible] did not take away any dead horses. The percentage of deaths does not [illegible] in spite of the horses being in the brickfields, in fact they appear to die in greater numbers there than in the open. [illegible] with [illegible] & [illegible] [illegible] Lieut. HILL & 200 [illegible] for England, [illegible] for [illegible] hospital.	
	Remaining 976 – admitted 44 – died 9 – destroyed 6 – discharged 36 – total 973.	
31st Dec.	Went round Dunkerque brickfields with Base Commandant but the sheds are not worth taking over & the expense & complications connected with them. New sheds to be built in place of old ones at [illegible] [illegible] for A.D.V.S. re disposal of manure – replied [illegible] [illegible] removal by carts. Visited D.V.S. [illegible] where 800 horses could [illegible]	
	Remaining 973 – admitted 63 – died 1 – total 1035	
		D. V. L.

(73989) W4141—463. 400,000. 9/14. H.&J.Ltd. Forms/C. 2118/10.

1st Div

No 2. Mobile Vety: Section.

Vol I.

January & February 1915

Instructions regarding War Diaries and Intelligence Summaries are contained in F. S. Regs., Part II. and the Staff Manual respectively. Title pages will be prepared in manuscript.

WAR DIARY
or
~~INTELLIGENCE SUMMARY.~~
(*Erase heading not required.*)

No 2 Mobile Vety Section

Army Form C. 2118.

Hour, Date, Place	Summary of Events and Information	Remarks and references to Appendices
Jany 24th 1915	Received orders to take over command of No 2 Mobile Veterinary Section. Proceeded to BETHUNE and took over command from Captain Lawrie A.V.C.	App 1
25th	Evacuated 43 horses from CHOCQUES station to No 10 Field Veterinary Hospital. Horses consisted of 32 ordinary sick cases, 11 cases of skin disease. Conducting party of 1 NCO and 5 men. 7 horses received cured	
27th	Conducting party rejoined from Base	
28th	Evacuated 28 horses from CHOCQUES Station consisting of 20 ordinary sick & 8 skin disease cases, conducting party of 1 NCO and 3 men	
30th	Conducting party rejoined Evacuated 25 horses from CHOCQUES Station consisting of 21 ordinary sick and 4 skin cases, conducting party of one NCO and 3 men. 5 horses received cured	

(9 29 6) W 3332–1107 100,000 10/13 H W V Forms/C. 2118/10.

Army Form C. [illegible]118.

WAR DIARY
or
INTELLIGENCE SUMMARY.
(*Erase heading not required.*)

Instructions regarding War Diaries and Intelligence Summaries are contained in F. S. Regs., Part II. and the Staff Manual respectively. Title pages will be prepared in manuscript.

Hour, Date, Place	Summary of Events and Information	Remarks and references to Appendices
February 1st 1915	Conducting party of Jan 30th returned. 4 horses reissued cured	
3rd	Sgt Ford AVC sent to England authority 1st Corps telegram A 530 of 2nd inst	App 2
4th	Evacuated from CHOCQUES Station 47 horses consisting of 32 ordinary sick and 15 skin cases, conducting party of a N C O and 3 men	
5	Left Bethune and marched to AUCHEL 15 kilometres Good accomodation for sick horses and skin cases	
	No 424 Cpl Stafford promoted Sgt dated 1.1.15. ~~[illegible]~~	
7	Conducting party of 4th inst rejoined	
10th	6 Horses reissued cured	
12th	3 Horses reissued cured	
13th	Evacuated from CHOCQUES Station 19 horses consisting of 16 ordinary sick and 3 skin disease cases, conducting party of an N C O and 2 men	
16th	Reissued cured 3 horses Conducting party of 13th returned	
25th	Evacuated from CHOCQUES Station 42 horses consisting of 23 ordinary sick, 7 skin diseases cases, 10 cast for Veterinary reasons, and 2 for cast for Remount	

(9 29 6) W 3332 -1107 100,000 10/13 H W V Forms/C. 2118/10.

Army Form C. [illegible]118.

Instructions regarding War Diaries and Intelligence Summaries are contained in F. S. Regs., Part II. and the Staff Manual respectively. Title pages will be prepared in manuscript.

WAR DIARY
or
INTELLIGENCE SUMMARY.
(Erase heading not required.)

Hour, Date, Place	Summary of Events and Information	Remarks and references to Appendices
25th (cont)	reasons, the last mentioned going to No 2 Remount Depot	
	Conducting party consisted of 1 NCO and 6 men	
27th	1 Horse reissued cured. Conducting party returned	
28th	moved from AUCHEL to LA VALLE 8 kilometres	
	Fair accommodation for sick horses	

121/5022

1st. Division

No 2 Mobile Vety: Section.

Vol II 3 — 30.3.15

No. 2 Mobile Veterinary Section

WAR DIARY
or
~~INTELLIGENCE~~ SUMMARY.
(*Erase heading not required.*)

Army Form C. 2118.

Instructions regarding War Diaries and Intelligence Summaries are contained in F. S. Regs., Part II. and the Staff Manual respectively. Title pages will be prepared in manuscript.

Hour, Date, Place	Summary of Events and Information	Remarks and references to Appendices
March 3rd 1915	21 sick horses evacuated from CHOCQUES under NCO & 3 men	
6th	Conducting party returned	
	[illegible] joining the Section have [illegible] their [illegible] fire arms [illegible] as [illegible], so that rifle drill and musketry instruction [illegible]	
10th	A party of 1 NCO & 3 men under my personal supervision formed advanced collecting and dressing station at SERVINGHE [illegible] [illegible] was [illegible] [illegible] returned to BUSNETTES at night	
12th	Collecting party of 1 NCO and 3 men sent to SERVINGHE daily to collect sick [illegible] [illegible] to Section at night.	
15th	17 sick horses evacuated from CHOCQUES under NCO & 2 men	
16th	Conducting party returned	
	17 sick horses evacuated from CHOCQUES under NCO & 2 men.	
18th	Conducting party returned	

(9 29 6) W 3332—1107 100,000 10/13 H W V Forms/C. 2118/10.

Instructions regarding War Diaries and Intelligence Summaries are contained in F. S. Regs., Part II. and the Staff Manual respectively. Title pages will be prepared in manuscript.

WAR DIARY
or
INTELLIGENCE SUMMARY.
(Erase heading not required.)

Army Form C. 2118.

Hour, Date, Place	Summary of Events and Information	Remarks and references to Appendices
March 21st 1915	Evacuated 26 sick & cast horses from CHOCQUES under a NCO & 3 men	
23rd	Conducting party returned	
	Marched to SEVELINGAE 2 kilometres to take up position there in fairly good situation	
27th	Sgt [illegible] & Cpl Brand posted away from section	
	Strength of section in NCOs changed from 6 to 4	
28th	20 sick & cast horses evacuated from CHOCQUES under NCO & 3 men	
30th	It is found extremely difficult to carry on the work of the section with the reduced number of NCOs	
	Conducting party returned	

1st Division

121/6306

No 2 Mobile Vety: Section

Vol III

April May & June 1915

No 2 Mobile Veterinary Section 1st Division

Army Form C. 2118.

Instructions regarding War Diaries and Intelligence Summaries are contained in F. S. Regs., Part II. and the Staff Manual respectively. Title pages will be prepared in manuscript.

WAR DIARY
or
~~INTELLIGENCE SUMMARY.~~
(Erase heading not required.)

Hour, Date, Place	Summary of Events and Information	Remarks and references to Appendices
SEVELINGAE 1.4.15.	5 horses collected from farmers in the neighbourhood [illegible] these horses having been left with them since October 1914.	
3.4.15	Evacuated 17 sick horses.	
5.4.15	2 more horses collected from farmers having been left for several months.	
6.4.15	Evacuated 26 sick horses.	
9.4.15	Moved section to good billets in village of LOCON, good accommodation for horses and men.	
LOCON 14.4.15	Evacuated 17 sick horses.	
16.4.15	Inspected by Brigadier General Moore C.B. A.V.S. [illegible]	
17.4.15	35 horses suffering from debility admitted from 39th Bde R.F.A. [illegible] admitted from this brigade [illegible] for the purpose of [illegible]	

(9 29 6) W 3332—1107 100,000 10/13 H W V Forms/C. 2118/10.

Instructions regarding War Diaries and Intelligence Summaries are contained in F. S. Regs., Part II. and the Staff Manual respectively. Title pages will be prepared in manuscript.

WAR DIARY
or
INTELLIGENCE SUMMARY.
(Erase heading not required.)

Army Form C. 2118.

Hour, Date, Place	Summary of Events and Information	Remarks and references to Appendices
LOCON. 19.4.15	39 [illegible]	
26.4.15	[illegible]	
30.4.15	Several [illegible] and [illegible]	
	[illegible]	
	[illegible]	
	[illegible]	
	Total [illegible] for the month.	
	[illegible]	
	[illegible] 6	
	[illegible] 4	

(9 29 6) W 3332–1107 100,000 10/13 H W V Forms/C. 2118/10.

No 2 Mobile Veterinary Section

Army Form C. 2118.

WAR DIARY
or
~~INTELLIGENCE SUMMARY.~~
(Erase heading not required.)

Instructions regarding War Diaries and Intelligence Summaries are contained in F. S. Regs., Part II. and the Staff Manual respectively. Title pages will be prepared in manuscript.

Hour, Date, Place	Summary of Events and Information	Remarks and references to Appendices
LOCON 7.5.15	Evacuated 26 sick horses.	
9.5.15	Attack by 1st Division. Advanced party from section consisting of [illegible] marched at 2.30 a.m. to a position [illegible] 1 kilometre S.E. LACOUTURE on the LACOUTURE–[illegible] ST VAAST road [illegible] capable of dealing with [illegible] wounded horses. Only 5 casualties [illegible] during the [illegible] of the [illegible]. Returned at [illegible] to LOCON.	
12.5.15	Evacuated [illegible] sick horses. Moved section to BETHUNE [illegible] more [illegible] for horses.	
BETHUNE 15.5.15	Evacuated 3[illegible] sick horses.	
16.5.15	BETHUNE heavily shelled [illegible] shells in [illegible]	
20.5.15	BETHUNE [illegible]	
22.5.15	Evacuated 32 sick horses.	

Instructions regarding War Diaries and Intelligence Summaries are contained in F. S. Regs., Part II. and the Staff Manual respectively. Title pages will be prepared in manuscript.

WAR DIARY
or
INTELLIGENCE SUMMARY.

(*Erase heading not required.*)

Army Form C. 2118.

Hour, Date, Place	Summary of Events and Information	Remarks and references to Appendices
BETHUNE 25.5.15	Evacuated 24 sick [illegible]	
26.5.15	Ordered by 1st Corps to remove section from BETHUNE moved to FOUQUIERES had accommodation for [illegible] [illegible] owing to village being crowded with troops	
FOUQUIERES 31.5.15	Total evacuations for the month	
	Sick 129	
	[illegible] 1	
	[illegible] 3	
	[illegible] DDR 14	

No 2 Mobile Veterinary Sect[illegible]

WAR DIARY
or
INTELLIGENCE SUMMARY.
(*Erase heading not required.*)

Army Form C. 2118.

Instructions regarding War Diaries and Intelligence Summaries are contained in F. S. Regs., Part II. and the Staff Manual respectively. Title pages will be prepared in manuscript.

Hour, Date, Place	Summary of Events and Information	Remarks and references to Appendices
FOUQUIERES 1.6.15	Evacuated 25 horses	
2.6.15	[illegible] good accommodation for horses [illegible]	
4.6.15	[illegible] 1 [illegible] SE BEUVRY [illegible]	
8.6.15	Evacuated 20 sick horses	
10.6.15	[illegible] R V S [illegible] continually [illegible] Routine Order No 310	
16.6.15	Evacuated 32 sick horses	
20.6.15	[illegible]	
	Evacuated [illegible] horses	
25.6.15	[illegible] ECOLE [illegible] accommodation [illegible]	

(9 29 6) W 3332 –1107 100,000 10/13 H W V Forms/C. 2118/10.

Instructions regarding War Diaries and Intelligence Summaries are contained in F. S. Regs., Part II. and the Staff Manual respectively. Title pages will be prepared in manuscript.

WAR DIARY
or
INTELLIGENCE SUMMARY.
(Erase heading not required.)

Army Form C. 2118.

Hour, Date, Place	Summary of Events and Information	Remarks and references to Appendices
BECKE 21.6.15	[illegible]	
22 6.15	Returned to [illegible] billets in FOUQUIERES	
FOUQUIERES 30.6.15	Total Evacuations for month	
	[illegible] 47	
	[illegible] 42	
	The [illegible] this month [illegible]	
	[illegible]	

(9 29 6) W 3332—1107 100,000 10/13 H W V Forms/C. 2118/10.

1st Division

No. 2 Mob. Vet Sec.

121/7437

H

Aug 15

No 2 M.V.S. for
J U L Y missing

Vol IV

2. Mobile Veterinary Section

WAR DIARY

or

~~INTELLIGENCE SUMMARY.~~

(*Erase heading not required.*)

Instructions regarding War Diaries and Intelligence Summaries are contained in F. S. Regs., Part II. and the Staff Manual respectively. Title pages will be prepared in manuscript.

Army Form C. 2118.

Hour, Date, Place		Summary of Events and Information	Remarks and references to Appendices
FOUQUIERES. LES BETHUNE	4·8·15	Evacuated 32 ordinary sick horses from CHOCQUES.	
"	6·8·15.	Conducting party returned.	
"	13·8·15.	Evacuated 16 sick horses and 6 Mange cases from CHOCQUES.	
"	15·8·15	Conducting party returned.	
"	17·8·15.	Evacuated 31 ordinary sick horses from CHOCQUES.	
"	19·8·15	Conducting party returned	
"	21·8·15.	Evacuated 15 ordinary sick horses & 9 cast for Remount reasons, from CHOCQUES.	
"	23·8·15	Conducting party returned.	
"	25·8·15.	Evacuated 24 ordinary sick horses from CHOCQUES.	
	27·8·15	Conducting party returned.	
	28·8·15.	Evacuated 20 ordinary sick horses & 3 cast for Remount reasons, from CHOCQUES	
	30·8·15	Conducting party returned	

G. Marriott

(9 29 6) W 3332–1107 100,000 10/13 H W V Forms/C. 2118/10.

1st Division

121/7107

No 2 Mobile Vety: Section

Vol V

Sep 1. 15

No 2 Mobile Veterinary Section

WAR DIARY

or

~~INTELLIGENCE SUMMARY~~.

(Erase heading not required.)

Army Form C. 2118.

Instructions regarding War Diaries and Intelligence Summaries are contained in F. S. Regs., Part II. and the Staff Manual respectively. Title pages will be prepared in manuscript.

Hour, Date, Place	Summary of Events and Information	Remarks and references to Appendices
September 2nd	Evacuated 12 horses from CHOCQUES	
	Marched with 3rd Infantry Brigade to LOZINGHEM	
	Division going into reserve	
LOZINGHEM 8th	Evacuated 25 sick & 2 cast horses from CHOCQUES	
16th	Evacuated 24 sick horses	
DROUVIN 19th	Evacuated 15 sick horses	
	Moved Section to DROUVIN K.4.c.9.9 x(i)	x(i) BETHUNE sheet 1/40.000
21st	Opened advanced collecting & dressing station at K.6.d.10.c x(i)	
	of an N.C.O. & 5 men which remained there till 25th inst	
24th	Evacuated 24 sick horses	
25th	At 9 a.m. moved advanced post of one officer 2 NCOs & 7 men	
	to L.17.d.1.9 x(i)	
	LIEUT G H BUTCHER A.V.C. was posted to the Section for	
	temporary duty during the operations 25-30th	
26th	At 6 a.m. moved advanced post to PHILOSOPHE L.18.c.9.6 x(i)	
	collecting 11 horses there 4 from 15th Division	

(9 29 6) W 3332-1107 100,000 10/13 H W V Forms/C. 2118/10.

Instructions regarding War Diaries and Intelligence Summaries are contained in F. S. Regs., Part II. and the Staff Manual respectively. Title pages will be prepared in manuscript.

WAR DIARY
or
~~INTELLIGENCE SUMMARY.~~
(Erase heading not required.)

Army Form C. 2118.

Hour, Date, Place		Summary of Events and Information	Remarks and references to Appendices
DROUVIN.	27th	Lieut BUTCHER took over advanced section	
		Evacuated 37 sick wounded horses including horses from 15	
		21st Guards Division also 3rd Cavalry Division	
MAZINGARB.	28th	Evacuated 19 wounded horses from NOEUX les MINES	
		Moved main section to MAZINGARB L17 c 83.	
	29th	Admitted 11 wounded practically all from 21st Division	
NOEUX les MINES	30th	Evacuated 28 sick wounded horses.	
		Main part of Section moved to NOEUX les MINES advanced	
		Party still remained at PHILOSOPHE under Lieut G. H.	
		BUTCHER.	
		Total wounded horses evacuated during operations	
		25th to 30th 84	
		Attached copy of A.V.C. Operation orders & route map.	

(9 29 6) W 3332–1107 100,000 10/13 H W V Forms/C. 2118/10.

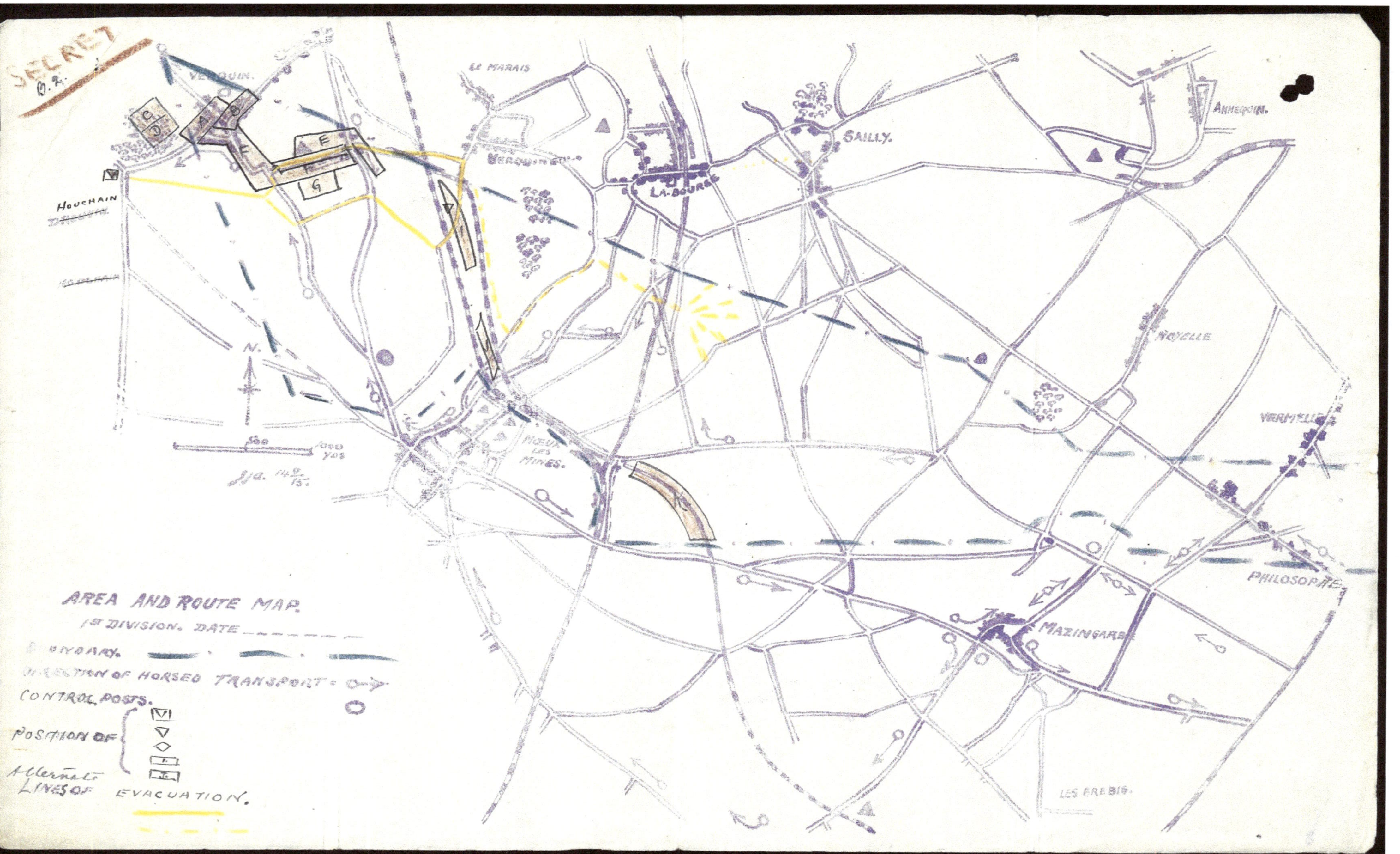
SECRET
B.2.
VERQUIN.
HOUCHAIN
LE MARAIS
VERQUINEUL
LA BOURSE
SAILLY.
ANNEQUIN.
NOYELLE
VERMELLES
NOEUX LES MINES.
MAZINGARBE
PHILOSOPHE
LES BREBIS.
N.
500
1000 YDS
AREA AND ROUTE MAP.
1ST DIVISION. DATE
BOUNDARY.
DIRECTION OF HORSED TRANSPORT
CONTROL POSTS.
POSITION OF
Alternate
LINES OF EVACUATION.

Operation Orders. A V C 1st Division
Ref 1-40000 36 & 4C.

To O C
No 2 Mobile Sec A V C.

The contents of these orders are Secret.

I am informed that on the ——
the Division will assume the offensive.
supported on the left by the 7th & on
the right by the 18th Divisions. The
Frontal area of the 1st Div is from
The junction of G 10 & 16. C D A B.. to
16 A. 2-0..
The attack will be preceded by a
prolonged bombardment.
On the 21st prior to the bombardment
you will proceed with a small party (about
9 NCOs & men) in marching order taking with
you one days full ration of forage, a pack
animal. dressings & a short length of rope.
to K. 6 d 4 10. Timing your arrival
to be ~~at~~ before 9. am.
You will proceed by following route.
Cross Country due E. to K 5 10.10.
thence by road NE by E to E 30 ~~c~~ 3.
thence E to E 30 d 2 8 thence SE to
K 6 B 10.10. thence S.W. to your position

Op orders A.V.C. 1st Div 10 Sheet 2.

arrival at the place indicated you will open a Veterinary collecting and dressing station. Indicating its position by a board with a white triangle on a red ground. fastened to some prominent tree or wall.

The position of this station has been notified in Div Operation orders.

You will dress all wounded animals received & evacuate same to Mobile Sec HQ from time to time. Evacuation will be by the route you came by.

During the period of the bombardment your Collecting Station will remain in this situation and as such will last over some days you must arrange reliefs of NCOs & men.

You will hold yourself in readiness to find a small collecting post to proceed at night to an advanced position on the main horse traffic route (night traffic only will take place thereon).

Immediately after the actual assault has taken place you will hold in readiness a party of 1 NCO & 9 men (Marching order 1 days rations) to follow up any advance of mounted troops.

Op. orders A.V.C. [illegible] Sheet 3.

[illegible] instructions will be issued regarding this party.

Instructions have been issued to the V.O. i/c train to assist you during the bombardment. You will mutually arrange for relieving one another at the collecting posts.

You will report to me nightly the number of casualties received on the V.E.S. that day and the number evacuated to rail head.

During the Bombardment my H.Qrs will be at VERQUIN. Please arrange that at least two orderlies acquaint themselves with the route there from all posts.

The following points should be borne in mind.
It is most important that at no time should roads be blocked by sick or wounded horses even momentarily.

Orders regarding lights at night & smoking must be strictly enforced

It is essential that all wounds be dressed prior to evacuation. and when possible all foreign bodies removed.

Orders in force in the Division against the using of water in washing wounds & regarding the antiseptics to be used must be enforced.

The greatest value of a Veterinary Service in the field during active operations lies in its ability to relieve Units of the [illegible] of wounded horses at the earliest possible moment and without interfering with any military movement of Troops.

~~To~~ Carry out this effectively it is essential that OCs of collecting units take over wounded horses immediately on arrival & send back the men in whose charge they arrived to their Units with the least possible delay. When possible men should be sent back under one of their own NCOs. & not allowed to straggle.

A traffic route map is attached on which is clearly marked the position during the Bombardment of all horse lines.

Op. Orders AVC no. Sheet 5.

The H^d Qrs of the mobile Sec will remain at K 4. a. pending further orders.

Note.

In the event of horse casualties being great or of a marked and continued advance taking place. The DDVS of the army will probably make arrangements to utilise the mobile secs of one Corps. as follows 1 or 2 to accompany advance & collect all wounded. 1 or 2 with the Division in support or the most rearward Division to evacuate to railhead. At railhead it is possible a party from L of C hospitals will take over & allow Section men to return to unit without delay. You will please consider therefore the most efficient method of carrying out either of these duties if such falls to the lot of the Sections under your command.

J Hulkes [illegible]
ADVS 1st [illegible]

Copy to:
Diary
DDVS. 1st/Army.

1st Division

121/7520

No. 2. Mobile Vet. Sect.

Oct 1915

Vol VI

H

No 2. Mobile Veterinary Section.

Army Form C. 2118.

Instructions regarding War Diaries and Intelligence Summaries are contained in F. S. Regs., Part II. and the Staff Manual respectively. Title pages will be prepared in manuscript.

WAR DIARY

or

~~INTELLIGENCE SUMMARY~~.

(Erase heading not required.)

Hour, Date, Place	Summary of Events and Information	Remarks and references to Appendices
NOEUX les MINES. 2·10·15.	Evacuated from NOEUX station 32 sick horses, 19 of which were from other divisions than 1st	
4·10·15.	Conducting Party returned.	
6·10·15.	Evacuated from NOEUX 24 ordinary sick and one mare and foal.	
MAZINGARB. 7·10·15.	Moved to MAZINGARB. poor place for section all men in bivouacs.	
8·10·15.	Conducting party returned.	
9·10·15.	Advanced collecting station formed at PHILOSOPHE consisting of an NCO and 4 men.	
10·10·15.	Evacuated 32 ordinary sick from NOEUX.	
12·10·15.	Conducting Party returned. The majority of the horses admitted by the Section were not at this time from our division	

10/13 H W V Forms/C. 2118/10.

No 2 Mobile Veterinary Section.

Army Form C. 2118.

WAR DIARY
or
~~INTELLIGENCE SUMMARY.~~
(*Erase heading not required.*)

Instructions regarding War Diaries and Intelligence Summaries are contained in F. S. Regs., Part II. and the Staff Manual respectively. Title pages will be prepared in manuscript.

Hour, Date, Place	Summary of Events and Information	Remarks and references to Appendices
MAZINGARB 13·10·15.	Under instructions of D.D.V.S. 1st Army 21 ordinary sick cases & 2 suspicious mange cases evacuated to No 2 8 Mobile Veterinary Section at VERQUIN.	
" 15·10·15.	Evacuated from NOEUX 15 ordinary sick.	
	Moved to LOZINGHEM 19 kilometres, good camp & billets for men.	
LOZINGHEM. 17·10·15.	Conducting Party returned.	
	~~Sgt~~ Corp. Hood promoted Sergeant, No 96 Sgt Albans posted to No 35 Mobile Veterinary Section, No 943 Pte. Quinn promoted Corporal.	
" 20·10·15.	Evacuated from LILLERS to No 10 Veterinary Hospital 24 ordinary sick & 1 cast by D.D.V.S.	
22·10·15.	Conducting Party returned.	
24·10·15.	Lieut F.J. DELANE assumed command of the Section during my absence on 7 days leave.	

(9 29 6) W 3332—1107 100,000 10/13 H W V Forms/C. 2118/10.

No2 Mobile Veterinary Section

Army Form C. 2118.

Instructions regarding War Diaries and Intelligence Summaries are contained in F. S. Regs., Part II. and the Staff Manual respectively. Title pages will be prepared in manuscript.

WAR DIARY

or

~~INTELLIGENCE SUMMARY~~.

(Erase heading not required.)

Hour, Date, Place	Summary of Events and Information	Remarks and references to Appendices
LOZINGHEM. 26.10.15	Evacuated from LILLERS 24 ordinary sick cases and 3 ringworm cases.	
28.10.15.	Conducting Party returned.	
29.10.15.	Evacuated from LILLERS. 16 ordinary sick cases and 1 suspicious mange case.	
31.10.15.	Returned from leave & resumed command of Section. Conducting Party returned.	

[illegible] Lieut A.V.C.

1ST DIVISION
DIVISIONAL TROOPS

NO.2 MOBILE VETERINARY SECTION

~~JAN - DEC 1916~~

1916 JAN - 1919 AUG

H.Q.

1st Division

Herewith War Diary from

No 1 Mobile Veterinary Section

[illegible]

Capt.

O.C. No 1 Mobile Veterinary Section

1/9/16.

January 1916.

Instructions regarding War Diaries and Intelligence Summaries are contained in F. S. Regs., Part II. and the Staff Manual respectively. Title Pages will be prepared in manuscript.

WAR DIARY
or
~~INTELLIGENCE SUMMARY~~
(Erase heading not required.)

No 2 Mobile Veterinary Section.

Army Form C. 2118

Place	Date	Hour	Summary of Events and Information	Remarks and references to Appendices
NOEUX les MINES.	Jany 1st 1916.		Helped to mallein horses of 2nd Inf Bde at MAZINGARB.	
— —	3rd		Mallienied horses at Divisional Train.	
— —	4th		Evacuated 4 mange cases & 28 ordinary sick & one cast for Vice.	
— —	5th		Mallienied horses at Divisional Train.	
			During the last week or ten days a very large number of laminitis cases have been admitted to Section practically all in heavy draught horses. 170th Coy R.E. having 5 cases out of 11 horses.	
	8th		Malleined horses of 1st Infantry Bde at MAZINGARB.	
	10th		Evacuated 30 ordinary sick, 4 mange cases 2 cast by DDVS 1st Army.	
	12th		Mallenid 2nd Reserve Park	
	14th		Evacuated 31 ordinary sick 8 mange cases.	
	15th		Moved to LILLERS. taking over place formerly occupied by 27 M.V.S who replaced this section.	
			Section was in a wood yard with large open sheds giving accomodation for section horses & about 24 sick.	

1875 Wt. W593/826 1,000,000 4/15 J.B.C. & A. A.D.S.S./Forms/C. 2118.

Instructions regarding War Diaries and Intelligence Summaries are contained in F. S. Regs., Part II. and the Staff Manual respectively. Title Pages will be prepared in manuscript.

WAR DIARY

or

~~INTELLIGENCE SUMMARY~~

(Erase heading not required.)

Army Form C. 2118

Place	Date	Hour	Summary of Events and Information	Remarks and references to Appendices
LILLERS.	16th		Evacuated 16 ordinary & 8 mange cases.	
"	20th		Evacuated 24 ordinary sick & 8 mange cases.	
			Considerable increase in the number of mange cases during the last fortnight	
	22nd		Cpl Quinn sent to ABBEVILLE to exchange a G S limbered waggon for a float.	
	24th		Evacuated 40 ordinary sick cases.	
	25th		Proceeded on 4 days leave Major England A.V.C. assumed command of Section during my absence	
	27th		Evacuated 40 ordinary sick & 8 mange cases.	
	31st		Evacuated 32 ordinary sick & 4 mange cases.	
			Cpl Quinn returned from ABBEVILLE with float.	
			S W Mansell Capt A.V.C.	
			Cmdg 2nd Mobile Veterinary Section	

1875 Wt. W593/826 1,000,000 4/15 J.B.C. & A. A.D.S.S./Forms/C. 2118.

February 1916.

Instructions regarding War Diaries and Intelligence Summaries are contained in F. S. Regs., Part II. and the Staff Manual respectively. Title Pages will be prepared in manuscript.

WAR DIARY

or

~~INTELLIGENCE~~ SUMMARY No 2 Mobile Veterinary Section

(Erase heading not required.)

Army Form C. 2118.

Place	Date	Hour	Summary of Events and Information	Remarks and references to Appendices
LILLERS.	Feb 2nd		Returned from leave took over the Section.	
"	6th		Evacuated 29 ordinary sick & 5 mange cases.	
"	7th		Divisional practice concentration route march of one day only no casualties in horses. No 2685 Pte CHARLTON AVC. posted to England being nominated for a commission in 3/6th North Stafford Regiment.	
"	11th		Evacuated Ordinary cases 31, mange 5, mare & foal 1.	
"	13th		Evacuated Ordinary 48, mange 4, cast by DDR 1st Army 3. During the rest period most units evacuated many debility cases this accounting for the large number of horses evacuated.	
"	16th		Marched to DROUVIN taking over place vacated by 47th Divisional M.V.S. good accomodation for section & sick horses. I left 2 cases for 47th Division who left 30 to be evacuated by me.	
DROUVIN.	18th		Evacuated 28 ordinary cases and 6 skin cases.	
	21st		Heavy fall of snow followed by frost, roads becoming slippery & bad for horse transport.	

1875 Wt. W593/826 1,000,000 4/15 J.B.C. & A. A.D.S.S./Forms/C. 2118.

Army Form C. 2118

Instructions regarding War Diaries and Intelligence Summaries are contained in F. S. Regs., Part II. and the Staff Manual respectively. Title Pages will be prepared in manuscript.

WAR DIARY or ~~INTELLIGENCE SUMMARY~~

No 2 Mobile Veterinary Section

(Erase heading not required.)

Place	Date	Hour	Summary of Events and Information	Remarks and references to Appendices
DROUVIN.	Feby. 23rd		Evacuated 38 Ordinary sick (including 16 from 47th Division) and 10 cast by DDR 1st Army from 1st D.A.C	
"	25th		Snow & frost continued roads impossible unless horses are frost cogged.	
"	27.		Thaw set in roads again possible for horse transport.	
"	28.		Evacuated 8 mange cases, 29 ordinary sick	
			~~Pu~~ Took over Veterinary charge of 1st Divisional Train owing to illness of Lieut Foust A.V.C.	
	29.		23 debility cases received from 1st D.A.C. & 11 from 116th Bty	

S W Mason (?) Capt A.V.C.
Cmdg No 2 Mobile Veterinary Section

1875 Wt. W593/826 1,000,000 4/15 J.B.C. & A. A.D.S.S./Forms/C. 2118.

Army Form C. 2118

Instructions regarding War Diaries and Intelligence Summaries are contained in F. S. Regs., Part II. and the Staff Manual respectively. Title Pages will be prepared in manuscript.

WAR DIARY
or
~~INTELLIGENCE~~ SUMMARY

No 2 Mobile Veterinary Section

(Erase heading not required.)

Place	Date	Hour	Summary of Events and Information	Remarks and references to Appendices
DROUVIN	1/3/16		Evacuated 55 ordinary sick and 1 mare in foal.	
"	3/3/16		Evacuated 36 ordinary sick and 5 mange cases. During the last six days over 140 cases were admitted to the Section over 100 being debility cases from the Artillery which points to great neglect and bad horsemastership.	
"	6/3/16		Two men received from No 1 Veterinary Hospital as reinforcements.	
"	7/3/16		Evacuated Ordinary 47, mange 7	
"	8/3/16		Inspected by Lieut Colonel Tulloch AA&QMG 1st Division	
"	11/3/16		Evacuated 30 ordinary sick & 2 cast by DDR 1st Army.	
"	13/3/16		It is noticed that owing to the Section now having a float many more horses are now received that have to be slaughtered than formerly	
"	16/3/16		Evacuated 23 ordinary sick & 4 mange cases.	

1875 Wt. W593/826 1,000,000 4/15 J.B.C. & A. A.D.S.S./Forms/C. 2118.

Army Form C. 2118

Instructions regarding War Diaries and Intelligence Summaries are contained in F. S. Regs., Part II. and the Staff Manual respectively. Title Pages will be prepared in manuscript.

WAR DIARY No 2 Mobile Veterinary Section 1st Division
or
~~INTELLIGENCE SUMMARY~~

(Erase heading not required.)

Place	Date	Hour	Summary of Events and Information	Remarks and references to Appendices
Drouvin	19/3/16		Inspected by Lieut Colonel Martin A.V.C. D.D.V.S 1st Division	
"	21/3/16		Evacuated 29 ordinary sick & 6 mange cases.	
"	28/3/16		Evacuated 22 ordinary sick and 6 mange cases.	

[signature] Capt A.V.C.
Cmg No 2 Mobile Veterinary Section

1875 Wt. W593/826 1,000,000 4/15 J.B.C. & A. A.D.S.S./Forms/C.2118.

Instructions regarding War Diaries and Intelligence Summaries are contained in F. S. Regs., Part II. and the Staff Manual respectively. Title Pages will be prepared in manuscript.

Army Form C. 2118

WAR DIARY

or

~~INTELLIGENCE SUMMARY~~

(*Erase heading not required.*)

No 2 Mobile Veterinary Section

Place	Date	Hour	Summary of Events and Information	Remarks and references to Appendices
DROUVIN	4/4/16		Evacuated 18 ordinary sick, 6 mange cases & 2 cast by DDR 1st Army.	
"	9/4/16		Evacuated 22 ordinary sick.	
"	11/4/16		A large proportion of the horses admitted to the Section are now shell wounds many of which have to be destroyed.	
"	17/4/16		Evacuated 19 Ordinary sick 1 mare in foal.	
"	19/4/16		B. Squadron Northumberland Hussars proceed today to 1st Cavalry Division for training, horses inspected before proceeding & found to be in good condition but rather soft owing to the majority of the men having been employed on trench maintenance & the horses not getting much exercise.	
"	22/4/16		Evacuated 22 ordinary sick & 1 cast by DDR 1st Army	

Instructions regarding War Diaries and Intelligence Summaries are contained in F. S. Regs., Part II. and the Staff Manual respectively. Title Pages will be prepared in manuscript.

Army Form C. 2118

WAR DIARY
or
INTELLIGENCE SUMMARY

(*Erase heading not required.*)

No 2 Mobile Veterinary Section

Place	Date	Hour	Summary of Events and Information	Remarks and references to Appendices
Drouvin	27/4/16		Evacuated 21 ordinary sick, 4 mange cases 2 destroyed by D.D.R. 1st Army	
	30/7/16.		The number of cases admitted to the Section has been the smallest this month since July 1915. The general improvement in the horses of the Division owing to the good weather being very noticeable. Except for the high percentage of shell wound cases (over 20% of horses admitted to Section) the total would have been much lower.	

S W Marriott Capt A.V.C.
O.C. No 2 Mobile Veterinary Section

Instructions regarding War Diaries and Intelligence Summaries are contained in F. S. Regs., Part II. and the Staff Manual respectively. Title Pages will be prepared in manuscript.

IV

No 2 Mobile **WAR DIARY** Veterinary Section

or

INTELLIGENCE SUMMARY

(Erase heading not required.)

Army Form C. 2118

1

Vol 10

Place	Date	Hour	Summary of Events and Information	Remarks and references to Appendices
DROUVIN	1/5/16		Granted 7 days leave to England. Captain BARR A.V.C. assumed command of Section during my absence.	
"	3/5/16		Evacuated 23 ordinary sick	
"	10/5/16		Evacuated 20 ordinary sick, 3 mange cases and 1 mare in foal. Resumed command of Section.	
"	19/5/16		Evacuated 5 skin cases (mange), 22 ordinary sick, 2 remount cases.	
"	24/5/16		Evacuated 21 ordinary sick. Inspected by Lieut Colonel [illegible] A.D.V.S. 1st Division.	
"	26/5/16		Received 33 lame & debility cases from 1st D.A.C. which was being reorganised; inspected 150 horses of 1st D.A.C. prior to their proceeding to Calais.	

1875 Wt. W593/826 1,000,000 4/15 J.B.C. & A. A.D.S.S./Forms/C. 2118.

Instructions regarding War Diaries and Intelligence Summaries are contained in F. S. Regs., Part II. and the Staff Manual respectively. Title Pages will be prepared in manuscript.

Army Form C. 2118

No 2 Mobile WAR DIARY Veterinary Section
or
INTELLIGENCE SUMMARY
(Erase heading not required.)

Place	Date	Hour	Summary of Events and Information	Remarks and references to Appendices
27/5/16.			Evacuated 38 ordinary sick cases	
DROUVIN	31/5/16		Total number of evacuations for the month was again low being only 133 considerably lower than the corresponding month last year although the percentage of [wounded] was again very high (about 20%)	
			[illegible] Capt A.V.C.	
			O.C. No 2 Mobile Vety Section	

1875 Wt. W593/826 1,000,000 4/15 J.B.C. & A. A.D.S.S./Forms/C. 2118.

Instructions regarding War Diaries and Intelligence Summaries are contained in F. S. Regs., Part II. and the Staff Manual respectively. Title Pages will be prepared in manuscript.

Army Form C. 2118

WAR DIARY or ~~INTELLIGENCE SUMMARY~~

(Erase heading not required.)

No 2 Mobile Veterinary Section

JUNE 1916.

Vol XI

Place	Date	Hour	Summary of Events and Information	Remarks and references to Appendices
DROUVIN.	2/6/16.		One artillery brigade & 1 Section of 12 D.A.C. from 12th Division attached to 1st Division	
	4/6/16.		Acting A.D.V.S. during leave of Major England A.V.C.	
	5/6/16.		Evacuated 16 ordinary sick and 2 mange cases.	
	6/6/16.		One brigade of Artillery from 40th Division attached this making the number of evacuations more but 1st Division percentage remained low.	
	11/6/16.		Several units from 40th Division attached increasing divisional strength by over 2000 horses & mules.	
	12/6/16		Most of 12th Division units return to their own division	
			Evacuated 29 Ordinary sick & 30 skin cases	
			Major England returned.	
	16/6/16.		Many horses being received from 40th Division including a number of float cases several of which have to be destroyed	
	19/6/16		Evacuated 31 ordinary sick.	
	20/6/16		1st Corps Heavy Artillery now evacuating their sick through this Section	

1875 Wt. W593/826 1,000,000 4/15 J.B.C. & A. A.D.S.S./Forms/C. 2118.

Army Form C. 2118

Instructions regarding War Diaries and Intelligence Summaries are contained in F. S. Regs., Part II. and the Staff Manual respectively. Title Pages will be prepared in manuscript.

WAR DIARY
or
~~INTELLIGENCE SUMMARY~~
(Erase heading not required.)

No 2 Mobile Veterinary Section

JUNE 1916

Place	Date	Hour	Summary of Events and Information	Remarks and references to Appendices
DROUVIN.	23/6/16		Evacuated 24 ordinary sick 3 skin cases & 2 sent by D.D.R. 1st Army	
	28/6/16		Evacuated 26 ordinary sick, 4 skin cases.	
			During the month only 96 cases were evacuated from 1st Division for Veterinary reasons this being the lowest total since July 1915. The total evacuations were higher than the two previous months owing to the large number of attached units	
			[signature] Capt A.V.C.	
			O.C. No 2 Mobile Veterinary Section	

1875 Wt. W593/826 1,000,000 4/15 J.B.C. & A. A.D.S.S./Forms/C. 2118.

Instructions regarding War Diaries and Intelligence Summaries are contained in F. S. Regs., Part II. and the Staff Manual respectively. Title Pages will be prepared in manuscript.

WAR DIARY
or
~~INTELLIGENCE~~ SUMMARY

(*Erase heading not required.*) No 2 MOBILE VETERINARY SECTION JULY

Army Form C. 2118

Vol 12

Place	Date	Hour	Summary of Events and Information	Remarks and references to Appendices
DROUVIN	3/7/16		Evacuated 32 ordinary sick cases.	
	4/7/16		Marched to BRUAY relieving 51st M.V.S. who also relieved their Section poor accomodation for horses & men.	
BRUAY	6/7/16		Evacuated 13 ordinary cases to No 57 Mobile Veterinary Section, as we had received orders to move next day.	
VIGNACOURT	7/7/16.		Left BRUAY at 1 am marched to FOUQUEREUIL Station entrained leaving station 6 am good accomodation for horses & waggons.	
			Arrived DOULLENS 10 am detrained, no casualties marched to VIGNACOURT 16 miles arrived 6.30 p.m billetted in ruins.	
ST GRATIEN	8/7/16		Marched at 2 p.m to ST. GRATIEN 12 miles arrived 7 p.m billetted in a field left one sick horse unable to walk at FLESSELLES.	
	9/7/16		Stopped at ST GRATIEN inspected by D.D.V.S. 4th Army.	
			Sent party to L'ETOILE 20 miles to see about horses left behind by 25th Bde R.F.A.	
	10/7/16		Remained at ST GRATIEN.	

1875 Wt. W593/826 1,000,000 4/15 J.B.C. & A. A.D.S.S./Forms/C. 2118.

Instructions regarding War Diaries and Intelligence Summaries are contained in F. S. Regs., Part II. and the Staff Manual respectively. Title Pages will be prepared in manuscript.

WAR DIARY
or
INTELLIGENCE SUMMARY
(Erase heading not required.)

Army Form C. 2118

No 2 Mobile Veterinary Section. JULY

Place	Date	Hour	Summary of Events and Information	Remarks and references to Appendices
DERNANCOURT	11/7/16		Marched to DERNANCOURT arrived [illegible] p.m.	
"	12/7/16		Moved on to the plain just outside DERNANCOURT village	
"	14/7/16		Admitted horses from 7 different divisions	
"	16/7/16		Evacuated 16 ordinary sick and 3 skin cases from MERICOURT Station	
"	19/7/16		Evacuated 9 ordinary sick cases moved to field just outside ALBERT but on arrival received orders to return to old camp.	
"	24/7/16		Evacuated 13 ordinary sick (10 wounded) & 7 skin cases (6 from other divisions than the 1st)	
"	26/7/16		All the Division except the Artillery went back into reserve; Section remained to receive horses from the Artillery	
"	28/7/16		Evacuated 31 ordinary sick cases.	
			During the month the number of horses admitted to the Section for diseases & injuries (other than shell wounds) was very small	
			[illegible] Capt. A.V.C.	
			O.C. No 2 Mobile Veterinary Section	

1875 Wt. W593/826 1,000,000 4/15 J.B.C. & A. A.D.S.S./Forms/C. 2118.

2 Mob Vet Sec
Vol. 13

Army Form C. 2118

Instructions regarding War Diaries and Intelligence Summaries are contained in F. S. Regs., Part II. and the Staff Manual respectively. Title Pages will be prepared in manuscript.

WAR DIARY
or
~~INTELLIGENCE SUMMARY~~
(Erase heading not required.)

No 2 MOBILE VETERINARY SECTION. AUGUST.

Place	Date	Hour	Summary of Events and Information	Remarks and references to Appendices
DERNACOURT	1/8/16		Assumed Veterinary charge of III Corps Heavy Artillery owing to illness of Captain Maconachie A.V.C.	
"	7/8/16		Evacuated 22 ordinary sick & 2 skin cases.	
"	14/8/16		Evacuated 19 ordinary sick & 1 cast by DDR 4th Army	
"	15/8/16		Remainder of Division returned to the line.	
"	18/8/16		No 928 Corporal Owen promoted Sergeant, No S.E. 662 Pte Gowing promoted Corporal	
	20/8/16		Evacuated 28 ordinary sick & 4 skin cases.	
	21/8/16		No 448 Sergeant Hood posted to No 5 Convalescent Horse Depot	
	26/8/16		Relinquished Veterinary charge of III Corps Heavy Artillery	
	27/8/16		Evacuated 31 ordinary sick cases & 1 skin case	

[signature] Capt AVC
O.C. No 2 Mobile Veterinary Section

A.Q. Gphy.
1st Division

Herewith War Diary for No 2 Mobile Veterinary Section for the month of September 1916.

[signature]

CAPTAIN, A.V.C.
O.C. 2 MOBILE VETERINARY SECTION.

4/10/16

Instructions regarding War Diaries and Intelligence Summaries are contained in F. S. Regs., Part II. and the Staff Manual respectively. Title Pages will be prepared in manuscript.

WAR DIARY
or
INTELLIGENCE SUMMARY
(Erase heading not required.)

Army Form C. 2118

Mob Vety Sec

No 2 MOBILE VETERINARY SECTION — SEPTEMBER

Vol 14

Place	Date	Hour	Summary of Events and Information	Remarks and references to Appendices
DERNANCOURT	2/9/16		Evacuated 24 ordinary sick & 2 remount cases from EDGEHILL	
	6/9/16		Captain Maconachie returned to duty & resumed Veterinary charge of III Corps Heavy Artillery.	
	10/9/16		Evacuated 31 ordinary sick cases.	
	14/9/16		Evacuated 32 ordinary sick, one remount case & one skin disease case	
			Moved section to BEHENCOURT. poor accommodation for men & horses.	
BEHENCOURT	20/9/16		Evacuated 17 ordinary cases & 4 remount cases	
ALBERT			Moved Section to ALBERT.	
BECORDEL	22/9/16		Moved section to BECORDEL on main PERONNE - ALBERT road. fair camping ground.	
			A Veterinary Casualty Clearing Station was opened at MEAULTE to which horses were sent by the Mobile Veterinary Sections for evacuation.	

1875 Wt. W593/826 1,000,000 4/15 J.B.C. & A. A.D.S.S./Forms/C. 2118.

Instructions regarding War Diaries and Intelligence Summaries are contained in F. S. Regs., Part II. and the Staff Manual respectively. Title Pages will be prepared in manuscript.

WAR DIARY
or
~~INTELLIGENCE~~ SUMMARY
(Erase heading not required.)

Army Form C. 2118

No 2 MOBILE VETERINARY SECTION SEPTEMBER

Place	Date	Hour	Summary of Events and Information	Remarks and references to Appendices
BECORDEL.	22/9/16.		Each Section at the time sent 2 men to the C.C.S. the rest of the personnel being found by the Base Hospitals	
	23/9/16		Evacuated 7 ordinary sick	
	25/9/16		Evacuated 6 ordinary sick	
	26/9/16.		Evacuated 7 ordinary sick 4 remount cases.	
	29/9/16.		Evacuated 8 ordinary sick.	

[signature] Capt A.V.C.
O.C. No 2 Mobile Veterinary Section

1875 Wt. W593/826 1,000,000 4/15 J.B.C. & A. A.D.S.S./Forms/C. 2118.

Army Form C. 2118 1

Mob Vety Sec

WAR DIARY
or
~~INTELLIGENCE SUMMARY~~
(Erase heading not required.)

Instructions regarding War Diaries and Intelligence Summaries are contained in F. S. Regs., Part II. and the Staff Manual respectively. Title Pages will be prepared in manuscript.

No 2 Mobile Veterinary Section October 1916

Vol 15 & 16

Place	Date	Hour	Summary of Events and Information	Remarks and references to Appendices
Buordel	1/10/16.		Evacuated. 6 ordinary sick cases withdrew man from Veterinary Casualty Clearing Station.	SWR
"	2/10/16		Marched with Section to LaCHAUSSIE. 24 miles joining the transport of the Division at AMIENS.	SWR
	3/10/16		Marched in rear of the Divisional transport to CHEPY via HANGEST, AIRAINES OISEMONT 31 miles arriving at destination 8 30p.m. Good accomodation for men & horses. One horse of Section left behind at LaCHAUSSIE with COLIC also one of the Company Train handed over to Section in route with colic left with a farmer at ALLERY	SWR
CHEPY	4/10/16		Information received that two other horses were left behind being unable to travel	
"	6/10/16.		Party sent to find out condition of horses left behind. Horse of Section left at LaCHAUSSIE died same day & also horse of 2nd Bde HQ left at YZEUX died same day 3rd. Horse left at ALLERY fit to walk. Unable to find horse left at AIRAINES	SWR

1875 Wt. W593/826 1,000,000 4/15 J.B.C. & A. A.D.S.S./Forms/C. 2118.

Army Form C. 2118

Instructions regarding War Diaries and Intelligence Summaries are contained in F. S. Regs., Part II. and the Staff Manual respectively. Title Pages will be prepared in manuscript.

WAR DIARY
or
INTELLIGENCE SUMMARY

(Erase heading not required.)

Place	Date	Hour	Summary of Events and Information	Remarks and references to Appendices
CHEPY	9/10/16		Major England A.V.C. proceeded on leave assumed duties of A.D.V.S.	[illegible]
"	10/10/16		Evacuated to ABBEVILLE (No 22 Veterinary Hospital) by road 15 ordinary sick cases & 2 cast by D.D.R. 4th Army.	[illegible]
"	12/10/16		Collected horse left at ALLERY	[illegible]
"	13/10/16		Collected horse left at AIRAINE in float	[illegible]
"	15/10/16		Evacuated to ABBEVILLE 6 ordinary cases	
"	22/10/16		Evacuated to ABBEVILLE 9 ordinary and 2 mange cases. Major England returned from leave	
"	23/10/16		Proceeded on 10 days leave to England. Captain G. H. Pollock assumed command of Section	[illegible]
"	29/10/16		Evacuated 10 cases to ABBEVILLE.	
"	30/10/16		Section marched to ST SAUVEUR 35 miles and joined the [illegible] Division there	[illegible]

1875 Wt. W593/826 1,000,000 4/15 J.B.C. & A. A.D.S.S./Forms/C. 2118.

Army Form C. 2118.

WAR DIARY
or
INTELLIGENCE SUMMARY.
(Erase heading not required.)

Instructions regarding War Diaries and Intelligence Summaries are contained in F. S. Regs., Part II. and the Staff Manual respectively. Title pages will be prepared in manuscript.

No 2 Mobile Veterinary Section

Hour, Date, Place	Summary of Events and Information	Remarks and references to Appendices
31/10/16	Section marched with Division to BAIZEU relieving the Section of 4th Division in moderate billets	[illegible]

[signature]

CAPTAIN, A.V.C.
O.C. 2 MOBILE VETERINARY SECTION

Instructions regarding War Diaries and Intelligence Summaries are contained in F. S. Regs., Part II. and the Staff Manual respectively. Title Pages will be prepared in manuscript.

Army Form C. 2118

WAR DIARY
or
~~INTELLIGENCE SUMMARY~~

(*Erase heading not required.*)

No 2 MOBILE Veterinary Section. November 1916

Place	Date	Hour	Summary of Events and Information	Remarks and references to Appendices
BAIZEU.	4/11/16		Captain Marriott returned from leave and assumed command of Section.	
	5/11/16		Evacuated 13 odinary sick and 1 mange case.	
BECORDEL.	6/11/16		Section marched to BECORDEL no accomodation or standings for horses watering poor.	
"	10/11/16		Owing to measles breaking out in the Section of 40th Division the evacuations for that Division were done by this Section.	[illegible]
"	11/11/16		Evacuated 48 ordinary sick.	
"	13/11/16		Obtained a working party of 10 men for burying horses & building stables. Evacuated 32 ordinary sick.	
"	16/11/16		Evacuated 64 ordinary sick	
"	18/11/16		Evacuated 71 ordinary sick and 9 cast by D.D.R.	[illegible]
"	20/11/16		Evacuated 80 ordinary sick.	
	22/11/16		Evacuated 96 ordinary sick	[illegible]

Army Form C. 2118

Instructions regarding War Diaries and Intelligence Summaries are contained in F. S. Regs., Part II. and the Staff Manual respectively. Title Pages will be prepared in manuscript.

WAR DIARY
or
~~INTELLIGENCE SUMMARY~~

(Erase heading not required.)

No 2 Mobile Veterinary Section

Place	Date	Hour	Summary of Events and Information	Remarks and references to Appendices
23/11/16 Becordel			The very high number of evacuations were largely due to ~~[illegible]~~ many horses being received from 48th & 5th Divisions & 23rd Divisional R.A. & Corps troops but the number from the 1st Division Artillery was very high particularly from 25th Bde R.F.A.	[illegible]
	24/11/16		Evacuated 80 ordinary sick	
	27/11/16		Evacuated 63 ordinary sick One stable for 32 horses completed.	
	29/11/16		Evacuated 109 ordinary sick. During November 707 horses were admitted to the Section of which 325 were not from the 1st Division. The number of horses evacuated during the month was more than double that of any previous month in 1915 or 1916.	[illegible]

[signature]
CAPTAIN, A.V.C.
O.C. 2 MOBILE VETERINARY SECTION.

1875 Wt. W593/826 1,000,000 4/15 J.B.C. & A. A.D.S.S./Forms/C. 2118.

Instructions regarding War Diaries and Intelligence Summaries are contained in F. S. Regs., Part II. and the Staff Manual respectively. Title Pages will be prepared in manuscript.

WAR DIARY
or
~~INTELLIGENCE SUMMARY~~
(Erase heading not required.) No 2 Mobile Veterinary Section.

Army Form C. 2118

Vol 17

Place	Date	Hour	Summary of Events and Information	Remarks and references to Appendices
BECORDEL	2/12/16		Evacuated 46 ordinary sick	
	5/12/16.		Evacuated 45 ordinary sick	
			Second stable for 50 horses completed.	
	6/12/16.		Horse Rest Camp for the Division opened for 50 horses requiring a rest but not badly enough debilitated to be ~~sent to~~ evacuated	
			15 men from infantry and 5 gunners sent as personnel	
			Allotment of horses 10 from each Artillery brigade 5 from each infantry brigade, 5 from other units.	[illegible]
	9/12/16		Evacuated 61 ordinary sick cases	
			Horse Rest Camp filled.	
	13/12/16		Evacuated 30 ordinary sick	
	17/12/16		Evacuated 48 ordinary sick	
	22/12/16		Evacuated 46 ordinary sick	

Instructions regarding War Diaries and Intelligence Summaries are contained in F. S. Regs., Part II. and the Staff Manual respectively. Title Pages will be prepared in manuscript.

WAR DIARY
or
~~INTELLIGENCE SUMMARY~~
(Erase heading not required.)

Army Form C. 2118

Place	Date	Hour	Summary of Events and Information	Remarks and references to Appendices
Beçordel.	24/12/16		The evacuations still continue to be high largely due to the number of horses admitted from units not in the Division	
	27/12/16		Evacuated 48 ordinary sick & 3 mange cases	
	30/12/16		Twelve horses from the Horse Rest Camp returned to their units as fit for work replaced by tired horses.	
			Evacuated 48 ordinary sick & two mange cases.	
			During the month 438 horses were evacuated the highest total for any month (except November 1916) for two years.	

[signature] Marrett

CAPTAIN, A.V.C.
O.C. 2 MOBILE VETERINARY SECTION.

1875 Wt. W593/826 1,000,000 4/15 J.B.C. & A. A.D.S.S./Forms/C. 2118.

Army Form C. 2118

Instructions regarding War Diaries and Intelligence Summaries are contained in F. S. Regs., Part II. and the Staff Manual respectively. Title Pages will be prepared in manuscript.

WAR DIARY
or
INTELLIGENCE ~~SUMMARY~~

No 2 Mobile Veterinary Section (*Erase heading not required.*) January 1917.

Vol 18

Place	Date	Hour	Summary of Events and Information	Remarks and references to Appendices
~~3/1/17~~ BECORDEL	3/1/17		Evacuated 64 ordinary sick cases. 42 from other units than 1st Division.	
	6/1/17		Evacuated 32 ordinary cases	
	8/1/17		20 horses from Horse Rest Camp returned to units as fit for work.	
	10/1/17		Evacuated 46 ordinary ~~[illegible]~~ sick cases & 2 mange cases	
	12/1/17		10 horses from Horse Rest Camp returned to units	
	16/1/17		29 ordinary sick cases evacuated.	
	21/1/17		11 horses from Horse Rest Camp returned to units	
	23/1/17		Evacuated 44 ordinary sick.	

1875 Wt. W593/826 1,000,000 4/15 J.B.C. & A. A.D.S.S./Forms/C. 2118.

Instructions regarding War Diaries and Intelligence Summaries are contained in F. S. Regs., Part II. and the Staff Manual respectively. Title Pages will be prepared in manuscript.

WAR DIARY
or
~~INTELLIGENCE SUMMARY~~
(Erase heading not required.)

Army Form C. 2118

January 1917

Place	Date	Hour	Summary of Events and Information	Remarks and references to Appendices
BECORDEL	27/1/17		Horse Rest Camp closed all horses remaining returned to Units	
			Total figures of horses admitted	
			Admitted 80.	
			Returned to units fit for work 71.	
			Evacuated 9	
			Average number of days in rest camp 30.	

[illegible] Capt. A.V.C.
O.C. No [illegible] Mobile Veterinary Section

1875 Wt. W593/826 1,000,000 4/15 J.B.C. & A. A.D.S.S./Forms/C. 2118.

Army Form C. 2118

Instructions regarding War Diaries and Intelligence Summaries are contained in F. S. Regs., Part II. and the Staff Manual respectively. Title Pages will be prepared in manuscript.

WAR DIARY
or
~~INTELLIGENCE SUMMARY~~

(Erase heading not required.)

No. 2 Mobile Vety. Section

Vol 19

Place	Date	Hour	Summary of Events and Information	Remarks and references to Appendices
BECORDEL	4/2/17		Handed over 23 ordinary sick & 5 mange cases to 5th Australian [illegible] as I was unable to get trucks owing to the stoppage of railway traffic.	
	5/2/17		Marched to FOUILLOY moderate accomodation for horses & men	
	7/2/17		Marched to R 9 a (Sheet 62D) good accomodation for men fair for horses but not enough for Horse Rest Camp	
R.9.a. (Sheet 62D)	10/2/17		Moved to larger building at R 9 a (Sheet 62D) good accomodation for men & for horses; stables very dirty & no road into camp, water a long way from Camp.	
	17/2/17		Horse Rest Camp reopened. 12 horses admitted.	
	21/2/17		18 more horses admitted to Horse Rest Camp.	
	24/2/17		Evacuated 35 ordinary sick & 5 mange cases.	

1875 Wt. W593/826 1,000,000 4/15 J.B.C. & A. A.D.S.S./Forms/C. 2118.

Army Form C. 2118

Instructions regarding War Diaries and Intelligence Summaries are contained in F. S. Regs., Part II. and the Staff Manual respectively. Title Pages will be prepared in manuscript.

WAR DIARY
or
~~INTELLIGENCE SUMMARY~~
(Erase heading not required.)

Place	Date	Hour	Summary of Events and Information	Remarks and references to Appendices
R.q.a.	28/2/17.		During this month very few horses were evacuated a great reduction on the three previous months.	

[signature]

1875 Wt. W593/826 1,000,000 4/15 J.B.C. & A. A.D.S.S./Forms/C. 2118.

Army Form C. 2118

WAR DIARY
or
~~INTELLIGENCE SUMMARY~~
(Erase heading not required.)

Instructions regarding War Diaries and Intelligence Summaries are contained in F. S. Regs., Part II. and the Staff Manual respectively. Title Pages will be prepared in manuscript.

No 2 MOBILE VETERINARY SECTION. MARCH 1917.

Vol 20

Place	Date	Hour	Summary of Events and Information	Remarks and references to Appendices
R. 9. a. (Sheet 62D)	2-3-17.		Major England A.V.C. returned & resumed duties of A.D.V.S	
	3-3-17.		Evacuated from BRAY 15 ordinary sick & 8 mange cases	
	5-3-17.		Inspected 25th Bde & 39th Bde R.F.A. with Major England	
	7-3-17.		Assumed Veterinary charge of 1st Field Ambulance at CERISY; inspected their horses condition very fair with the exception of [illegible] & [illegible] - poor condition	
	9-3-17.		Conference of V.O's at A.D.V.S office.	
	10-3-17.		Evacuated from CHUIGNES 15 mange cases and 11 ordinary sick	
	12-3-17.		Horse Rest Camp inspected by A.Q. & Chief 1st Division	
	13-3-17		Inspection by A.D.V.S. 1st Division.	
	16-3-17		Conference of V.O's at A.D.V.S. Office	
	17-3-17.		Evacuated from CHUIGNES 8 mange cases & 16 ordinary sick.	
	19-3-17.		Inspected by A.D.V.S. 1st Division.	
	20-3-17.		Evacuated 6 mange cases & 3 ordinary sick.	

1875 Wt. W593/826 1,000,000 4/15 J.B.C. & A. A.D.S.S./Forms/C. 2118.

Army Form C. 2118

WAR DIARY
or
~~INTELLIGENCE SUMMARY~~
(Erase heading not required.)

Instructions regarding War Diaries and Intelligence Summaries are contained in F. S. Regs., Part II. and the Staff Manual respectively. Title Pages will be prepared in manuscript.

No 2 Mobile Veterinary Section — March

Place	Date	Hour	Summary of Events and Information	Remarks and references to Appendices
R.9.a. (Sht. 62 D.)	23-3-17.		Conference of V.O's at A.D.V.S.'s Office	
	24-3-17.		Evacuated 6 mange cases & 6 ordinary sick.	
	27-3-17.		Evacuated 4 mange cases.	
	30-3-17.		Conference of V.O's.	
	31-3-17		Evacuated 23 ordinary sick & 8 mange cases.	
			During the month the evacuations, except for mange cases, were slight being only 40 from 1st Division units.	

S. W. Marriott
CAPTAIN
O.C. 2 MOBILE VETERINARY SEC.

1875 Wt. W593/826 1,000,000 4/15 J.B.C. & A. A.D.S.S./Forms/C. 2118.

Army Form C. 2118

Mob Vety Sec

Instructions regarding War Diaries and Intelligence Summaries are contained in F. S. Regs., Part II. and the Staff Manual respectively. Title Pages will be prepared in manuscript.

WAR DIARY
or
~~INTELLIGENCE~~ SUMMARY

(Erase heading not required.)

No 2 Mobile Veterinary Section.

April 1917.

Vol 21

Place	Date	Hour	Summary of Events and Information	Remarks and references to Appendices
~~3/4/17~~ R.G.A (Sheet 62D) 1/40000	3/4/17		Inspected by A.D.V.S 1st Division	
	6/4/17.		Conference of V.O's at A.D.V.S Office.	
	7/4/17.		Evacuated 21 ordinary sick & 4 mange cases	
	12/4/17		Returned 8 horses from Rest Camp to their units	
	13/4/17.		Conference of VO's at A.D.V.S Office.	
	14/4/17.		Evacuated 20 ordinary sick & 4 mange cases.	
	18/4/17.		Large increase in number of cases of mange sent to the Section especially from 3rd Inf Bde & 6th Welsh.	
	20/4/17.		Conference of VO's.	
	21/4/17.		Evacuated 14 ordinary & 20 mange cases	
	22/4/17.		Admitted 14 cases from 42 Division who were moving.	
	22/4/17.		Evacuated 16 ordinary sick & 8 mange cases. Inspected by D.D.V.S. 4th Army.	

1875 Wt. W593/826 1,000,000 4/15 J.B.C. & A. A.D.S.S./Forms/C. 2118.

Army Form C. 2118

WAR DIARY
or
~~INTELLIGENCE~~ SUMMARY

Instructions regarding War Diaries and Intelligence Summaries are contained in F. S. Regs., Part II. and the Staff Manual respectively. Title Pages will be prepared in manuscript. No 2 MOBILE VETERINARY Section

(Erase heading not required.)

April 1917

Place	Date	Hour	Summary of Events and Information	Remarks and references to Appendices
R.Q.a (Sheet 62D) 1/40000	28/4/17		Evacuated ordinary 6 mange 12	
			During the month the number of horses evacuated for Veterinary reasons has been small with the exception of mange cases which have considerably increased being higher this month than any previous month except January 1915.	
			[signature] Marriott CAPTAIN, A.V.C. O.C. 2 MOBILE VETERINARY SECTION.	

Army Form C. 2118

WAR DIARY
or
INTELLIGENCE SUMMARY
(Erase heading not required.)

Instructions regarding War Diaries and Intelligence Summaries are contained in F. S. Regs., Part II. and the Staff Manual respectively. Title Pages will be prepared in manuscript.

No 2 Mobile Veterinary Section — May 1917

Vol 22

Place	Date	Hour	Summary of Events and Information	Remarks and references to Appendices
R.Q.a (Sheet 62D)	5/5/17		Evacuated 9 ordinary sick, 2 [illegible] cases + 3 mange cases.	
	9/5/17		All horses belonging to the Artillery that were in the Rest Camp fit for work were returned & all [illegible] artillery attached for duty were returned.	
	10/5/17		24 ordinary sick evacuated + [illegible] mange cases. 6 horses destroyed by order of D.D.V.S. 4th Army for [illegible]	
	16/5/17		Horse Rest Camp closed [illegible] returned to their units. Since 17-2-17 92 horses were admitted, 61 were returned to their units fit for work, 27 evacuated or destroyed.	
	19/5/17		Evacuated 16 ordinary sick.	
	20/5/17		Moved to VILLIERS BRETONNEUX.	
VILLERS BRETONNEUX	26/5/17		Evacuated 8 ordinary sick.	
	24/5/17		Entrained at GUILLACOURT for Second Army.	

1875 Wt. W593/826 1,000,000 4/15 J.B.C. & A. A.D.S.S./Forms/C. 2118.

Instructions regarding War Diaries and Intelligence Summaries are contained in F. S. Regs., Part II. and the Staff Manual respectively. Title Pages will be prepared in manuscript.

WAR DIARY
or
~~INTELLIGENCE~~ SUMMARY
(Erase heading not required.)

Army Form C. 2118

May 1917

Place	Date	Hour	Summary of Events and Information	Remarks and references to Appendices
VILLERS BRETONNEUX	24/5/17		All horses entrained well watering accomodation on journey good.	
BERTHER.	28/5/17		Detrained at CASTRE marched to BERTHEN good accomodation	
	29/5/17		Major England assumed charge of the Section during my absence on leave to England	
			During the month the evacuations were very light partly owing to the Artillery being detached; mange was entirely stamped out in the Division by the end of the month	

[signature]
CAPTAIN, A.V.C.
O.C. 2 MOBILE VETERINARY SECTION.

1875 Wt. W593/826 1,000,000 4/15 J.B.C. & A. A.D.S.S./Forms/C. 2118.

Instructions regarding War Diaries and Intelligence Summaries are contained in F. S. Regs., Part II. and the Staff Manual respectively. Title Pages will be prepared in manuscript.

WAR DIARY

or

~~INTELLIGENCE SUMMARY~~

(Erase heading not required.)

No 2 Mobile Veterinary Section

Army Form C. 2118

2 Mob Vety Sec

June

Vol 23

Place	Date	Hour	Summary of Events and Information	Remarks and references to Appendices
BERTHEN	10/6/17		Captain Marriott resumed command vice Major A. England.	
	11/6/17		Section marched to & road to CINQ RUES about 2 miles west of HAZEBROUCK 14 miles.	
	19/6/17		Major England proceeded to VIII Corps Captain S.W. Marriott assumed duties of A.D.V.S. as well as O.C. Section	
			Evacuated 17 ordinary sick by road to ST OMER 15 miles.	
			Section marched to ST MARIE CAPPEL 7 miles	
	20/6/17		Section marched under orders of G.O.C. 2nd Infantry Bde to WORMHOUDT 12 miles.	
	21/6/17		Section marched to COUDEKERQUE-BRANCHE 15 miles	
	24/6/17		Section marched to COXIDE-BAINS 18 miles good accomodation	
	28/6/17		A few cases of mange admitted. These were horses that had had mange during the winter that have recurred.	

S.W. Marriott

CAPTAIN, A.V.C.
O.C. 2 MOBILE VETERINARY SECTION.

1875 Wt. W593/826 1,000,000 4/15 J.B.C. & A. A.D.S.S./Forms/C. 2118.

Army Form C. 2118

Instructions regarding War Diaries and Intelligence Summaries are contained in F. S. Regs., Part II. and the Staff Manual respectively. Title Pages will be prepared in manuscript.

WAR DIARY
or
~~INTELLIGENCE SUMMARY~~

(Erase heading not required.)

No 2 Mobile Veterinary Section July 1917. Vol 2

Place	Date	Hour	Summary of Events and Information	Remarks and references to Appendices
COXYDE BAINS (Sheet 11.)	6/7/17		Conference of V.O's at A.D.V.S's Offices	
			Evacuated 20 ordinary sick & 6 mange cases from ST IDESBAUD RD Station	
	7/7/17		Assumed Veterinary charge of 1st D.A.C, 1st Divisional Train & 1st D.H.Q owing to illness of Capt Pollock A.V.C.	
	10/7/17		Several wounded horses admitted to the Section.	
	13/7/17		Conference of V.O's.	
	17/7/17		Evacuated 26 ordinary sick (including 21 cases of shell wounds) and 5 mange cases.	
	18 7 17		Section marched to COUDEKERQUE-BRANCHE 20 miles.	
	19 7 17		Section marched to level crossing east of LOOM-BLAGE village (Sheet 5A HAZEBROOK) fair accomodation for horses & men but rather cramped.	
	20.7.17.		Conference of V.O's.	

1875 Wt. W593/826 1,000,000 4/15 J.B.C. & A. A.D.S.S./Forms/C. 2118.

Army Form C. 2118

Instructions regarding War Diaries and Intelligence Summaries are contained in F. S. Regs., Part II. and the Staff Manual respectively. Title Pages will be prepared in manuscript.

WAR DIARY
or
~~INTELLIGENCE SUMMARY~~
(Erase heading not required.)

No 2 Mobile Veterinary Section — July 1917

Place	Date	Hour	Summary of Events and Information	Remarks and references to Appendices
LECLIPON WAGGON LINES.	21.7.17		Inspected by D.A.D.V.S 1st Division	
			Conference of V.O's	
	24.7.17		Evacuated 5 mange + 3 ordinary sick from DUNKERQUE (8 miles)	
			During the month the evacuations from 1st Division were very low & 60% of the cases evacuated were shell wounds.	

S W Mannett[?] Capt AVC
OC No 2 Mobile Veterinary Section

1875 Wt. W593/826 1,000,000 4/15 J.B.C. & A. A.D.S.S./Forms/C. 2118.

WAR DIARY.

2/ MOBILE VETERINARY SECTION. AUGUST,1917.

Leclipon Waggon Lines.

3. 8. 17.	Conference of Veterinary Officers re Sand Colic.
10, 8. 17.	Evacuated 6 ordinary sick and 2 mange cases by road, to No.4 Veterinary Hospital,CALAIS also 21 remount cases to No.5 Base Remount Depot, CALAIS. Distance 23 miles, time taken 8 hours.
11. 8. 17	Returned to camp 5 hours journey.
16. 8. 17.	Moved camp to DANES close to LECLIPON Camp, good accomodation but sandy ground for standings. Assumed Veterinary charge of all horses outside LECLIPON Camp.
21.8. 17.	Evacuated 8 ordinary sick from LOOM PLAGE Station.
24. 8. 17.	Many cases of Sand Colic now occurred. in all units standing on the sand. High lines and muzzles adopted. Conference of Veterinary Officers.

During the month the evacuations from the Division werethe lowest since January,1915.

Instructions regarding War Diaries and Intelligence Summaries are contained in F. S. Regs., Part II. and the Staff Manual respectively. Title Pages will be prepared in manuscript.

WAR DIARY
or
~~INTELLIGENCE~~ SUMMARY
(Erase heading not required.)

Army Form C. 2118

No 2 Mobile Veterinary Section September

Place	Date	Hour	Summary of Events and Information	Remarks and references to Appendices
LECLIPON CAMP	4-9-17		Evacuated 20 ordinary sick from LOON PLAGE STATION.	
WAGGONDRIES	7-9-17		Conference of VOs at DADVS Office	
			Handed over Veterinary charge of Infantry units of Division to Capt. Barr A.V.C.	
	14-9-17		Conference of V.O's	
	18-9-17		Evacuated 12 ordinary sick cases	
	19-9-17		No S.E. 7275 Pte JETCOFFIED accidentally drowned whilst fishing.	
	26-9-17		Assumed Veterinary charge of all horses in ZE CLIDON Waggon lines.	
			During the month only 22 horses were evacuated from the division for Veterinary reasons	

[signature]
Captain A.V.C.

C.O. 2 Mobile V... Section

1875 Wt. W593/826 1,000,000 4/15 J.B.C. & A. A.D.S.S./Forms/C. 2118.

Army Form C. 2118.

Instructions regarding War Diaries and Intelligence Summaries are contained in F. S. Regs. Part II. and the Staff Manual respectively. Title pages will be prepared in manuscript.

WAR DIARY
or
~~INTELLIGENCE SUMMARY.~~

(Erase heading not required.)

Place	Date	Hour	Summary of Events and Information	Remarks and references to Appendices
	[illegible] 3		Evacuated 20 ordinary sick from [illegible] STATION	
	[illegible]		Conference of OCs and ADVS Office	
			Handed over Veterinary charge of Infantry units of	
			Division to Capt Barr AVC	
	[illegible] 10		Conference of O.Cs	
	[illegible] 14		Evacuated 12 ordinary sick horses	
	[illegible] 14		Pte SE 4245 Pte BETCHFIELD accidentally drowned whilst [illegible]	
	[illegible]		Resumed Veterinary charge of all horses in the [illegible]	
			Division lines	
			During the month only 22 horses were evacuated	
			[illegible] for Veterinary reasons	

Army Form C. 2118.

WAR DIARY
or
~~INTELLIGENCE SUMMARY.~~
(Erase heading not required.)

Instructions regarding War Diaries and Intelligence Summaries are contained in F. S. Regs., Part II. and the Staff Manual respectively. Title pages will be prepared in manuscript.

No 2 Mobile Veterinary Section. October 1917 + Nov

Place	Date	Hour	Summary of Events and Information	Remarks and references to Appendices
LECLIPON CAMP	2-10-17.		Evacuated 8 ordinary sick from LOON PLAGE.	Vol 27 + 28
WAGGON Lines	9-10-17.		Handed over command of Section to Capt BARR AVC during absence on leave from 10-10-17 to 20-10-17	
	16.10.17		Evacuated 7 ordinary sick from LOON PLAGE.	
	21.10.17		~~Resum~~ Capt S. W. MARRIOTT A.V.C. assumed command of Section on return from leave.	
			Evacuated 2 ordinary sick by motor ambulance to No 2 Veterinary Hospital	
	22.10.17.		Section marched to LEDERZEELE 18 miles.	
LEDERZEELE	23.10.17		Capt BARR. A.V.C. assumed command of Section vice Capt S.W. MARRIOTT who proceeded to ABBEVILLE for duty at No 3 Veterinary Hospital	
			Capt [illegible] Barr AVC assumes command of Section whilst also retaining Veterinary charge of 1st Inf Bde until Brigades get closer together	

D. D. & L., London, E.C. (A8c04) Wt W1771/M2031 750,000 5/17 Sch. 52 Forms/C2118/14

Army Form C. 2118.

Instructions regarding War Diaries and Intelligence Summaries are contained in F. S. Regs., Part II. and the Staff Manual respectively. Title pages will be prepared in manuscript.

WAR DIARY
or
INTELLIGENCE SUMMARY.

(Erase heading not required.)

No 2 Mobile Veterinary Section — October 1917

Place	Date	Hour	Summary of Events and Information	Remarks and references to Appendices
[illegible]	26.10.17		Section marches to Wormhout 10 miles — good accomodation for Horses & Men.	
Wormhout			Remain there until 30th. Take in 4 cases from other Divisions.	
	29.10.17		Sends advanced party to Quebec Farm (Sheet 28 A 25 a 4.7) to take over Billets from 30th MVS. Quebec Farm is 2 miles beyond Poperinghe.	
	30.10.17		Section marches to Quebec Farm. 15 miles from Wormhout — Billets for Horses & Men good. Overhead cover for 50 horses & brick flooring. Entrance to Quebec Farm (distance 300 yds) very bad. On 30th & 31st receive 16 horses. All from other Divisions.	

Andrew Barr

CAPTAIN. A.V.C.
O.C. 2 MOBILE VETERINARY SECTION.

D. D. & L., London, E.C.
(A8c04) Wt W1771/M2031 750,000 5/17 Sch. 52 Forms/C2118/14

Instructions regarding War Diaries and Intelligence Summaries are contained in F. S. Regs., Part II. and the Staff Manual respectively. Title pages will be prepared in manuscript.

WAR DIARY
or
INTELLIGENCE SUMMARY.
(Erase heading not required.)

Army Form C. 2118.

No 2 Mobile Veterinary Section — November 1917

Place	Date	Hour	Summary of Events and Information	Remarks and references to Appendices
Gwent Farm (2 miles beyond Poperinghe)	2.11.17		2nd Corps takes over from 18th Corps. Colonel Griffiths (DDVS 2nd Corps) takes over from Colonel Nicholls (DDVS 18th Corps)	
	3.11.17		Colonel Griffiths inspects Section.	
	4.11.17		Sick & casualties now number over 100 in Section & unable to get any evacuated. All other Divisional MVSs & Corps Detached Mobiles found here crammed full too. Many debility & minor casualties having to return to Units for a few days.	
	6.11.17		Take over Advanced Aid Post (at H [illegible] central. Sheet 28) from 63rd M.V.S. A Lance Corporal & Private remain there. DDVS visits Section & inspects cases for evacuation.	
	7.11.17		Evacuate 48 to Hosp. [illegible] by rail from [illegible]. Same afternoon evacuate 46 to 19th Corps Detached Mobile Section	
	9.11.17		7 PB men attached to Section for Temporary Duty from 1st Inf [illegible]	
	12.11.17		Evacuate 46 by rail to Hosp [illegible]	
	14.11.17		Get 15 men from [illegible] RE to make protection walls around Horse Lines to prevent [illegible] wounds.	
	15.11.17		Put up wind screens [illegible] [illegible] in Billet	
	17.11.17		ADVS shows new Billet for Section on main road to Poperinghe & about 2 kilometres from present one. Accommodation with [illegible] [illegible] for 40 animals & great advantage of being on side of main road. Map location, Sheet 28 A 28 c 2.4	

D. D. & L., London, E.C.
(A8604) Wt W1771/M2031 750,000 5/17 Sch. 52 Forms/C2118/14

Army Form C. 2118.

Instructions regarding War Diaries and Intelligence Summaries are contained in F. S. Regs., Part II. and the Staff Manual respectively. Title pages will be prepared in manuscript.

WAR DIARY
or
INTELLIGENCE SUMMARY.
(Erase heading not required.)

No 2 Mobile Veterinary Sect. November 1917

Place	Date	Hour	Summary of Events and Information	Remarks and references to Appendices
Poperinghe L.28.c.2.4	17.11.17		Move to new Billet.	
			Floors, roofing & drainage requiring much repair. [illegible] repaired it will make an excellent Billet for M.V.S. Huts [illegible] good.	
	19.11.17		[illegible] of R.E. ([illegible]) commence to repair Billet.	
			Evacuate 59 animals from International Railhead	
	23.11.17		Evacuate 64 animals from Proven? Railhead.	
	26.11.17		Section moves to Hamhoek & takes over Billet (F.30.a.5.5 Sheet 27) from 42 M.V.S. An excellent M.V.S. Billet.	
Hamhoek				
	27.11.17		Section moves to XIV Corps Area & takes over Billet (E.[illegible] Sheet 27) [illegible]	
			[illegible]	
Proven.	28.11.17		[illegible]	
	29.11.17		Private W.D. Dunsday? & Pte. [illegible] join Section to complete strength: Sent from No 2 Vet Hosp.	
	30.11.17		Inspection of Rifles, Gas Helmets & Box respirators of Section.	
			Inspection of clothing of Section & half of Section go to baths.	
			30 sick animals admitted since arrival at [illegible]	
			ADVS inspects Billet.	
			Private [illegible] leaves for No 22 Vet Hosp. to go through 6 weeks course of Farriery	
			[illegible] Capt.	
			CAPTAIN, A.V.C.	
			O.C. 2 MOBILE VETERINARY SECTION.	

D. D. & L., London, E.C.
(A8004) Wt W1771/M2031 750,000 5/17 Sch. 52 Forms/C2118/14

2 Mob Vet Sec

Army Form C. 2118.

Vol 29

WAR DIARY
or
INTELLIGENCE SUMMARY.
(Erase heading not required.)

Instructions regarding War Diaries and Intelligence Summaries are contained in F. S. Regs., Part II. and the Staff Manual respectively. Title pages will be prepared in manuscript.

No 2 Mobile Vet Sect — December 1917

Place	Date	Hour	Summary of Events and Information	Remarks and references to Appendices
[illegible]	1.12.17		Commence to dress wounds with oily dressing [illegible] [illegible]	
			[illegible] with [illegible]	
	2.12.17		Prepare horses for evacuation	
	3.12.17		Evacuate from [illegible] 53 animals [illegible]	
	5.12.17		Section moves to new Divisional Area. Taken over Billet from 29th MVS [illegible]	
Meaulte			29th MVS [illegible] 75 animals [illegible]	
			[illegible] Billet situated [illegible]	
			Accommodation for men very good.	
			[illegible]	
	6.12.17		[illegible]	
			Evacuate 77 animals [illegible]	
			[illegible]	
	7.12.17		[illegible]	
			[illegible]	

D. D. & L., London, E.C.
(A8004) Wt W1771/M2031 750,000 5/17 Sch. 52 Forms/C2118/14

Army Form C. 2118.

WAR DIARY
or
INTELLIGENCE SUMMARY.
(*Erase heading not required.*)

Instructions regarding War Diaries and Intelligence Summaries are contained in F. S. Regs., Part II. and the Staff Manual respectively. Title pages will be prepared in manuscript.

Place	Date	Hour	Summary of Events and Information — No 2 Mobile Veterinary Section — December 1917	Remarks and references to Appendices
Ondank	9.12.17		Very wet day & unable to get on with Horse standings	
			Prepare animals for evacuation	
	10.12.17		Evacuate 40 animals from Peselhoek Railhead	
	12.12.17		DADVS returns from leave.	
	13.12.17		Evacuate 27 animals to SSS VII Corps — 26 of which are debility	
	14.12.17		DADVS inspects Section	
	15.12.17		Receive orders that a draft of 13 men are being sent from No 22 Hospital to relieve 13 B class & men in Section who have to proceed to No 2 Hospital	
	16.12.17		Attend conference of VOs at DADVS	
			Prepare animals for evacuation	
	17.12.17		Evacuate 30 animals. Return 7 Ophthalmia cases.	
	18.12.17		New covered standing for Horses practically finished. Held up to get proper flooring done until arrival of concrete blocks. Do some temporary flooring with timber [illegible] [illegible] [illegible] as precaution against [illegible] [illegible] [illegible] road around horse standing [illegible] [illegible] [illegible] [illegible] [illegible] [illegible]	
	19.12.17		Draft of 13 men arrive from No 22 Hospital [illegible] [illegible] [illegible] [illegible]	
			Send off 13 B class men from Section to No 2 Veterinary Hospital	
	20.12.17		Leave increased to 1 per day until the [illegible]	
	21.12.17		Evacuate 25 animals from Peselhoek Railhead [illegible] [illegible] [illegible]	
			[illegible] animals [illegible] [illegible] [illegible]	
	25.12.17		Have a quiet time over Xmas. Do as little work as possible on Xmas Day. NCOs & men have Xmas Dinner at 3 o'clock. DADVS comes up & gives a few cheering words at commencement. Mess Room is made very cosy & everyone seems thoroughly satisfied.	

D. D. & L., London, E.C.
(A8004) Wt W1771/M2031 750,000 5/17 Sch. 52 Forms/C2118/14

Army Form C. 2118.

WAR DIARY
or
INTELLIGENCE SUMMARY.

(Erase heading not required.)

Instructions regarding War Diaries and Intelligence Summaries are contained in F. S. Regs., Part II. and the Staff Manual respectively. Title pages will be prepared in manuscript.

No 2 Mobile Veterinary Section — December 1917

Place	Date	Hour	Summary of Events and Information	Remarks and references to Appendices
[illegible]	26.12.17		Evacuate 25 Horses from [illegible] Railhead including 2 Mange & 5 [illegible] Had to wait 3 hours at Railhead for [illegible]	
	27.12.17 to 30.12.17		Quiet time at Section not many cases coming in Seven men on Leave including Staff Sergeant & two Corporals	
	31.12.17		Evacuate 13 Horses from [illegible] Railhead — including 2 Mange ADVS visits & goes all round the Section Expresses satisfaction	

Andrew Barr

CAPTAIN, A.V.C.
No. 2 MOBILE VETERINARY SECTION.

D. D. & L., London, E.C.
(A8004) Wt W1771/M2031 750,000 5/17 Sch. 52 Forms/C2118/14

Vol 30

Confidential.

War Diary

of

No. 2 M. V. S. 1st Div.

From Jany 1st 1918 To Jany 31st 1918.

(Vol 1.)

Instructions regarding War Diaries and Intelligence Summaries are contained in F. S. Regs., Part II. and the Staff Manual respectively. Title pages will be prepared in manuscript.

WAR DIARY

or

~~INTELLIGENCE SUMMARY.~~

(Erase heading not required.)

Army Form C. 2118.

Place	Date	Hour	Summary of Events and Information	Remarks and references to Appendices
			No 2 Mobile Veterinary Sect. January 1918	
[illegible]	1–6/1/18		During first six days taken in 71 suspected mange cases but in only 3 of these was actually able to find mange parasite. Practically every one had been dressed with Calcium Sulphide prep. All continue to [illegible] themselves [illegible]. Evacuate all as mange. Majority are from [illegible] D.A.	
	7.1.18		Evacuate 69 animals from [illegible] Railhead.	
	12.1.18		[illegible] inspects Section & expresses satisfaction.	
	13.1.18		Frost having gone we commence to lay floor of stable with concrete blocks	
	14.1.18		Evacuate 36 sick horses including 6 mange – 5 of these are from [illegible]	
"	20·1·18.		Assumed command of No 2 M.V.S. – Temporarily. Routine work.	
"	21·1·18.		Routine work and laying floor of new Stable. Evacuated from Peselhoek Station	
"	–	–	73 animals, including 5 cases mange and 2 cases Ulcerative Cellulitis.	
"	22·1·18		Routine work. Hauling broken brick and laying [illegible] bricks in Stable.	
"	–	–	Collected by float horse suffering a fracture of Humerus.	
"	23·1·18		Routine work. Hauling bricks and laying stable floors. Sent horse to Butcher's	
"	" –	–	and collected horse by float. Visited by A.D.V.S. XIX Corps. Slipped 2 chargers [illegible] 1st Div	
"	24·1·18		Routine work. Hauling sand. Repairing and laying stable floors. Moved mange lines.	[illegible] Capt. A.V.C.

D. D. & L., London, E.C.
(A8co4) Wt W1771/M2031 750,000 5/17 Sch. 52 Forms/C2118/14

Instructions regarding War Diaries and Intelligence Summaries are contained in F. S. Regs., Part II. and the Staff Manual respectively. Title pages will be prepared in manuscript.

WAR DIARY
or
~~INTELLIGENCE SUMMARY.~~
(Erase heading not required.)

Army Form C. 2118.

Place	Date	Hour	Summary of Events and Information	Remarks and references to Appendices
			No. 2 M. V. Section.	
	Jany.	1918		
Oosthoek	25-1-18		Routine work. Took over Veterinary charge of 95th Bgde R.F.A. and 2 Sect. B Echl. 1st DAC	
"	26-1-18		Routine work. Laying stable floors and building up new mange line.	
"	28-1-18		Evacuated from Peselhoek Railhead 73 animals including 45 mange, 2 cellulitis	
			Visited by A.D.V.S. XIX and II Corps. Visited lines of B Echelon 1st D A C	
"	29-1-18		Routine work. Visited lines of 113th and 114th Bdes R.F.A.	
"	30-1-18		Routine work. Visited lines of 95th Bde. R.F.A.	
"	31-1-18		Routine work. Hauling trials for standings. Visited by the D.D.V.S. II Corps. Collected horse by	[illegible] Capt. O.C. No. 2 M.V.S.
			float from 1st Divl Train	

D. D. & L., London, E.C. (A8004) Wt W1771/M2031 750,000 5/17 Sch. 52 Forms/C2118/14

Army Form C. 2118.

WAR DIARY
or
~~INTELLIGENCE SUMMARY.~~

(Erase heading not required.)

Instructions regarding War Diaries and Intelligence Summaries are contained in F. S. Regs., Part II. and the Staff Manual respectively. Title pages will be prepared in manuscript.

Place	Date	Hour	Summary of Events and Information	Remarks and references to Appendices
			No. 2 M. V. S.	
OUDDANK	Feb. 1st	1918	Routine work. Hauling broken fuel. Visited lines of 113th & 114th RFA Btys. (Destroyed 2 animals at PROVEN.)	[illegible]
"	2nd		" " . Visited lines of 115th and 40th Btys R.F.A.	
"	3rd		" " Visited lines of 2 Btys 23rd A.F.A. Bgde.	
"	4th		– – Evacuated 51 Animals from Peselhoek Stn. Visited sick lines 114th Bty.	
"	5th		" " Preparing portion of ground for cultivation of vegetables. Visited lines of 23rd Bgde A.F.A. and destroyed mule at Amm. Col.	
"	6th		Routine work. Visited horse lines of 124th Bty, and 65th How. Bty. Selected 25 cases of mange from latter for evacuation. Arranged for Unit to keep animals until trucks available. Visited lines of 23rd Bgde Amm Col and 216 M.G.C. Destroyed 1 mule at each place.	
"	7th		Routine work. Completed garden patch. Visited lines of 113th & 114th Btys.	
"	8th		Routine work. Two men of R.Es reconstructing kitchen grate. Collected 3 horses by float. One Tetanus case and one Pneumonia died in the M.V.S. Visited lines of 123rd Bty, and sent in 4 cases mange also 2 cases mange from 124th Bty.	

D. D. & L., London, E.C.
(A8004) Wt W1771/M2031 750,000 5/17 Sch. 52 Forms/C2118/14

Army Form C. 2118.

WAR DIARY
or
~~INTELLIGENCE SUMMARY.~~
(Erase heading not required.)

Instructions regarding War Diaries and Intelligence Summaries are contained in F. S. Regs., Part II. and the Staff Manual respectively. Title pages will be prepared in manuscript.

Place	Date	Hour	Summary of Events and Information No. 2. M. V. S.	Remarks and references to Appendices
ONDANK	FEB 8th	1918 (Contd)	Accompanied A/D.A.D.V.S. in search of suitable location for M.V.S. in event of moving. No where approaching a suitable place seen. Visited by D.A.D.V.S. 32nd Div	
"	9th	"	Routine work. Completing work on kitchen grate and constructing wind screen for mange line. Collected one horse by float.	
"	10th	"	Routine work. Visited No 2 F. Amb. at Crombeke and 95th Bde R.F.A	
"	11th	"	Evacuated 77 animals from Proven ... including 72 mange ... which were in contact ... sent ... by ... ... from 1st D.A.C. ...	
"	12th	"	Changed location to near Elverdinghe. Visited all Co. Div. Train and Co. Cleaning out sleeping huts and preparing horse line. Covered accommodation for 80 horses.	
"	13th	"	Routine work. Hauled bricks and iron for new grate, also timber for mange-line. Started construction of dining place for Section. Collected 2 horses by float. Visited No 1 Co. Train and No 1. Field Ambulance.	
"	14th		Routine. Hauling timber for Mange line. Visited Co. hire and ... Section.	[illegible] Capt. A.V.C.

D. D. & L., London, E.C.
(A8co4) Wt W1771/M2031 750,000 5/17 Sch. 52 Forms/C2118/14

Instructions regarding War Diaries and Intelligence Summaries are contained in F. S. Regs., Part II. and the Staff Manual respectively. Title pages will be prepared in manuscript.

WAR DIARY
or
~~INTELLIGENCE SUMMARY.~~
(Erase heading not required.)

Army Form C. 2118.

Place	Date	Hour	Summary of Events and Information	Remarks and references to Appendices
	Feb 1917		No 2 M.V.S.	
ELVERDINGE	15th		Routine Hauling bricks and timber Visited No 2. and 4 Co Train	
"	16th		Routine Hauling brick and timber for forkhouse, mange line and stables. Visited Nos 2 and 4 Co. Train. Sent in 2 horses from No 2 Co. for evacuation. One mange.	
"	17th		Routine work. Inspected wallets. Completed manure standing and laying of water pipes to horse troughs, and dining room for Section	
"	18th		Evacuated 30 animals from Peselhoek Stn including 17 cases of mange. Started work on wind screen round interior lines.	
"	19th		Routine work. Washing vehicles and going on with general improvements of camp. Visited Nos 4 and 2 Co. Train and sent in 4 cases mange from latter unit to M.V.S. Visited by Maj Gen Moore D.V.S. also by D.D.V.S. Army and A.D.V.S. II Corps. The D.V.S. declared himself very well satisfied with location, general appearance and work being carried on by M.V.S.	[signature] Capt. O.C. No 2 M.V.S.
"	20th		Routine work. Hauling duck boards and laying floor in Sick Horse Stable. Visited No 1 F. Amb and Nos 1 and 3 Co. Train.	

D. D. & L., London, E.C. (A8004) Wt W1771/M2031 750,000 5/17 Sch. 52 Forms/C2118/14

Instructions regarding War Diaries and Intelligence Summaries are contained in F. S. Regs., Part II. and the Staff Manual respectively. Title pages will be prepared in manuscript.

WAR DIARY

or

~~INTELLIGENCE SUMMARY.~~

(Erase heading not required.)

Army Form C. 2118.

Place	Date	Hour	Summary of Events and Information	Remarks and references to Appendices
	Feb	1918		
ELVERDINGE	21st		Routine work. Hauling pit-props. Forwarded smear from Ulcer on Crest of base of [illegible] Dvr. Main, to Mob. V.S. II Corps for microscopical examination.	
"	"	"	Visited No 4 and 2 Co. Train	
"	22nd	"	Routine work. Erected new shelters round manger line. Hauled posts from Ordnance.	
"	23rd		Routine work. Cpl Gwyn admitted to No 10 Gen. Hosp.	
"	25th		Evacuated 60 animals from [illegible] Stn including 40 mangy, mostly from 1st Div and [illegible] horses to be returned to England. Visited 108th & 4th Siege Btys.	
"	26th		Routine work, constructing Ablution bench. Visited 4th Siege & 108th Bty. Corps Arty.	
"	27th		Routine work. Visited 108th & 4th Siege Btys. Sent up in 2 cases mangy. Visited also 142 Bty.	
"	28th		Routine work. Capt Barr A.V.C. rejoined his Unit. Visited 4th Siege & 108th Bty.	[signature] Capt. A.V.C.

D. D. & L., London, E.C. (A8004) Wt W1771/M2031 750,000 5/17 Sch. 52 Forms/C2118/14

Army Form C. 2118.

Instructions regarding War Diaries and Intelligence Summaries are contained in F. S. Regs., Part II. and the Staff Manual respectively. Title pages will be prepared in manuscript.

WAR DIARY
or
INTELLIGENCE SUMMARY.
(Erase heading not required.)

Place	Date	Hour	Summary of Events and Information	Remarks and references to Appendices
			No 2 Mob Vet Sect — March 1918	
Everdinge	1.3.18		Capt [illegible] AVC resumes command of Section. Also V.O. for 1st [illegible] Train	
			No 1 Field Ambulance [illegible] whilst Capt [illegible] AVC is on leave. 1st [illegible]	
			1st/2 RGA; 6th Siege & 33rd Reserve Park	
			Visit Field Section & paid Section	
	2.3.18		[illegible] from No 4 Train	
	3.3.18		Prepare animals for evacuation	
	4.3.18		No Train for sick horses & not likely to be one until Friday	
			[illegible] today to give me [illegible] Section [illegible]	
	4/5/6.3.18		General routine in Section	
	8.3.18		Evacuate 41 animals from [illegible] railhead including 22 Mange	
	10.3.18		Bath Parade to Baths at Siege Camp	
	11.3.18		Visit Field Section & paid Section	
	13.3.18		Got leave to England for 14 days. Lieut Bond AVC in charge of	
			Section during my absence	

D. D. & L., London, E.C.
(A8001) Wt. W1771/M2031 750,000 5/17 Sch. 52 Forms/C2118/14.

Instructions regarding War Diaries and Intelligence Summaries are contained in F. S. Regs., Part II. and the Staff Manual respectively. Title pages will be prepared in manuscript.

Army Form C. 2118.

WAR DIARY
or
~~INTELLIGENCE SUMMARY.~~
(Erase heading not required.)

Place	Date	Hour	Summary of Events and Information — No 2 Mob. Vet. Sect. — March 1918	Remarks and references to Appendices
Elverdinge	21.3.18		Much shelling all day around the Section	
	22.3.18		Shelling continued. Evacuated 35 animals from Peselhoek Railhead 14 of these were Mange cases; 9 of which were from 1st Durs. Notified that in future animals for evacuation will be sent to the VIII Corps Veterinary Evac. Station.	
	18.3.18		Pte Bottomley No 30433 arrived from No 4 Vet Hosp. to do work in Office in place of Corpl. Gunn who has been evacuated sick to England.	[illegible]
	19.3.18		Pte Long No 32332 being surplus to strength is sent to No 2 Vet Hosp.	
	22.3.18		Pte Luscott No 14876 who has been at Base sick since end of December last is returned to Section by special request of OC No 2 MVS to the AVC Records	
	25.3.18		23 Animals evacuated to VIII Corps Vet Evac Stat including 4 Mange four of which are from 1st Durhams	
	27.3.18		Pte Dransu No 34236 who suffers from Shell Shock is sent to No 2 Veterinary Hosp. as has never been completely sheltered since big Shelling on 21st & 22nd. A very good man but absolutely no use when any shelling near. Evacuated 7 animals on 27th to VIII Corps V E S.	

D. D. & L., London, E.C.
(A8c04) Wt W1771/M2031 750,000 5/17 Sch. 52 Forms/C2118/14

Instructions regarding War Diaries and Intelligence Summaries are contained in F. S. Regs., Part II. and the Staff Manual respectively. Title pages will be prepared in manuscript.

WAR DIARY
or
~~INTELLIGENCE SUMMARY.~~
(Erase heading not required.)

Army Form C. 2118.

Place	Date	Hour	Summary of Events and Information — No 2 Mob. Vet. Sect. — March 1918	Remarks and references to Appendices
Elverdinghe	28.3.17		Evacuated 10 animals to V.E.S.	
	30.3.17		Evacuated 21 animals to V.E.S.	
			Privates Chapman, Ford, Earp, Blundy, Stirling, Dykes sent from Section to VIII Corps V.E.S. for duty.	
			Capt. A.D. [illegible] AVC resumes command of Sect. being two days late in returning from leave having been held up one day at Calais going & one day returning.	
			Besides taking over charge as before of Train & 7th [illegible] [illegible] by DADVS to the 14th Glosters, 11th R. Lanc. Fus., 16th Cheshires, 15th Lancs Fusiliers & 17th H.L.I. which Transport has been attached to Div.	
	31.3.17		Visit Field Cashier at II Corps re pay Section	
			Routine work of Section during past 17 days consisted of repairing floors of stables, repairing canvas shelters along sides of stables so that they can be rolled up in day time; white washing stables; white washing fence at entrance. Making fences along pathways in Section & white washing these. Levelling up shell holes. Preparing ground for seeds & vegetable plants.	
	31.3.18		Evacuated 8 animals to V.E.S.	

D. D. & L., London, E.C.
(A8004) Wt W1771/M2031 750,000 5/17 Sch. 52 Forms/C2118/14

Instructions regarding War Diaries and Intelligence Summaries are contained in F. S. Regs., Part II. and the Staff Manual respectively. Title pages will be prepared in manuscript.

WAR DIARY

or

~~INTELLIGENCE SUMMARY.~~

(Erase heading not required.)

Army Form C. 2118.

Place	Date	Hour	Summary of Events and Information — No 2 Mob. Vet. Sect. — April 1918	Remarks and references to Appendices
Everdinge	1.4.18		Evac. 13 animals including 2 Mange to V.E.S.	
			Inspect detached horses of Divisional Train at Poperinghe, Vlam. Houtkerque, Proven, IInd Corps Hqrs	
	2.4.18		Evacuate 11 animals including 4 Mange (2 from 1st Divn) to V.E.S	
	3.4.18		Notified that Division is moving to another Army in a few days.	
			DADVS inspects skin cases with me at No 1, 2 & 3 Train & gives authority to treat 3.	
	4.4.18		ADVS visits Section. Evact 13 animals including 9 Mange (5 from 1st Divn) to V.E.S.	
	6.4.18		Parade of Section to Baths at Siege Camp.	
			6 men attached to 5th Corps V.E.S. return to Section	
			Evact 7 animals to V.E.S. including 3 Mange (two from 1st Divn)	
	7.4.18		Evac 5 animals to V.E.S including 1 Mange from 1st Divn	
			Send surplus stores to Divn Dump at Proven. Hand in one blanket per man to Salvage Dump; also quantity of Salvage from Section	
			Get orders at midday to be ready to move off at 4 pm to Godewaersvelde.	
			Move off at 4 p (sharp). 48th Mob. Vet. Sect. come in Billet & take over two sick cases & 3 stray animals. Water & feed on way & arrive at Billet 3 miles beyond Godewaersvelde at 10 pm. Horses stand out in open. Good Billet for men in a barn.	
				OC No 2 MVS Capt. AVC [illegible signature]

D. D. & L., London, E.C.
(A8004) Wt W1771/M2031 750,000 5/17 Sch. 52 Forms/C2118/14

WAR DIARY
or
~~INTELLIGENCE SUMMARY.~~
(Erase heading not required.)

Army Form C. 2118.

Instructions regarding War Diaries and Intelligence Summaries are contained in F. S. Regs., Part II. and the Staff Manual respectively. Title pages will be prepared in manuscript.

Place	Date	Hour	Summary of Events and Information	Remarks and references to Appendices
			No 2 Mob. Vet. Sect. April 1918	
VENDIN	8.4.18		Reveille at 4 am & parade at 6.30. Marched with 3rd Cav Bde via Caestre, Hazebrouck St Venant, Robecq arriving at Billet at Vendin at 6.30 pm. Water [illegible] on route & feed were halting for 1 hour at midday. Standings for horses very dirty & poor other accommodation. Men billeted in lofts which are also very dirty.	
	9.4.18		Cleaning up lines, Billets & Harness. DADVS visits Section. Germans attack at Givenchy at 4 am & much shelling all day of Bethune, Beuvry & main roads around these parts.	
	10.4.18		18 Shell ~~wounds~~ cases received at Section on 9th & 10th 6 of these from 12th Divn others from 55th.	
LAPUGNOY	11.4.18		At 9 am receive telegram from Divn HdQrs to move Section to Lapugnoy. Move off at 12.30 taking all sick except 1 float case. At Lapugnoy get as Billet for Section place vacated by CCS a few days ago. Good accommodation.	
	12.4.18		Evacuate 13 animals by road to Aire to be met there by men from 23 Vet Hosp who will take them over for completion of journey. Keep 4 horses which are too lame to do journey. All vehicles of Section washed & good day at harness. Take in 13 animals (shell wounds) from 12th Divn. ADVS 1st Corps visits Section.	[illegible] Capt AVC OC No 2 MVS

D. D. & L., London, E.C.
(A8004) Wt W1771/M2031 750,000 5/17 Sch. 52 Forms/C2118/14

Instructions regarding War Diaries and Intelligence Summaries are contained in F. S. Regs., Part II. and the Staff Manual respectively. Title pages will be prepared in manuscript.

WAR DIARY
or
~~INTELLIGENCE SUMMARY.~~
(Erase heading not required.)

Army Form C. 2118.

No 2 Mob. Vet. Sect. — April 1918

Place	Date	Hour	Summary of Events and Information	Remarks and references to Appendices
Lapugnoy	13.4.17		Men return who took animals to Aire & report all correct	
			Send a Corporal & Private to Burbure Concentration Camp by order from Corps	
			to look after animals brought there by refugees. Get Corporal	
			returned to Section next day because there is nothing for him to do	
	14.4.17		Visit 1st Corps Cashier & get money to pay Section	
	15.4.17		Ordered to find new Billet for Section as present site required for a Dump	
			Evacuate 17 animals by road to Aire in charge of a Corporal & 3 Privates	
			Retain 7 not fit to travel distance	
Fouquières	16.4.17		Section moves to Fouquières. Leave two Float cases behind.	
			Send two mounted men to Aire to assist in evacuating animals to 23 V.H.	
			(by order from Corps)	
Hesdigneul	17.4.17		Section moves to Veterinary Lines at Headquarters (by order from Division)	
			Good accommodation for men & horses	
			Send the Float for two horses left at Lapugnoy	
			By order of ADVS 2 Stomatitis cases brought to Section left behind	
			by 15th Bde AFA at Lapugnoy. They are isolated, and at the far	
			end of Section & the two Artillery men retained to look after them	
			who are also kept apart from Section men	

D. D. & L., London, E.C.
(A8604) Wt W1771/M2031 750,000 5/17 Sch. 52 Forms/C2118/14

Instructions regarding War Diaries and Intelligence Summaries are contained in F. S. Regs., Part II. and the Staff Manual respectively. Title pages will be prepared in manuscript.

WAR DIARY

or

~~INTELLIGENCE SUMMARY.~~

(Erase heading not required.)

Army Form C. 2118.

Place	Date	Hour	Summary of Events and Information	Remarks and references to Appendices
			No 2 Mob. Vet. Section — April 1918	
Hersignenl	17.4.18		DDVS & ADVS visit Section	
	19.4.18		DAQMG visits Section & expresses satisfaction. DADVS inspects Section	
			Harness inspection & indent for several new pieces to replace worn out: &	
			make note of several other parts requiring repair	
	20.4.18		Commence to rebuild cookhouse; get bricklayers from No 6 Sanitary Section	
			also some material required. Visit CRE's & get authority to draw	
			corrugated iron & wood necessary for cookhouse	
			Send man to Sanitary Section (No 6) to assist making a meat safe	
			for Section. Get 2 latrine buckets & seats from Sanitary Section for latrines	
			12 Corps V.E.S. [illegible] at Borden. Send 18 animals	
	21.4.18		Men have Sunday afternoon off	
			Four pigs brought to Section which had been left behind in evacuated	
			areas; also two calves. SSO of Division takes over charge of them.	
	22.4.18		Parade of Section to Corps Baths in Hersignenl	
			Finish cookhouse & meat-safe. Repair Horse standings with broken bricks	
	23.4.18		Evacuate 12 ordinary cases (mostly shell wounds) & 1 mange to V.E.S.	
			Saddler from No 6 [illegible] spends day at Section repairing harness	
			Inspection of rifles & ammunition	

Remarks: [signature] Capt AVC, OC No 2 MVS

D. D. & L., London, E.C. (A8004) Wt W1771/M2031 750,000 5/17 Sch. 52 Forms/C2118/14

Instructions regarding War Diaries and Intelligence Summaries are contained in F. S. Regs., Part II. and the Staff Manual respectively. Title pages will be prepared in manuscript.

WAR DIARY
or
~~INTELLIGENCE SUMMARY.~~
(Erase heading not required.)

Army Form C. 2118.

Place	Date	Hour	Summary of Events and Information	Remarks and references to Appendices
			No. 2 Mobile Vet. Sect. April 1918	
Hinges	24.4.18		Evacuate 7 ordinary cases to V.E.S.	
			Orders from Divn to move in afternoon to Barlin	
BARLIN			Move Section to Veterinary Lines at Barlin (Map loc K 33 c 8). 1st Corps	
			V.E.S. in ~~adjoining~~ Billet. All section horses in covered standing.	
			Sick lines of Section in open & accomodation for about twenty	
			Sick cases for evacuation will be handed over to V.E.S.	
			Good accomodation for men.	
	25.4.18		Two men sent from Section to Corps V.E.S. for duty	
	26.4.18		Evacuate 5 animals to V.E.S. Send Float with horses unable to walk	
			to Barlin Station for V.E.S. V.E.S. not yet got a Float.	
	27.4.18		Take over Veterinary Charge of all the Divn Train: 1st Inf Bde	
			& 1st Battalion Mach. Gun Corps & No. 2 Field Ambul.	
			Cleaning up all vehicles of Section	
	28.4.18		Evacuate 4 animals to V.E.S.	
	29.4.18		Visit Field Cashier & pay out Section. Prepare vehicle for painting –	
			burn off old paint with blow lamp & scrape. Evac. 13 animals including	
			1 Mange to V.E.S.	
			Remove tumours from French civilian's Horse's shoulder	
	30.4.18		Exam. carcases of 2 cows on 29 & 30th for French civilians re being fit for food.	
			Give Certif. for both.	

D. D. & L., London, E.C. (A8004) Wt. W1771/M2031 750,000 5/17 Sch. 52 Forms/C2118/14

Army Form C. 2118.

WAR DIARY
or
~~INTELLIGENCE SUMMARY.~~

(Erase heading not required.)

Instructions regarding War Diaries and Intelligence Summaries are contained in F. S. Regs., Part II. and the Staff Manual respectively. Title pages will be prepared in manuscript.

No 2 M. Vet Sect. — May 1918

Place	Date	Hour	Summary of Events and Information	Remarks and references to Appendices
BARLIN	22.5.18		Remove placenta from cow for French civilian	
	23.5.18		Admit French civilian's horse to Section for treatment. Evac. [illegible] animals to V.E.S.	
	24.5.18		Musketry Instructor instructs Section in musketry for one hour	
			Harness & saddlery inspection. Sent 3 float cases to Station for V.E.S.	
	25.5.18		Half an hour's rifle drill	
	26.5.18		Section have Sunday afternoon off	
	27.5.18		Evacuate 7 animals to V.E.S. including 5 Mange	
	28.5.18		Take 3 float cases to Station for V.E.S.	
			Corporal & private return to Section from Refugee animal Concentration Camp	
			[illegible] to repair road.	
			SE 11716 S Smith [illegible] arrived yesterday from No 2 Vet Hosp to relieve SE 3949	
			[illegible] posted to No 7 Vet Hosp. [illegible] leaves Section today	
	29.5.18		Musketry Instructor instructs Sect. in musketry for 1 hour	
	30.5.18		" " " " " " "	
			Evacuate 7 animals to V.E.S.	
	31.5.18		[illegible] leaves for 14 days leave to England. Sect. in his absence [illegible]	
			Parade by Section to Baths at [illegible] 7	
			Stripped harness inspection	
			Andrew Barr	Andrew Barr

CAPTAIN, A.V.C.
O.C. 2 MOBILE VETERINARY SECTION.

D. D. & L., London, E.C.
(A8004) Wt W1771/M2031 750,000 5/17 Sch. 52 Forms/C2118/14

WAR DIARY
or
~~INTELLIGENCE SUMMARY.~~
(Erase heading not required.)

Army Form C. 2118.

Instructions regarding War Diaries and Intelligence Summaries are contained in F. S. Regs., Part II. and the Staff Manual respectively. Title pages will be prepared in manuscript.

No 2 Mobile Vet Sect — May 1918

Place	Date	Hour	Summary of Events and Information	Remarks and references to Appendices
BARLIN	14.5.18		[illegible]	
			[illegible]	
			[illegible] clenches to be left much stronger	
	15.5.18		Capt [illegible] V.E.S. [illegible]	
			[illegible]	
			to take over command of [illegible]	
			of No 2 M.V.S.	
			[illegible] to V.E.S.	
	16.5.18		Evact [illegible] animals to V.E.S. [illegible] drill by Serg Major [illegible]	
			all personnel of Section on parade.	
	17.5.18		Harness inspection & washing of vehicles	
			Commence a small Dry Canteen in Section.	
	18.5.18		Get surplus stores back from Divis Dumps.	
	19.5.18		Section have Sunday afternoon off. I go to Corps Headqtrs have tea & spend	
			a couple of hours with ADVS (Col McDougall & Capt J Stone	
	20.5.18		Evacuate 11 animals to V.E.S. [illegible]	
			Water off in afternoon owing to Bruay having been shelled & pumping arrangement	
			upset. Have to water horses at well in Town	
	21.5.18		Water on again. [illegible] of Section to Baths at [illegible]	

D. D. & L., London, E.C.
(A8004) Wt W1771/M2031 750,000 5/17 Sch. 52 Forms/C2118/14

Instructions regarding War Diaries and Intelligence Summaries are contained in F. S. Regs., Part II. and the Staff Manual respectively. Title pages will be prepared in manuscript.

WAR DIARY
or
INTELLIGENCE SUMMARY.
(Erase heading not required.)

Army Form C. 2118.

Place	Date	Hour	Summary of Events and Information	Remarks and references to Appendices
			No 2 Mob. Vet. Sect. May 1918	
BARLIN	8.5.18		1 Serg & 1 Pte leave for No 2 Vet Hosp. as being surplus to Establishment of Sect. The remaining 2 Privates sent to 1st V.E.S. as 3rd Echelon attached, are being transferred. Thus making the New Establishment strength of Divisional Mob. Vet. Sectn — 1 Officer 1 Serg 2 Corporals 12 Privates with 3 A.S.C. Drivers attached.	
			Erecting Shelters for repairing Horse Standings	
	9.5.18		Lime wash stables	
	10.5.18		Stripped inspection of harness & saddlery of Section.	
			DADVS has meeting of all Transport Officers at Section & gives lecture & Demonstration on Shoeing	
			Corporal & two men inoculated. Remainder of Section have been inoculated under 12 months.	
	11.5.18		Got inoculated myself by M.O. of 1st D.A.C.	
	12.5.18		No sick cases received at Section during past two days. Section have Sunday afternoon off	
	13.5.18		Accompany DADVS at inspection of Horses in Nos 2, 3 & 4 Cos. 1st Div Train. Evact 3 animals to V.E.S.	
	14.5.18		DADVS makes a thorough inspection of Section — men, horses, harness, [illegible] [illegible] [illegible] [illegible]	

D. D. & L., London, E.C. (A8004) Wt W1771/M2031 750,000 5/17 Sch. 52 Forms/C2118/14

Army Form C.2118.

WAR DIARY
or
INTELLIGENCE SUMMARY.

(Erase heading not required.)

Instructions regarding War Diaries and Intelligence Summaries are contained in F. S. Regs., Part II. and the Staff Manual respectively. Title pages will be prepared in manuscript.

No 2 Mob. Vet Sect — May 1918

Place	Date	Hour	Summary of Events and Information	Remarks and references to Appendices
BARLIN	1.5.	18	Continue with painting of Section Vehicles: water tins & steel helmets	
			Evacuate 10 animals to VES including 5 [illegible] from 1st Divn	
	2.5.	18	Receive two Riders & one LD Mule issued to Units in Division	
			Visit D.A.G. & inspect RA Remounts with DADVS	
	3.5.	18	[illegible] DADVS 1st Divn visit Section on way to VES	
			Visit Bruay & see Mule [illegible]	
	4.5.	18	Commence to have those men in Section, who have not been inoculated with TAB for 12 months, inoculated. Capt Loyd RAMC [illegible] 3 [illegible] duty for 24 hrs.	
	5.5.	18	DADVS [illegible] inspects Section. [illegible] have Sunday afternoon off	
			Visit 1st S.W.B. Transport lines & inspect Mare with Capt [illegible] that has passed no faeces for 17 days. Has now drawn [illegible] & drinks small quantities. Suspect [illegible]	
	6.5.	18	DDVS has Conference at Section of VOs. Three more men of Section inoculated.	
			5 [illegible] cases evac to VES. [illegible]	
	7.5.	18	Parade of Section to Baths. Impromptu inspection of all kits [illegible]	
	8.5.	18	Every one in Section fitted out with clothing required, old garments being handed in in place of new issued.	
			Attend with DADVS at inspection of 1st Divn [illegible] good	
			Evacuate 19 animals to VES including 4 Mange from 1st Divn	

D. D. & L., London, E.C. (A8004) Wt W1771/M2031 750,000 5/17 Sch. 52 Forms/C2118/14

Army Form C. 2118.

Instructions regarding War Diaries and Intelligence Summaries are contained in F. S. Regs., Part II, and the Staff Manual respectively. Title pages will be prepared in manuscript.

WAR DIARY
or
~~INTELLIGENCE SUMMARY.~~
(Erase heading not required.)

Place	Date	Hour	Summary of Events and Information	Remarks and references to Appendices
			No 2 Mob. Vet. Sect. June 1918	
BARLIN	1.6.18		Capt. Hutton returns today from Hospital & again takes over command of V.E.S.	
			from me. Evacuate 6 ordinary cases & 1 Mange to V.E.S.	
	2.6.18		Section go to Range & under instruction from Serg. Hendy (Instructor) fire 10 rounds each	
			While acting DADVS have charge of all H.Q. [illegible] horses	
	3.6.18		Evacuate 19 animals to V.E.S. including 10 Mange from 1st Divn. [illegible] from 52nd [illegible]	
	4.6.18		Commence to build bomb shelter for horse lines. [illegible] & expanding	
			metal. Fill up spaces with earth.	
			Make thorough inspection of all horses in Train Co. in the evening	
	5.6.18		Section has 3 hours rifle practice on Range	
			Evacuate 1 ordinary & 6 Mange to V.E.S. 6 Mange cases from 1st Divn.	
	6.6.18		Evacuate 14 Mange & 11 ordinary to V.E.S. All Mange from 1st Divn. [illegible]	
	7.6.18		Receive & evacuate to V.E.S. [illegible] animals from 66th Divn. [illegible] of these are Mange	
			Debility & also 6 Mange from No 2 Sect. D.A.C.	
			D.D.V.S. 1st Army inspect horses & mules from Divn. for casting	
			A/ADVS spent afternoon between Sect. & V.E.S.	
	8.6.18		Parade of Section to [illegible] [illegible] Form 7.	

D. D. & L., London, E.C.
(A7883) Wt. W803/M1672 350,000 4/17 Sch. 52a Forms/C/2118/14

Instructions regarding War Diaries and Intelligence Summaries are contained in F. S. Regs., Part II, and the Staff Manual respectively. Title pages will be prepared in manuscript.

WAR DIARY
or
INTELLIGENCE SUMMARY.

(Erase heading not required.)

Army Form C. 2118.

Place	Date	Hour	Summary of Events and Information	Remarks and references to Appendices
			No 2 Mobile Vet. Sec. June 1918	
Berlin	9.6.	18	Section have Sunday afternoon off.	
			Attend 3rd Inf Bde Horse Show & judge horses in limbers, water carts, cookers & pack animals.	
			Evacuate 7 animals to VES	
			Visit Field Bakery & pay Section in evening.	
	11.6.	18	Evacuate 3 Mange & 2 ordinary to VES. Mange cases from 1st DAC	
	12.6.	18	Evacuate 23 Mange (all from 1st DA) & 5 others to VES.	
			Corporal Walker & two men take 5 cast Horses from Divn to Field Remount Sect at Noyelles. Bring back 2 LD Mules & 2 LD Horses in exchange for LD	
	13.6.	18	Have Kit inspection of Section.	
			Evacuate 4 Mange & 3 ordinary to V.E.S. Mange from D.A.	
			DDVS 1st Army visit Section & inspect Mange cases that are being evacuated	
	14.6.	18	Have Marching Order inspection of Section	
			Notified that Riders in Section will be reduced to 11 as a temporary measure.	
	15.6.	18	Baths Parade of Section to baths at [illegible]	
	16.6.	18	Men have Sunday afternoon off.	

D. D. & L., London, E.C.
(A7883) Wt. W809/M1672 350,000 4/17 Sch. 52a Forms/C/2118/14

Instructions regarding War Diaries and Intelligence Summaries are contained in F. S. Regs., Part II, and the Staff Manual respectively. Title pages will be prepared in manuscript.

WAR DIARY
or
INTELLIGENCE SUMMARY.
(Erase heading not required.)

Army Form C. 2118.

Place	Date	Hour	Summary of Events and Information — No 2 Mob Vet Sect. June 1918	Remarks and references to Appendices
BARLIN	16.6.18		Attend 1st Inf Bde Horse Show & Sports. Judge Heavy & Light Draught horses	
	17.6.18		DADVS returns from leave & visits Section. Musketry Instructor instructs Section for 1½ hours	
	18.6.18		Spare time in Section being employed repairing Horse Standings. [illegible]	
	20.6.18		Several motor lorry loads of slag brought by V.E.S. motor lorry	
	20.6.18		Four surplus Riders on strength of Section drawn by AMP 1st Northumbrian	
			1st Signal Co RE & 23rd F Co RE. DADVS attends distribution	
			Surplus saddlery returned to Ordnance.	
	21.6.18		Sergt Owen awarded the Meritorious Medal (London Gazette June 17th)	
	22.6.18		Musketry Instructor from Div HdQrs instructs Section in Musketry for 1½ hours	
			Evacuate 5 Ordinary cases to V.E.S	
			AD 6 Charger admitted to Section with lacerated heel	
	23.6.18		Section have two hours rifle practice on Range. Instructor with them	
	24.6.18		Four men off duty with P.U.O.	
			Visit Field Cashier & pay out Section	
	25.6.18		2 NCOs & 6 men off duty with P.U.O. [illegible]	
	26.6.18		1 NCO & 6 men off duty with P.U.O.	[illegible]

D. D. & L., London, E.C. (A7883) Wt. W809/M1672 350,000 4/17 Sch. 52a Forms/C/2118/14

Instructions regarding War Diaries and Intelligence Summaries are contained in F. S. Regs., Part II, and the Staff Manual respectively. Title pages will be prepared in manuscript.

WAR DIARY
or
INTELLIGENCE SUMMARY.
(Erase heading not required.)

Army Form C. 2118.

Place	Date	Hour	Summary of Events and Information	Remarks and references to Appendices
			No. 2 Mob. Vet. Sect. June 1918	
BARLIN	27.6.18		1 NCO & 5 men off duty with P.U.O. 1 man [illegible] [illegible]	
			[illegible]	
			[illegible] 3 Mange [illegible] 3 Mange from 1st Division.	
	28.6.18		1 NCO & 5 men off duty with P.U.O.	
			2 of Section go to Baths at [illegible]	
	29.6.18		All Section back to duty except 2.	
			Evacuate 7 ordinary cases.	
	30.6.18		Section have 2 hours rifle practice on Range.	
			Shoeing-smith has relapse of P.U.O. & admitted to Hospital. M.O. does not consider he	[illegible]
			will be fit for duty for 3 or 4 weeks. Wire to Base AVC Records for [illegible]	

[illegible signature]
CAPTAIN A.V.C.
O.C. 2 MOBILE VETERINARY SECTION

D. D. & L., London, E.C.
(A7883) Wt. W803/M1672 350,000 4/17 Sch. 52a Forms/C/2118/14

Instructions regarding War Diaries and Intelligence Summaries are contained in F. S. Regs., Part II, and the Staff Manual respectively. Title pages will be prepared in manuscript.

WAR DIARY
or
~~INTELLIGENCE SUMMARY.~~
(Erase heading not required.)

Army Form C. 2118.

Place	Date	Hour	Summary of Events and Information	Remarks and references to Appendices
			No 2 Mob. Vet. Sect. July 1918	
BARLIN	1.7.	18	All Section Horses put through Horse-dip	
			Repair horse standings & lime wash Saddle Shed	
	2.7.	18	Wash vehicles of Section. Repairing horse standings & [illegible] woodwork of	
	3.7	18	[illegible] stables	
	4.7	18	Rifle, bandolier & box respirator inspection of Section	
			Accompany DADVS at inspection of all horses in Nos 1, 2, 3, 4 Coy Train.	
			Still a great many Horses in each Coy with broken walls of feet.	
			Evacuate 3 ordinary cases & 2 Mange to V.E.S.	
	5.7	18	Evacuate 3 ordinary cases & 1 Mange to V.E.S. Saddlery & harness inspection	
	6.7.	18	Two men off duty with P.U.O.	
			Bath Parade of Section to baths at Barlin	
	7.7.	18	Section have two hours rifle practice on Range	
			Assist in judging horses to represent Div Train at Divisional Horse Show	
	8.7.	18	Return surplus bits & harness to No 1 Coy A.S.C. as directed by order from Div HdQrs	
			Visit Field Cashier & pay Section	
			Corpl Walker admitted to Hospital with Urticaria & Pte Paxton with P.U.O.	

[illegible signature] Capt. A.V.C.

D. D. & L., London, E.C.
(A7883) Wt. W803/M1672 350,000 4/17 Sch. 52a Forms/C/2118/14

Army Form C. 2118.

Instructions regarding War Diaries and Intelligence Summaries are contained in F. S. Regs., Part II. and the Staff Manual respectively. Title pages will be prepared in manuscript.

WAR DIARY
or
~~INTELLIGENCE SUMMARY.~~
(Erase heading not required.)

Place	Date	Hour	Summary of Events and Information — No 2 Mob. Vet. Sect. — July 1918	Remarks and references to Appendices
BARLIN	9.7.	18	Corpl Walker & Pte Preston returned to Section & resumed duty for two days.	
			Shoeing Smith arrived at Divn Reception Camp on 8th but detained for 3 days	
			for inoculation & to go through Gas Parade.	
	10.7.	18	Sect. chloroform & operate on Horse from 114 Btty RFA	
	11.7.	18	Shoeing smith arrives at Section for duty	
	12.7.	18	DDR 1st Army inspects Horses prepared for [illegible] at Section.	
			Mare [illegible] was in box for [illegible]: she makes good recovery.	
	13.7.	18	Bath Parade of all Section to baths at Barlin.	
	14.7.	18	During past fortnight have evacuated 45 animals to V.E.S. & [illegible] two	
			Section have Sunday afternoon off	
	15.7.	18	On account of 39th Bde RFA moving out & Capt Bartlett AVC going with them to	
			take over charge of 2nd & 3rd Inf Bdes	[illegible] Capt AVC
	16.7.	18	Material received for making a ~~Forge~~ stalls for shoeing horses in	
			~~Fore~~ float came to bring from Houdain from 470 Field Coy RE lines as	
			result of bombing last night.	
	17.7.	18	Make shed to be used as Forge & Dressing shed.	
			~~6 Sacks~~	
			6 Sacks of Bran received for Division — for Veterinary use only.	

D. D. & L., London, E.C. (A7883) Wt. W809/M1672 350,000 4/17 Sch. 52a Forms/C/2118/14

Instructions regarding War Diaries and Intelligence Summaries are contained in F. S. Regs., Part II, and the Staff Manual respectively. Title pages will be prepared in manuscript.

WAR DIARY
or
~~INTELLIGENCE SUMMARY.~~
(Erase heading not required.)

Army Form C. 2118.

Place	Date	Hour	Summary of Events and Information	Remarks and references to Appendices
			No 2 Mobile Veterinary Sect. July 1918.	
BARLIN	18.7	.18	Inspect Horses in Train Coy with OC of Train	
	20.7	.18	Section have 1½ hours rifle practice on Range. owing to thunderstorm they had to leave off before finished	
	21.7	.18	Parade of Section to Baths	
			Capt Hartigan AVC OC 8th Div MVS calls & has lunch. Passing through on way to take over from 52nd Div MVS	
	22.7	.18	Two horses cured reissued to 6th Welsh	
			View Field Cashier & pay Section	
	23.7	.18	Clothing inspection of section. Cancel rifle inspection on account of heavy rain.	
	25.7	.18	DADVS inspects Section – full marching order – Well satisfied with turnout.	
	27.7	.18	Receive 5 sacks of Bran for the Divn (for veterinary use only)	
			1 lb of Sodium Bicarb supplied to each AVC Sergeant in Division to be retained for use in case of Gas poisoning	
			Parade of Section to Baths	
	28.7	.18	Attend Conference of VOs at DADVS office	
			Men have Sunday afternoon off	

D. D. & L., London, E.C. (A7883) Wt. W809/M1672 350,000 4/17 Sch. 52a Forms/C/2118/14

Instructions regarding War Diaries and Intelligence Summaries are contained in F. S. Regs., Part II. and the Staff Manual respectively. Title pages will be prepared in manuscript.

WAR DIARY
or
~~INTELLIGENCE~~ SUMMARY.
(Erase heading not required.)

Army Form C. 2118.

Place	Date	Hour	Summary of Events and Information	Remarks and references to Appendices
			No 2 Mobile Vet. Sect. July 1918	
BARLIN	29.7.18		D.D.V.S. inspects horses for issuing through D.D.R. in Section	
	30.7.18		Draw sand & 20 sheets corrugated iron for making new cookhouse.	
			Attend eliminating jumping competition for Divisional Show on Sunday	
			& assist in judging Officers Class. Serg Owen & Corpl Walker enter their	
			Riders in NCO & Mens Class. Serg Owen's refuses to start; Corpl Walker	
			does round in good style	
	31.7.18		Build new cook-house for Section.	
			During past fortnight (since 14th inst) were evac. 37 animals to V.E.S. & butcher	
			5 incurables. Receive 5 wound cases.	
			Andrew Barr	
			CAPTAIN, A.V.C. O.C. 2 MOBILE VETERINARY SECTION.	

D. D. & L., London, E.C. (A7883) Wt. W803/M1672 350,000 4/17 Sch. 52a Forms/C/2118/14

Instructions regarding War Diaries and Intelligence Summaries are contained in F. S. Regs., Part II. and the Staff Manual respectively. Title pages will be prepared in manuscript.

WAR DIARY
or
INTELLIGENCE SUMMARY.
(Erase heading not required.)

Army Form C. 2118.

Place	Date	Hour	Summary of Events and Information — No 2 Mobile Vet: Sect. August 1918	Remarks and references to Appendices
BARLIN	1.8.18		Repairing Horse standings with thick sub-layer of chalk & thin layer of slag on top	
			GOC visits Section to see his charger	
	2&3.8.18		Continue repairing Horse standings	
	3.8.18		Parade of Section to Baths at Barlin.	
	4.8.18		Divisional Horse Show commencing at 9 a.m. Weather fine & Show a great success. Corpl Walker rides Capt [illegible] Mare in jumping Compet: for NCOs & men does two good rounds but not in first three. Give Section the day off 14 go to Show	
	5.8.18		Draw money from Field Cashier & pay Section	
	6.8.18		Inspect MMP horses at 2nd & 3rd Inf Bdes with ATRM. Issue two horses which have been under treatment from other Divisions to 23rd RE	
	8.8.18		Rifle, bandolier, box respirator inspection of Section	
			Sergt. Dunn takes out mounted men of Section to practise mounting & dismounting with rifle	
	9.8.18		Stripped harness inspection	

D. D. & L., London, E.C.
(A7883) Wt. W803/M1672 350,000 4/17 Sch. 52a Forms/C/2118/14

Army Form C. 2118.

Instructions regarding War Diaries and Intelligence Summaries are contained in F. S. Regs., Part II. and the Staff Manual respectively. Title pages will be prepared in manuscript.

WAR DIARY
or
INTELLIGENCE SUMMARY.
(Erase heading not required.)

Place	Date	Hour	Summary of Events and Information — No 2 Mob. Vet. Sect. — Aug. 1918.	Remarks and references to Appendices
BARLIN	10.8.18		Parade of Section to baths at Barlin	
	11.8.18		Inspect animals of 3rd Inf Bde individually for infectious diseases	
	12.8.18		Commence to make new horse standing for sick horses	
	11.8.18		Noeux les Mines badly shelled. 3 dropped in 3rd Inf Bde lines — No casualties	
	13.8.18		Inspect animals of 2nd Inf Bde individually for infectious diseases.	
	14.8.18		Admit 12 HD (shell cases) from 9th A.H.T.C. at Noeux les Mines. Send float for 3	
			Butcher 2 : evac 1 to 1st V.E.S. : treat remainder.	
			Privates W Berry, F Fairy(?), R J Skinner & G W Wright arrived from Base for duty	
	16.8.18		Corpl Walker Corpl Ambrose & Pte Fuller dispatched to No 2 Vet Hosp	
			by order from O/c AVC Base Records to be reclassified, being Category A(?) present(?)	
			1st MTC to make two front springs for my four wheeled van	
	17.8.18		Parade of all Section to Baths at Barlin.	
	18.8.18		Section have Sunday afternoon off	
			Judge showing at eliminating contest of 39th Bde RFA.	
	19.8.18		Take over veterinary charge 147 A.F.A Bde while Capt Thompson is on	
			leave to England.	

D. D. & L., London, E.C.
(A7883) Wt. W803/M1672 350,000 4/17 Sch. 52a Forms/C/2118/14

Instructions regarding War Diaries and Intelligence Summaries are contained in F. S. Regs., Part II. and the Staff Manual respectively. Title pages will be prepared in manuscript.

WAR DIARY
or
INTELLIGENCE SUMMARY.
(Erase heading not required.)

Army Form C. 2118.

Place	Date	Hour	Summary of Events and Information — No 2 Mob Vet Sect. Aug 1915.	Remarks and references to Appendices
BARLIN	20.8.15		Go to 1st Corps Horse Show in afternoon	
	21.8.15		Get vehicles loaded up & all put straight ready for moving early tomorrow morning	
	22.8.15		Reveille at 4 o'clock, move off at 6 to Billet at Dieval. Have good march in cool of morning & arrive at Dieval at 9.45. Horse line in open; billet for men in a barn. Pitch two tents – one for offices, other for Sergeants. Watering accommodation poor. Fix up canvas tank in waggon & cart one or two loads each day to fill troughs in lines. Take Section horses 3 times a day to stream to water. Division very scattered over many miles of training area	[illegible]
DIEVAL	23.8.15		[illegible] Section. Build oven, open fire for dixies & covering for cook house. Also forage shed & harness shed	
	24.8.15		Send a man to Sanitary Section to assist in making 3 latrine seats. Indent for 6 Rt. pumps. Draw Chaff & make new Horse line. From 22nd take over Veterinary charge of 25th Bde RFA & 2nd Inf Bde Group. Parade of Section to Baths at Dieval RE Camp. Corpl Walker, Corpl Ambrose & Pte Fuller return to Section from No 2 Vet Hosp having been classed in 'B' Category	

D. D. & L., London, E.C. (A7883) Wt. W809/M1672 350,000 4/17 Sch. 52a Forms/C/2118/14

Instructions regarding War Diaries and Intelligence Summaries are contained in F. S. Regs., Part II, and the Staff Manual respectively. Title pages will be prepared in manuscript.

WAR DIARY
or
INTELLIGENCE SUMMARY.
(Erase heading not required.)

Army Form C. 2118.

Place	Date	Hour	Summary of Events and Information	Remarks and references to Appendices
			No 2 Mob. Vet. Sect. August 1918	
Dieval	25.8.	18	Privates Hollam, Berry & Skinner sent to Base being now surplus to my Establishment	
			~~Section~~ have Sunday afternoon off.	
	26.8.	18	Inspection of ~~Sections~~ ~~kits~~ clothing	
	27.8.	18	Rifle & box respirator inspection	
			Corpl. Ambrose, Drivers Dugard & Pte Pearson inoculated at No 2 F.A.	
	29.8.	18	Ptes Stevens, Stanley & Ruffles inoculated at No 2 F.A.	
			Harness & Saddlery inspection. Sent two Riders with saddlery complete from Section to	
			Division H.d.qrs for mounted Infantry	
	30.8.	18	DVS & Col. Kendall visit & inspect Section	
	31.8.	18	During August evacuated 48 animals to 1st VES & 11 to 22nd VES	
			" " sold 6 to Butcher for consumption	
			" " issued 6 to 1st Division	
			Move with 2nd Inf Bde Group to Capelle Fermont leaving Dieval at 1pm arriving	
			at Capelle Fermont at 9. Very fine afternoon for march. Good standings for	
			Horses & good Billets for personnel of Section	

Andrew Bam[?]
Capt. AVC
OC No 2 MVS

D. D. & L., London, E.C.
(A7883) Wt. W809/M1672 350,000 4/17 Sch. 52a Forms/C/2118/14

Instructions regarding War Diaries and Intelligence Summaries are contained in F. S. Regs., Part II, and the Staff Manual respectively. Title pages will be prepared in manuscript.

WAR DIARY
or
~~INTELLIGENCE SUMMARY.~~
(Erase heading not required.)

Army Form C. 2118.

Place	Date	Hour	Summary of Events and Information — September 1918	Remarks and references to Appendices
Capelle-Fermont	1.9.18		Remain at Capelle Fermont until 5.30 pm when Section moves with 2nd Inf Bde Group to Arras Area. Sergt [illegible] goes on ahead to find new Billet.	
ARRAS.			Arrive at field allotted on outskirts of Arras on Bullecourt road [illegible] Sheet 51B at 10.30pm. Sleep out in open — night dry & fine.	
	2.9.18		Make lines, fix up trough for watering, Office in house adjoining, Mess room & Cookhouse adjoining Office. Men make bivouacs with salved corrugated iron etc. Send 1 NCO & 3 men forward with DADVS to Signal Co. [illegible] to [illegible] in 10 horses wounded by bomb during night.	[illegible] Capt AVC
	3.9.18		Send Corpl [illegible] & Pte Evans forward to establish an Advanced Post as arranged by DADVS.	
			Send Corpl Walker & 2 men to 1st Army Advanced Remount Depot at Noyelles to bring Remounts for Signal Co. as arranged by Q & DADVS. Taken to Noyelles in a motor lorry.	
			Cleaning up horses & vehicles. Visit Advanced Post.	
	4.9.18		Send for Chargers for Major General to Noyelles (No 1 Field Remount Sect)	
	5.9.18		Take over 5 animals unfit to walk from 4th Divn Mobile: 4th Div MVS is moving back	

D. D. & L., London, E.C.
(A7883) Wt. W803/M1672 350,000 4/17 Sch. 52a Forms/C/2118/14

Instructions regarding War Diaries and Intelligence Summaries are contained in F. S. Regs., Part II. and the Staff Manual respectively. Title pages will be prepared in manuscript.

WAR DIARY
or
~~INTELLIGENCE~~ SUMMARY.
(Erase heading not required.)

Army Form C. 2118.

Place	Date	Hour	Summary of Events and Information	Remarks and references to Appendices
			No 2 Mobile Vet. Sect. September 1918	
ARRAS	5.9.18		Evacuate 51 animals to Canadian V.E.S. at Ecoivres: each animal being dressed, & pieces of shell (yesterday) extracted where located. Majority of cases are casualties from bombs	
			Float has been out all day from 6 am bringing in cases unfit to walk	
	6.9.18		Evacuate 20 animals to 18th V.E.S. Destroy two incurables.	
			6 Vet Evac Stn move to [illegible]	
	7.9.18		Evacuate 14 walking & 3 Float cases to Canadian V.E.S. & bring in two Float cases from advanced Post.	Wm. W. Barr Capt. A.V.C.
			Pay out to Section on the 6th	
			Get notice of moving to new Area on the ~~9th~~ 10th	
	8.9.18		Evacuate 12 animals to 6. V.E.S. & [illegible] one H.D. (cured of G.S. wound) to No 1 [illegible] Train	
	10.9.18		Evacuate 16 animals to 6. V.E.S. Get vehicles packed up ready for moving	
			Move off at 5 pm to Marœuil Station. On arrival find entraining 3 hours behind	
			Get Section horses into a small covered standing close to station until entraining time	
	11.9.18		Commence to entrain at 11.30 pm with No 1 Field Ambul. Move off between 2 & 3 am. Very slow journey. Arrive at detraining station (Merville?) at 5.30 pm after detraining	

D. D. & L., London, E.C.
(A7883) Wt. W803/M1672 350,000 4/17 Sch. 52a Forms/C/2118/14

Instructions regarding War Diaries and Intelligence Summaries are contained in F. S. Regs., Part II, and the Staff Manual respectively. Title pages will be prepared in manuscript.

Army Form C. 2118.

~~WAR DIARY~~ WAR DIARY or ~~INTELLIGENCE SUMMARY.~~

(Erase heading not required.)

Place	Date	Hour	Summary of Events and Information — No 2 Mob. Vet. Sect. Sept. 1918.	Remarks and references to Appendices
Morcourt	11.9.18		March Section to billet at Morcourt arriving at 10.30 pm. Personnel get shelter in broken down buildings. Horses standing in open.	
	12.9.18		DADVS visits Section.	
			Thorough harness & saddlery cleaning & vehicles washed.	
	13.9.18		March in rear of Artillery Group to area S of Villers Carbonnel & bivouac for night.	
			Shoeingsmith granted leave to England from 12.9.18 – 26.9.18	
	14.9.18		March with Artillery Group to area between ~~[illegible]~~ Devise & Monchy-Lagache. Section bivouac	
DEVISE			by side of wood at V4C22. DADVS visits Section in afternoon.	
			Spread horses about in wood at night in case of bombing. Put them in pairs	
	15.9.18		Take in 27 animals to Section. Have to destroy & bury 3 cases of fracture, 1 open fetlock joint. 1 colic of intestine: and one peritonitis & 1 colic of intestine died.	
	15.9.18		Look out new site for Section a few miles further forward in Bouvincourt area	
			Put up 30 Remounts for Division & 15 men in attendance overnight at Section	
	16.9.18		~~Send~~ No 9 V.E.S moves forward close to Brie.	
	17.9.18		Send 35 animals to V.E.S. Prepare for moving Section in afternoon.	
			Remounts issued to Units between 8 & 9 am by DADVS.	

[Remarks column, handwritten signature:] Capt AVC

D. D. & L., London, E.C.
(A7883) Wt. W803/M1672 350,000 4/17 Sch. 52a Forms/C/2118/14

Army Form C. 2118.

Instructions regarding War Diaries and Intelligence Summaries are contained in F. S. Regs., Part II. and the Staff Manual respectively. Title pages will be prepared in manuscript.

WAR DIARY
or
INTELLIGENCE SUMMARY.
(Erase heading not required.)

Place	Date	Hour	Summary of Events and Information	Remarks and references to Appendices
			No 2 Mob. Vet. Sect. September 1918	
Coulincourt			Move Section forward to Coulincourt area W3a7.7 after dinner. Get good lines	
W3a7.7	17.9.18		made for horses behind bank. Men make bivouacs dug into banking.	
			Heavy bombing all round between 9 & 12 PM.	
	18.9.18		Take in 20 cases to Section majority result of previous nights bombing	
			Take over Veterinary charge of 1st DAC & Divisional Train by order of DADVS	
			Pay out Section. Destroy & bury 2 horses received with broken legs	
			Destroy & bury two horses (broken legs) brought in with Float.	
	19.9.18.		Send 22 animals to IX V.E.S.	
	20.9.18.		Accompany DADVS round 3 Sections of DAC.	
			Corpl Ambrose granted 14 days leave to England from 22nd inst.	
	21.9.18.		Evacuate 20 animals to V.E.S. Destroy & bury two: – one with ruptured tendon other	
			with open joint. Three men from Section go to IX V.E.S. for temporary duty by order of DDVS	
	22.9.18.		Take over Veterinary charge of 21st Labour Co & 77 Labour Co by order of DADVS	
	23.9.18.		Evacuate 17 animals to V.E.S. one Float case.	
	24.9.18		Dress all animals with wounds preparing for evacuation tomorrow morning	
	25.9.18		Evacuate 20 animals to IX V.E.S. 1 float case	
			Take over Vet. charge of 253, 254, 256 Tunnelling Cos.	
	26.9.18		Evacuate 17 animals to IX V.E.S.	Andrew Boyd Capt. AVC

D. D. & L., London E.C.
(10340) Wt W5300/P713 750,000 3/18 E 2688 Forms/C2118/16.

Army Form C. 2118.

WAR DIARY
or
INTELLIGENCE SUMMARY.

(Erase heading not required.)

Instructions regarding War Diaries and Intelligence Summaries are contained in F. S. Regs., Part II. and the Staff Manual respectively. Title pages will be prepared in manuscript.

Place	Date	Hour	Summary of Events and Information	Remarks and references to Appendices
			No 2 Mob. Vet. Sect. September 1915	
[illegible] W3A7.7	27.9.15		Call on Div Laundry Officer & arrange to draw new shirts & pair of socks for each man in Section in exchange for old. Parading Section to Baths as arranged, but unable to get a bath on account of 3rd Bde bathing.	
	25.9.15		Evacuate 20 animals to V.E.S. — one float case.	
	27.9.15		Three men of Section who have been on temporary duty at IX V.E.S returned.	
	29.9.15		Section have Sunday afternoon off.	
	30.9.15		Retain 25 animals in Section on account of V.E.S moving to [illegible] & not receiving any.	
			Visit Cashier & pay Section. 300 animals for evacuation passed thro Section during month.	
			Expecting orders to move Section forward.	
			[illegible] [illegible] Capt AVC O.C. No 2 M.V.S.	

D. D. & L., London E.C.
(10340) Wt W5300/P713 750,000 3/18 E 2688 Forms/C2118/16.

Instructions regarding War Diaries and Intelligence Summaries are contained in F. S. Regs., Part II. and the Staff Manual respectively. Title pages will be prepared in manuscript.

WAR DIARY
or
INTELLIGENCE SUMMARY.
(Erase heading not required.)

Army Form C. 2118.

Place	Date	Hour	Summary of Events and Information	Remarks and references to Appendices
			No 2 Mobile Vet Sect. October 1918	
Caulaincourt	1.10.18		Evacuate 24 animals to IX VES.	
VERMAND			Go to Vermand to look out new site for taking Section forward. While away Section gets all ready for moving. Pte Bottomley proceeds on 14 days leave. Section moves in afternoon to Vermand (R 32 d 9.7 Sheet 62c). A few good dugouts & bombproof shelter for men sleeping in. Handy for watering animals.	
	2.10.18		Take over 6 sick animals from 16th (Cavalry) MVS as they are moving. Dress all wounded cases.	
	3.10.18		Cleaning up harness & vehicles	
	4.10.18		Take over Veterinary charge of No 2 Siege Co RARE	
	5.10.18		VES moves up to Montigny Farm & close down for evacuation until afternoon. Evacuate 26 animals in afternoon to VES. Have to leave two men at VES for temporary duty	
	6.10.18		Commence to build protecting wall against bombs round standings. Visit & inspect all animals of SAA Section 1st DAC individually for infectious diseases; also [illegible] 13 horses & 4 mules attached.	
	~~6.10.18~~		Men have Sunday afternoon off	
	7.10.18		By order from Corps send 9 men & 2 NCOs to IX V.E.S. for duty. Evacuate 6 animals to VES. Take in 3 horses from 12th MVS Cavalry as they are moving forward.	

D. D. & L., London E.C. (10340) Wt W5300/P713 750,000 3/18 E 2688 Forms/C2118/16.

Army Form C. 2118.

WAR DIARY
or
INTELLIGENCE SUMMARY.
(Erase heading not required.)

Instructions regarding War Diaries and Intelligence Summaries are contained in F. S. Regs., Part II. and the Staff Manual respectively. Title pages will be prepared in manuscript.

October 1915 — No. 2 Mobile Vet. Section

Place	Date	Hour	Summary of Events and Information	Remarks and references to Appendices
VERMAND	9.10.15		Evacuate [illegible] animals to 9th V.E.S.	
	10.10.15		Inspect all animals of No 2 Sect. DAC individually for infectious diseases	
	11.10.15		Evacuate 15 animals to 9th VES. 3 of which are [illegible] cases.	
			NCO & men returned to Section from VES.	
			DADVS goes out to find new Position in forward area for Section	
PONTRU	12.10.15		Move Section to Pontru (Sheet 62 B. M.8.c.7.3.) about [illegible] kilometres forward arriving there about midday. Watering accommodation good & [illegible] [illegible] [illegible] [illegible] close to section lines. ADVS [illegible] today [illegible] [illegible] method of MVS & [illegible] from forward MVS backwards to VES by staging method. Take in 7 animals from 6th Div. MVS [illegible] forward MVS. No 4 [illegible] [illegible] [illegible] [illegible] [illegible] [illegible] for personnel of Section.	
	13.10.15		Evacuate 43 animals to 9th VES, 37 of which were received from forward MVS (46th Divn & 6 Divn & 7th Cavalry Mobile.	
	14.10.15		Evacuate 32 animals to 9th VES. 25 of these from forward Mobiles.	
	~~[illegible]~~		ADVS visits Section	
	15.10.15		Evacuate 82 animals to 9th VES. 80 of these from 6th & 46th Div. MVS.	
	16.10.15		Send NCO to new forward location for Section	
			Evacuate [illegible] animals to 9th VES. 20 of these from 6th Div. MVS.	

[illegible] Capt AVC

D. D. & L., London, E.C. (10340) Wt W5300/P715 750,000 3/15 E 2688 Forms/C2118/16.

Army Form C. 2118.

WAR DIARY
or
INTELLIGENCE SUMMARY.
(Erase heading not required.)

Instructions regarding War Diaries and Intelligence Summaries are contained in F. S. Regs., Part II. and the Staff Manual respectively. Title pages will be prepared in manuscript.

Place	Date	Hour	Summary of Events and Information — No. 2 Mobile Vet. Secn. — October 1918	Remarks and references to Appendices
Pont-ru.	16.10.18		Prepare for moving next morning	
Brancourt	17.10.18		Move off with Section to Brancourt (C.75.c Sheet 62B) at 9 o'clock. N.C.O. from 32nd Divn M.V.S. takes over Billet at Pont-ru. Arrive at Brancourt at [illegible] hrs. Site in open piece of field. Nearest watering place for horses a kilometre from Section. Men get comfortably fixed up in huts & tents.	
	18.10.18		ADVS visits Section	
	19.10.18		9th V.E.S. moves up to Fresnoy le Grand & occupy buildings near Station. Visit V.E.S. & arrange about evacuating early to them tomorrow morning on account of our moving.	
	20.10.18		Evacuate 21 Animals to 9th V.E.S.	
VAUX ANDIGNY			Move off with Section to Vaux Andigny at 10 o'clock arriving at location W25.b.3.7 Sheet 57B at 12 ~~hrs~~ o'clock. Occupy an small orchard. Water point for horses 1 kilometre distance. Make arrangements for carting water in tank & keeping our troughs filled in orchard. Very wet miserable day for moving. Take in 15 animals [illegible]. Personnel of Section [illegible] [illegible] Two Sergeants [illegible]	Andrew Barr Capt. AVC

D. D. & L., London E.C.
(10340) Wt W5300/P713 750,000 3/18 E 2688 Forms/C2118/16.

Army Form C. 2118.

WAR DIARY
or
INTELLIGENCE SUMMARY.
(Erase heading not required.)

Instructions regarding War Diaries and Intelligence Summaries are contained in F. S. Regs., Part II. and the Staff Manual respectively. Title pages will be prepared in manuscript.

Place	Date	Hour	Summary of Events and Information — No 2 Mob. Vet. Sect. October 1918	Remarks and references to Appendices
Vaux Andigny	21.10.18		Evacuate 25 animals to 9th V.E.S. 2 of these were captured German horses.	
			Two of the evacuated had ulcerated mouths. suspect [illegible]	
	23.10.18		Evacuate 23 animals to 9th V.E.S. one of these had [illegible] ulcerated mouth	
			[illegible] on 23rd [illegible] to [illegible] on [illegible] until [illegible]	
			returns to him from leave.	
	24.10.18		Parade of Section to Baths at Vaux Andigny at 8 o'clock. get very good bath.	
	25.10.18		Evacuate 27 animals to V.E.S. Receive 9 captured German horses in Section retain two Riders & test them with Mallein before reissuing	
	25.10.18		Have all vehicles washed. send [illegible] to [illegible] Train to be repaired & get [illegible] returned completed on 26th	
	26		Evacuate 20 Animals to V.E.S. [illegible]	
	26.10.18		Pay out Section	
	27.10.18		Evacuate 36 Animals to V.E.S. send one [illegible] Horse to APM [illegible] for human consumption by civilians. Section bury all Sunday afternoon	

Name [illegible] Capt. A.V.C.

D. D. & L., London E.C.
(10340) Wt W5300/P713 750,000 3/18 E 2688 Forms/C2118/16.

Army Form C. 2118.

Instructions regarding War Diaries and Intelligence Summaries are contained in F. S. Regs., Part II. and the Staff Manual respectively. Title pages will be prepared in manuscript.

WAR DIARY
or
INTELLIGENCE SUMMARY.
(Erase heading not required.)

Place	Date	Hour	Summary of Events and Information — No 2 Mobile Vet Sectn — October 1918	Remarks and references to Appendices
Vaux Andigny			Evacuated 71 animals to 9th V.E.S. Sent one fallen horse to A.D.M.	
	25.10.18		Taken for human consumption.	
	29.10.18		Evacuated 14 animals to 9th V.E.S. During past two days 12 of these evacuated [illegible]	
			[illegible]	
	30.10.18		Granted 14 days leave to England to [illegible] over on 31st. Leave Section at morning of 30th by car to Amiens. Got lift with the Lewis [illegible] Officer i/c Divn Field Supply Column. Capt. Shearman is put in charge of Section while I am on leave	

Andrew Barr

CAPTAIN, A.V.C.
O.C. 2 MOBILE VETERINARY SECTION

D. D. & L., London E.C.
(10340) Wt W5300/P713 750,000 3/18 E 2688 Forms/C2118/16.

Instructions regarding War Diaries and Intelligence Summaries are contained in F. S. Regs., Part II. and the Staff Manual respectively. Title pages will be prepared in manuscript.

WAR DIARY
or
INTELLIGENCE SUMMARY.
(Erase heading not required.)

Army Form C. 2118.

No 2 Mob. Vet. Sect. — November 1918

Place	Date	Hour	Summary of Events and Information	Remarks and references to Appendices
VAUX ANDIGNY	31.10.18		Evacuated 20 animals to No 9 V.E.S	
	1.11.18		Evacuated 22 animals to No 9 V.E.S.	
	2.11.18		Evacuated 15 animals to No 9 V.E.S	
	3.11.18		Quiet day.	
	4.11.18		Established advanced post for battle at Bellevue. Collected 4 animals. Evacuated 12 animals. Sent 1 NCO 1 S.S + 2 O.R as conducting party for remounts to Rossel	
	5.11.18		Evacuated 12 animals to No 9 V.E.S 48 remounts arrive and remain overnight	
	6.11.18		Evacuated 7 animals. Closed + withdrew advanced post at Bellevue. Section moved + opened at Fresnoy le Grand. D.A.D.V.S issued remounts to units	
Fresnoy le Grand	7.11.18		Evacuated 3 animals to V.E.S Mallein'd 8 captured animals	
	8.11.18		Visited by A.D.V.S Corps. Evacuated 7 animals including 1 Tetanus	
	9.11.18		Established advanced post at St SOUPLET. Evacuated 6 animals from Section	
	10.11.18		Collected + Evacuated 16 animals from advanced post to No 9 V.E.S.	
	11.11.18		Closed advanced post at St SOUPLET. Made arrangements for section to open at CATILLION. Visited by A.D.V.S Corps. Hostilities cease at 11 am to-day	
	12.11.18		Section less 1 NCO + 4 men move to Catillon. Good Billets for men + animals	
CATILLON	13.11.18		Remainder of Section personnel join Section. Evacuated 37 animals to 9 V.E.S. Received 20 animals, [illegible] 17 from 42nd M.V.S. [illegible] 11 from 11th North Midland [illegible] [illegible] from No 7 M.V.S	

[illegible]

D. D. & L., London E.C.
(10340) Wt W5300/P713 750,000 3/18 E 2688 Forms/C2118/16.

Army Form C. 2118.

Instructions regarding War Diaries and Intelligence Summaries are contained in F. S. Regs., Part II. and the Staff Manual respectively. Title pages will be prepared in manuscript.

WAR DIARY
or
INTELLIGENCE SUMMARY.
(Erase heading not required.)

No 2 Mob. Vet. Sect. — November 1918

Place	Date	Hour	Summary of Events and Information	Remarks and references to Appendices
Carillon	14.11.18		Evac. 54 animals to 9th V.E.S.	[illegible]
			Advanced party from 9th VES arrive to take over Billets as Section is moving off on 15th [illegible] with Division to occupy territory [illegible]	
	15.11.18		Evacuated [illegible] animals to 9th VES. Section marches to [illegible] [illegible] hours [illegible]. Good billets [illegible] horses	
			Captain [illegible] returns from Leave & takes over charge of Section again	
Semousies	16.11.18		Section marches to Semousies, distance about 20 kilometres. Billets for men very poor. Horses in the open.	
Sars le Chateau	17.11.18		Section marches to Sars le Chateau, distance about 13 kilometres. Good billets for men. Horses in the open. [illegible] [illegible] Evacuate [illegible] for [illegible]	
La Savate	18.11.18		Evacuate 17 animals to ~~[illegible]~~ 50th Div M.V.S. Section [illegible] at La Savate Station. Billeted with [illegible] Australian Light Horse. Good billets for men & horses	
[illegible]	19.11.18		Leave Sars le Chateau at [illegible] hours arrived La Savate at [illegible] hours. Section [illegible] Australian Light Horse to [illegible] arriving about midday. Good billets for men & stabling for horses. Taken up [illegible] in afternoon.	

(A7092). Wt. W12839/M1293. 750,000. 1/17. D. D. & L., Ltd. Forms/C.2118/14.

Instructions regarding War Diaries and Intelligence Summaries are contained in F. S. Regs., Part II. and the Staff Manual respectively. Title pages will be prepared in manuscript.

WAR DIARY

or

INTELLIGENCE SUMMARY.

(Erase heading not required.)

Army Form C. 2118.

No 7 Mobile Veterinary Sec — November 1918

Place	Date	Hour	Summary of Events and Information	Remarks and references to Appendices
Bousu lez Walcourt	20.11.18		Halt for day. Section clean up harness & saddlery. Draw money from Field Cashier at Walcourt to pay Section. DADVS gives me veterinary charge of Hdqr Groups while on march. Visit [illegible] Train [illegible] in 3 groups. [illegible] Horse Transport [illegible]	
	21.11.18		Section continues to clean up harness, saddlery & wash vehicles. Pay out Section. Visit 12 DAC.	
	22.11.18		Further moving forward deferred for a few days on account of rail & road transport. Section continues with cleaning up. Attend [illegible] for civilian [illegible] [illegible] Return [illegible] Visit [illegible] BAC RHA. Notified to be ready to move on morning of 23rd	
Vogenee	23.11.18		Section marches to billet at Vogenee — 2½ hours march arriving at 12.30. Good billets for men & stabling for horses. Leave horse with civilian at Bousu lez Walcourt to be picked up by motor float from 9th VES. Section spends afternoon in cleaning harness & vehicles.	
Stave	24.11.18		Send off Corporal & one man with 5 animals to advanced VES at Surry. Section marches to billets at Stave starting at 09.30 arriving at [illegible] 1½ hours. Roads for first 7 to 10 kilometres very hilly & slippery.	

(A7092). Wt. W12839/M1293. 750,000. 1/17. D. D. & L., Ltd. Forms/C.2118/14.

Instructions regarding War Diaries and Intelligence Summaries are contained in F. S. Regs., Part II. and the Staff Manual respectively. Title pages will be prepared in manuscript.

WAR DIARY
or
INTELLIGENCE SUMMARY.
(Erase heading not required.)

Army Form C. 2118.

Place	Date	Hour	Summary of Events and Information — No 2 Mob. Vet. Sec. — November 1918	Remarks and references to Appendices
SEAVE	24.11.18		remainder of march very good. Billeted in a farm. good billet for men & good stabling for horses. [illegible] which has paralysed [illegible] for farmer [illegible] slaughtering [illegible] for human consumption. DADVS visits Section	
	25.11.18		Send off Lance Corporal [illegible] & Private Wright to collect two animals left by Artillery Units. After collecting they will go on to VES with them. Group halt today. Clip 3 draught horses of Section, cleaning up [illegible] saddlery	
	26.11.18		Clip other 3 draught horses. Attend Conference of Brig. General for OC of Units in Div. Hdqrs Group. [illegible] & Pte Morley start on leave to England [illegible]	
	27.11.18		Evacuate 9 animals to 3rd MVS at [illegible]	
	28.11.18		DADVS & DAQMG visit Section	
	29.11.18		Visit [illegible] & with Belgian Interpreter inspect cows at B[illegible] for foot & mouth. Majority of cases are cured. what remain affected are very slight. [illegible] Test Horse for Glanders sent in today by order of DADVS as a suspected case — Negative reaction. Sent from 3 Bde AFA	[illegible]
	30.11.18		DADVS visits Section & inspects Horse which was malleined	

(A7092). Wt. W12839/M1293. 750,000. 1/17. D. D. & L., Ltd. Forms/C.2118/14.

Army Form C. 2118.

WAR DIARY
or
INTELLIGENCE SUMMARY.

(*Erase heading not required.*)

Instructions regarding War Diaries and Intelligence Summaries are contained in F. S. Regs., Part II. and the Staff Manual respectively. Title pages will be prepared in manuscript.

No 2 Mob Vet Sec. November 1918.

Place	Date	Hour	Summary of Events and Information	Remarks and references to Appendices
~~[illegible]~~ ST AVE	30.11.18		Receive 6 Horses for evacuation. Get warning notice to prepare to move forward [illegible] with Div Group. Moving to ANTHEE	

[illegible] Barr
Capt AVC
OC No 2 M V S

(A7092). Wt. W12839/M1293. 750,000. 1/17. D. D. & L., Ltd. Forms/C.2118/14.

WAR DIARY
or
~~INTELLIGENCE SUMMARY.~~

(Erase heading not required.)

Army Form C. 2118.

Instructions regarding War Diaries and Intelligence Summaries are contained in F. S. Regs., Part II. and the Staff Manual respectively. Title pages will be prepared in manuscript.

No. 2 Mobile Vet: Sec: December 1918.

Place	Date	Hour	Summary of Events and Information	Remarks and references to Appendices
Essig	30.12.18		Give Section Xmas Dinner which passes off very well every one appearing well satisfied.	
	31.12.18		Get notice that Sergt Owen, Warren & Corpl Ambrose having been recommended for a tour of home duty will be relieved at an early date by two Sergts & one Corporal from No 2 Vet Hosp	

Andrew Barr
Capt RAVC
OC No 2 M.V.S.

D. D. & L., London, E.C.
(10340) Wt W5300/P713 750,000 3/18 E 2668 Forms/C2118/16.

Army Form C. 2118.

WAR DIARY
or
INTELLIGENCE SUMMARY.
(Erase heading not required.)

Instructions regarding War Diaries and Intelligence Summaries are contained in F. S. Regs., Part II. and the Staff Manual respectively. Title pages will be prepared in manuscript.

Place	Date	Hour	Summary of Events and Information	Remarks and references to Appendices
			No 2 Mob Vet Sec — December 1918	
			Billet to which we move on 27th, where we hope to hold	
MUNSTER EIFEL	26.12.18		for several weeks.	
			Day spent in cleaning up saddlery, harness, preparing for GOC's inspection.	
			Visit from [illegible] of IX Corps, Capt. Harris (Mob Vet) to pay out Section.	
Essig	27.12.18		March to final Billet at Essig starting at 10.45 hrs behind No 1 Sec Train. GOC inspects Column during march through Rheinbach. Arrive Essig at 14 hours. Get good Billets for Section at two Farms at [illegible] points. Men all got comfortably billeted & all horses under cover.	
	28.12.18		Look round village to find better stabling for horses. Unload stores & clean out two places to make forage shed & place for stores. Pay out Section.	
	29.12.18		Men have Sunday afternoon off.	
	30.12.18		ADVS IX Corps & DADVS visit Section.	

D. D. & L., London E.C.
(10340) Wt W5300/P713 750,000 3/18 E 2638 Forms/C2118/16.

Instructions regarding War Diaries and Intelligence Summaries are contained in F. S. Regs., Part II. and the Staff Manual respectively. Title pages will be prepared in manuscript.

WAR DIARY
or
INTELLIGENCE SUMMARY.
(Erase heading not required.)

Army Form C. 2118.

Place	Date	Hour	Summary of Events and Information — No 2 Mobile Vet Sect — December 1918	Remarks and references to Appendices
Kronenburg	22.12.18		to ~~[illegible]~~ Kronenburg where the Section was to be billeted. Owing to bad accommodation was a poor [illegible] made up to billet so had to go on in search of a billet further on. Got well fixed up in a Tobacco factory four kilometres further on. Roads were very hilly & heavy going. Pick up horse at [illegible] left on 10th inst by 6 M.V.S.	[illegible] Capt. RAVC
Mulheim	23.12.18		Resume march at 10.30 behind H.Qrs 11th Bty H.T. & march to billets at MULHEIM. Very rough journey & heavy rain during march. Roads very heavy & hilly. Arrive Mulheim at 14.30 hours. Billets for men & accommodation for horses very fair.	
Munster Eifel	24.12.18		Resume march at 10 hours behind H.Qrs 15th A.H.T. & march to billets at MUNSTEREIFEL about 18 Kilos, arriving at 14 hours. Day clear & frosty. Good march, roads not too hilly. Good billets for men & stable accommodation for horses. Remainder stand out in open.	
	25.12.18		Xmas Day. Section do some cleaning up in morning & have afternoon off. "Xmas Dinner" postponed until we arrive at dest[illegible]	

D. D. & L., London E.C.
(10340) Wt W5300/P713 750,000 3/18 E 2688 Forms/C2118/16.

Instructions regarding War Diaries and Intelligence Summaries are contained in F. S. Regs., Part II. and the Staff Manual respectively. Title pages will be prepared in manuscript.

WAR DIARY
or
INTELLIGENCE SUMMARY.
(Erase heading not required.)

Army Form C. 2118.

Place	Date	Hour	Summary of Events and Information	Remarks and references to Appendices
			No 2 Mob. Vet. Sect. December 1918	
			Got good billets for men & covering for all horses. Arrived at BEHO	
BEHO	18.12.18		at 13.30 hours. Very rough weather all morning & [illegible] all	
			the way. Afternoon spent in washing saddlery harness & vehicles	
			Before leaving Fraiture Corpl Stevens & 2 men started out with 7 animals for	
			V.E.S at STAVELOT a distance of 32 Kilometres. They got back to Section	
			on morning of 19th before we leave BEHO: having stayed overnight at a village halfway	
	19.12.18		Resume march at 11 hours in rear of No 1 Sq Train & cross over frontier into Germany	
GRUFFLINGEN			marching to billets at GRUFFLINGEN, arriving at 13 hours. Heavy snowstorm	
			part of march. Got good billets for men & horses comfortably stabled	
			Find inhabitants quite willing to help us.	
	20.12.18		Halt for one day	
	21.12.18		Resume march at 09 hours in rear of No 1 Sq Train & march to billets	
ANDLER	22.12.18		at Andler a distance of 22 Kilometres arriving at 14.30 hours. Roads	
			hilly & heavy going	
			Resume march at 09.15 hours in rear of No 1 Sq Train & march	

D. D. & L., London E.C.
(10340) Wt W5300/P713 750,000 3/18 E 2638 Forms/C2118/16.

Instructions regarding War Diaries and Intelligence Summaries are contained in F. S. Regs., Part II. and the Staff Manual respectively. Title pages will be prepared in manuscript.

WAR DIARY
or
~~INTELLIGENCE SUMMARY.~~

(Erase heading not required.)

Army Form C. 2118.

Place	Date	Hour	Summary of Events and Information	Remarks and references to Appendices
			Section marches with No 1 Co Train 1 Hqrs 16 Aus HT to billets at	
Bomal	14.12.18		Bomal – a short march of 7 Kilometres arriving at midday.	
			Got men horses all comfortably fixed up.	
			Visit DADVS inspect Veterinary Sergeants [illegible]	
			[illegible] chests.	
	15.12.18		Halt for the day. Section spends forenoon in cleaning up [illegible]	
			[illegible]	
Erezee [illegible]			[illegible] 08 hours with No 1 Co Train & Hqrs 16 AHT to billets	
	16.12.18		at [illegible] at 13 hours [illegible]	
			[illegible] all [illegible]	
			Resume march at 10 hours with No 1 Co Train & 16 AHT & march to	
[illegible]	17.12.18		billets at [illegible] arriving at 13 hours. Weather very [illegible]	
			[illegible] snow & rain & much colder. Billets & shelter for	
			horses only fair. DADVS visits Section.	
~~[illegible]~~	18.12.18		Resume march at 08 hours with No 1 Co Train & 16 Aus HT & march to BEHO	[illegible]

D. D. & L., London E.C.
(10340) Wt W5300/P713 750,000 3/18 E 2688 Forms/C2118/16.

Army Form C. 2118.

WAR DIARY
or
INTELLIGENCE SUMMARY.
(Erase heading not required.)

Instructions regarding War Diaries and Intelligence Summaries are contained in F. S. Regs., Part II. and the Staff Manual respectively. Title pages will be prepared in manuscript.

Place	Date	Hour	Summary of Events and Information No 2 Mob. Vet. Sect. Dec 1915	Remarks and references to Appendices
HEROCK	7.12.15		DADVS visit Section. Section got fitted out with ankle boots & puttees in place of field boots which are returned to DADVS	
	9.12.15		Section marched to new billets with No 1 Co Train & HdQrs 16 Aux HT Transport	
Briquemont			at BRIQUEMONT. Section billeted near farm & men billeted in two empty rooms in farmhouse. Stabling for all horses	
SENSIN			Arrive in billet at midday after 2½ hours march.	
	10.12.15		March with No 1 Co Train & HdQrs 16 Aux HT to billets at SENSIN four hours march, arriving at 11.30 hours. Billets for men in two rooms of house. All horses under cover.	
PETIT HAN	11.12.15		Resume march at 10 hours, halt at 11.30 [illegible] & continue march in rear of No 1 Co Train. Arrive in billet at Petit Han at 15.30 hours. Billets in farm. Men & horses made very comfortable. Very wet day for march, roads in bad state & heavy going	
	12.12.15		Section halts for two days. Greater part of time spent in cleaning harness, saddlery & vehicles. Two very wet days. Inspect [illegible] sheets of No 1 Co Train HdQrs 16th A.H.T. & 5th BAC RHA.	

D. D. & L., London E.C.
(10340) Wt W5300/P713 750,000 3/18 E 2688 Forms/C2118/16.

Instructions regarding War Diaries and Intelligence Summaries are contained in F. S. Regs., Part II. and the Staff Manual respectively. Title pages will be prepared in manuscript.

WAR DIARY
or
~~INTELLIGENCE SUMMARY.~~
(Erase heading not required.)

Army Form C. 2118.

Place	Date	Hour	Summary of Events and Information — No 2 Mobile Vet. Sect. — December 1918	Remarks and references to Appendices
HEROCK	4.12.18		Divisional Group halts for a few days. Section spends day in cleaning up harness & ~~vehicles~~ saddles.	[illegible] Capt RAVC
	5.12.18		Inspect mares of 11 [?] Horse Transport re being suitable to send home for breeding. None found suitable.	
			Section continues cleaning up harness & vehicles.	
			Draw money from Field Cashier & pay out Sect.	
	6.12.18		Inspect mares of 14 Batn MGC re breeding – none found suitable. Give Section afternoon off after inspecting & [illegible]	
	7.12.18		Evacuate 9 animals to 9th V.E.S. at Boiselles [?]. Capt goes out to main station of V.E.S. at [illegible] & brings back D.A.D.V.S. [?] [illegible] was detained there for 4 weeks.	
			Inspect mares of 3rd D.A.C. & [illegible] R.F.A. re breeding	
			Dvr [illegible] returns from leave having been held up at Reception Camp for [illegible] days	

D. D. & L., London E.C.
(10340) Wt W5300/P713 750,000 3/18 E 2688 Forms/C2118/16.

Instructions regarding War Diaries and Intelligence Summaries are contained in F. S. Regs., Part II. and the Staff Manual respectively. Title pages will be prepared in manuscript.

WAR DIARY
or
~~INTELLIGENCE SUMMARY.~~
(Erase heading not required.)

Army Form C. 2118.

Place	Date	Hour	Summary of Events and Information	Remarks and references to Appendices
	1.12.18		Mov. Section with Divis HdQrs Group. March from ST AVE to billets at ANTHEE	
ANTHEE			Good billets for men & stabling for horses. Watering good & convenient.	
			Distance of march about 11 Kilometres; getting in about midday.	
	2.12.18		Continue march; march to billets at BLAIMONT going in front of No 1	
BLAIMONT			18 A.S.C. & rear of HdQrs Group going by another route.	
			Distance of march 11 Kilometres getting in about midday. Men	
			billeted in [illegible]. Section spent afternoon cleaning harness	
			saddlery & vehicles.	
			Evacuated 5 Horses to [illegible] VES at Dinant.	
	3.12.18		Continue march passing starting point at 09.00 hours. March to billets at	
			HERBUCK Station a distance of about 25 Kilos. reaching there 14.30 hours.	
			Very good billets for men & stabling for horses, good watering & handy.	
			[illegible] part of journey over very hilly roads. [illegible]	
			to Billet [illegible]	

D. D. & L., London, E.C.
(10340) Wt W5300/P713 750,000 3/18 E 2688 Forms/C2118/16.

16

VR 43

War Diary

of No 2 Mobile Veterinary Section

for January 1919

Army Form C. 2118.

Instructions regarding War Diaries and Intelligence Summaries are contained in F. S. Regs., Part II. and the Staff Manual respectively. Title pages will be prepared in manuscript.

WAR DIARY
or
INTELLIGENCE SUMMARY.
(Erase heading not required.)

Place	Date	Hour	Summary of Events and Information January 1919	Remarks and references to Appendices
Essig	1.1.19		Given veterinary charge of 3rd Cav Bde & the three R.E. Units	
			Sell [illegible] cases to Horse Butcher in Euskirchen who pays 1 Franc per Kilo	
	2.1.19		after animal is dressed up.	
			On 1st & 2nd receive many debility animals from Division majority	
			of which are from R.F.A. [illegible] cases from 23rd R.E.	
	3.1.19		Visit & inspect animals in Units of 3rd Cav Bde	
	4.1.19		Evacuate 37 Animals to V.E.S. (9th) Inspect R.E. Units	
	5.1.19		Give Pass to half of Section to visit Bonn & Cologne; go	
			by train from Odendorf.	
	6.1.19		With Capt. [illegible] to inspect all animals of 3rd & 5th [illegible] Batteries	
			& categorise them [illegible] for demobilisation	
			[illegible]	
			& warm.	
			With Capt. Barbet inspect all animals of [illegible] Batteries.	
			[illegible]	

D. D. & L., London E.C.
(10340) Wt W5300/P713 750,000 3/18 E 2688 Forms/C2118/16.

Instructions regarding War Diaries and Intelligence Summaries are contained in F. S. Regs., Part II. and the Staff Manual respectively. Title pages will be prepared in manuscript.

WAR DIARY
or
INTELLIGENCE SUMMARY.

(*Erase heading not required.*)

Army Form C. 2118.

Place	Date	Hour	Summary of Events and Information	Remarks and references to Appendices
Essig	7.1.19		Examined 12 animals [illegible]	
			[illegible] Section	
	8.1.19		Sergeant [illegible] leave today for Home [illegible] England	
	9.1.19		With Capt Burkets inspect all animals of S.A.A. Section [illegible]	
			[illegible] Capt Walker [illegible] leave [illegible]	
	10.1.19		With Capt Burketts inspect [illegible] all animals of No. [illegible] Sect [illegible]	
	11.1.19		Some of Section granted leave [illegible] to go to Bonn & Cologne	
	12.1.19		[illegible] Sunday [illegible]	
	13.1.19		With Capt Burketts inspect [illegible] all animals of [illegible]	
	14.1.19		With Capt Burketts inspect [illegible] all animals of [illegible]	
			Examined [illegible] animals [illegible]	
			[illegible] Field [illegible] R.E. [illegible] Pte. [illegible]	
			in hospital	
			With Capt Burketts inspect [illegible] animals of [illegible]	
	16.1.19		With [illegible] all animals of [illegible]	

D. D. & L., London E.C.
(10340) Wt W5300/P713 750,000 3/18 E 2688 Forms/C2118/16.

Army Form C. 2118.

WAR DIARY
or
INTELLIGENCE SUMMARY.
(Erase heading not required.)

Instructions regarding War Diaries and Intelligence Summaries are contained in F. S. Regs., Part II. and the Staff Manual respectively. Title pages will be prepared in manuscript.

Place	Date	Hour	Summary of Events and Information	Remarks and references to Appendices
			No 7 M.V. Sect [illegible]	
[illegible]	16.1.19		[illegible]	
			[illegible]	
			[illegible]	
			[illegible]	
			[illegible]	
	17.1.19		With D.A.D.V.S. & Capt. Bond inspect & category all animals of 1st Signal Coy	[illegible]
			Division HdQrs commencing at 7.30 hours	
			[illegible] 52 animals received in Section	
			(classed [illegible]) from units of 1st Division	
			Recd letter from Pte Fallin RAVC who went on leave from Sect on Dec 19th saying he	
			has been retained in England for demobilisation	
	18.1.19		Brand animals for Cologne with D on quarter	
			[illegible] Notified that Pte Morley has been sent to [illegible] C.C.S.	
	19.1.19		Send [illegible] animals to Cologne in charge of Corporal [illegible]	
			[illegible]	
			[illegible]	

D. D. & L., London E.C.
(10340) Wt W5300/P713 750,000 3/18 E 2688 Forms/C2118/16.

Army Form C. 2118.

Instructions regarding War Diaries and Intelligence Summaries are contained in F. S. Regs., Part II. and the Staff Manual respectively. Title pages will be prepared in manuscript.

WAR DIARY
or
INTELLIGENCE SUMMARY.
(Erase heading not required.)

Place	Date	Hour	Summary of Events and Information	Remarks and references to Appendices
			No 2 Mobile Vet Section Jany 1919	
[illegible]	[illegible].1.19		[illegible] D animals [illegible] Troops [illegible]	
			[illegible] on Friday [illegible]	
			[illegible] who went with animals to Cologne [illegible]	
			Mallein animals classified D received today	
	22.1.19		Evacuate [illegible] animals to 9th V.E.S.	
			Brand D animals	
			[illegible] Section	
	23.1.19		Send [illegible] animals ([illegible] 2 mules) to Cologne [illegible]	
			[illegible]	
	24.1.19		[illegible] to England [illegible]	
			[illegible] to England [illegible]	
	25.1.19		[illegible] D animals to Cologne [illegible]	
	[illegible].1.19		[illegible] Horses [illegible] 9th V.E.S. [illegible] Cologne [illegible]	
			[illegible]	
			[illegible] England [illegible]	
	27.1.19		Send 3 Men to [illegible] 9th V.E.S. [illegible] D Horses to Cologne	
			Corpl [illegible]	
	29.1.19		Three [illegible] who went to Cologne	

D. D. & L., London E.C.
(10340) Wt W5300/P713 750,000 3/18 E 2688 Forms/C2118/16.

Instructions regarding War Diaries and Intelligence Summaries are contained in F. S. Regs., Part II. and the Staff Manual respectively. Title pages will be prepared in manuscript.

WAR DIARY

or

~~INTELLIGENCE SUMMARY.~~

(Erase heading not required.)

Army Form C. 2118.

No. 2 Mobile Vet. Sect. — January 1919

Place	Date	Hour	Summary of Events and Information	Remarks and references to Appendices
Essay [illegible]	31.1.19		Evacuated 11 animals to 9th V.E.S. including one [illegible] case of mange. "Mange" case from [illegible] Bty RFA	
			[illegible] Capt. RAVC	

D. D. & L., London, E.C.
(10340) Wt W5300/P713 750,000 3/18 E 2688 Forms/C2118/16.

26

Vol 44

War Diary of No 2 Mobile Veterinary Section

for February 1919

Instructions regarding War Diaries and Intelligence Summaries are contained in F. S. Regs., Part II. and the Staff Manual respectively. Title pages will be prepared in manuscript.

WAR DIARY
or
INTELLIGENCE SUMMARY.
(Erase heading not required.)

Army Form C. 2118.

Place	Date	Hour	Summary of Events and Information ~~January~~ February 1919	Remarks and references to Appendices
ESSIG	1.2.	19	By order of ADVS send 3 men to 9th V.E.S to assist in evacuating 'D' animals to Cologne.	
			Corporal Walton returns from [illegible] having been [illegible] up at [illegible]	
			By order of ADVS no animals to be evacuated (except MVS in true mange) to V.E.S until number is over 30.	
	2.2.	19	Men have Sunday afternoon off.	
	3.2.	19	Lance Corporal R H White & Lance Corpl A Boniface leave for 28 days course in Veterinary Science & Cold shoeing. L/Corpl White from No 2 Field Ambul & L/Corpl Boniface from 2nd Survey(?)	
			The 3 men return from Cologne.	
			Send blankets to be deloused in Foden at Rheinbach(?)	
	4.2.	19	Mallein of Class D animals	
	5.2.	19	Driver Dugard(?) goes on leave to England returning on the 8th inst.	
			Visit Field Ambulance & pay out Section.	
	6.2.	19	Evacuate 7 Class D Horses (reclassified) to 9th V.E.S & one Mange	
	7.2.	19	Private Evans returns from Leave. Sergt Emmers(?) & Corpl Stevens have day off to go to Cologne	

D. D. & L., London E.C.
(10340) Wt W5300/P713 750,000 3/18 E 2688 Forms/C2118/16.

Instructions regarding War Diaries and Intelligence Summaries are contained in F. S. Regs., Part II. and the Staff Manual respectively. Title pages will be prepared in manuscript.

WAR DIARY
or
INTELLIGENCE SUMMARY.
(Erase heading not required.)

Army Form C. 2118.

Place	Date	Hour	Summary of Events and Information — No 2 Mobile Vet Sect — February 1919	Remarks and references to Appendices
Feb 19	8.2.19		Corpl Walker & Pte Facey have day off to go to Cologne	
			Remount Board (Lt Col West & Capt Hamilton) classify animals of Section	
			Brand all animals of section with broad arrow	
	9.2.19		Summary mark all animals [illegible] according to R.B. classification	
	10.2.19		Send one NCO & two men to 9th V.E.S. taking animals to Cologne	
	11.2.19		Driver Peace returns from leave – had seven days extension	
	12.2.19		Attend Corps Commanders Conference at Duisdorf	
	14.2.19		Evacuate 16 animals to 9th V.E.S. – 7 of these are Mange	
			Pte Gregory returns from leave – having had 7 days extension.	
	15.2.19		Mallein all [illegible] V&Z animals in 3rd Inf Bde – 12 mall.	
			Private [illegible] goes on leave to England	
	16.2.19		Inspect all animals malleined yesterday	
			Section have Sunday afternoon off	
	17.2.19		DADVS returns from leave	
	18.2.19		Have harness & saddlery inspection. Give Section 1½ hours off for football in afternoon	
	19.2.19		Rifle inspection	

D. D. & L., London, E.C.
(10340) Wt W5300/P713 750,000 3/18 E 2688 Forms/C2118/16.

Instructions regarding War Diaries and Intelligence Summaries are contained in F. S. Regs., Part II. and the Staff Manual respectively. Title pages will be prepared in manuscript.

WAR DIARY

or

INTELLIGENCE ~~SUMMARY.~~

(Erase heading not required.)

Army Form C. 2118.

Place	Date	Hour	Summary of Events and Information — No 2 Mob. Vet. Sec. — February 1919	Remarks and references to Appendices
Emq [illegible]	19.2.19		Visit Field Butchers [illegible]	
	21.2.19		Visit [illegible] & speak [illegible] of 2 animals for destruction	
	21.2.19		Pte Keyworth returns from leave.	
	22.2.19		Visit 7th Inf. Bde. & speak [illegible] of 2 animals for destruction for human consumption	
	23.2.19		Visit Sanitary Section & make arrangements for Meat Sup. made [illegible] works [illegible] for R.E. & get authority to draw materials for latrines.	
	24.2.19		Have Divisional Engineers Class Z horses paraded & speak [illegible] for destruction for human consumption.	
			Evacuate to 9th V.E.S. 3 Class D horses & two Mange	
	26.2.19		Sgt Evans admitted to hospital with [illegible]	
			[illegible] Pte [illegible] returns from Leave	
	27.2.19		Attend Funeral of [illegible] [illegible] Farewell Dinner [illegible] Hotel [illegible] which were reserved for officers who had been longest with Division	
			[illegible] Barr [illegible] Capt. R.A.V.C.	[illegible]

D. P. & L., London E.C.
(10340) Wt W5300/P713 750,000 3/18 E 2688 Forms/C2118/16.

19

Vol 45

War Diary.

for March.

No 2 Mobile. Veterinary Section.

Instructions regarding War Diaries and Intelligence Summaries are contained in F. S. Regs., Part II. and the Staff Manual respectively. Title pages will be prepared in manuscript.

WAR DIARY

or

~~INTELLIGENCE SUMMARY.~~

(Erase heading not required.)

Army Form C. 2118.

No [illegible] Mobile Vet. Sect. — March 1919

Place	Date	Hour	Summary of Events and Information	Remarks and references to Appendices
Essig	1.3.19		Mallein Class Y & Z animals of 409 (Lowland) Field Co RE & [illegible] Field Co RE. They took over yesterday from 2[illegible] & 23rd RE who are leaving Division to return to England.	
	2.3.19		DADVS visits Section & arranges for NCO & 5 men going to Cologne with 10 men from 2[illegible] Bde RFA taking 100 animals from that Bde for destruction for human consumption.	
	3.3.19		Send Corpl & 5 men to 2[illegible] Bde RFA Lines to Cologne with 100 animals to Evacuate. 13 animals including 1 Mange to 9th VES.	
			Mallein Y & Z animals of 76 Field [illegible] & 23 Field Co RE & [illegible] DADVS.	
			Mallein Y & Z of Divisional Signals, [illegible] & 121 FA.	
			Sergt Evans evacuated from No 3 [illegible] to Base.	
	4.3.19		Mallein Class Y & Z animals of 76 Field Co RE & pick out 9 [illegible] to be reclassified to D.	
			Visit No 1 [illegible] re [illegible] of [illegible] picketing lines for [illegible] animals to Cologne [illegible].	

D. D. & L., London E.C.
(10340) Wt W5300/P713 750,000 3/18 E 2688 Forms/C2118/16.

Army Form C. 2118.

WAR DIARY
or
INTELLIGENCE SUMMARY.
(Erase heading not required.)

Instructions regarding War Diaries and Intelligence Summaries are contained in F. S. Regs., Part II. and the Staff Manual respectively. Title pages will be prepared in manuscript.

No 2 Mob. Vet. Sect. — March 1919

Place	Date	Hour	Summary of Events and Information	Remarks and references to Appendices
Essig	5.3.19		Conducting party return from Cologne.	
	6.3.19		Bay horse which died of Pneumonia admitted from 1st [illegible] [illegible] [illegible] Vet. [illegible] [illegible] Section	
	7.3.19		Send 100 [illegible] D/2 [illegible] from Duren to Cologne [illegible] [illegible] [illegible] in charge of 5 men & 1 N.C.O.	
	9.3.19		Men return from Cologne.	
	9.3.19		Pte Thompson [illegible] from No 1 M.V.S. for duty	
	10.3.19		Attend Dransdorf Race Meeting	
	11.3.19		Ptes Clayton & Taylor [illegible] from No 17 Vet. Hosp. for duty. By order of DADVS [illegible] [illegible] & [illegible] two horses with advanced Mange & [illegible] belonging to a German civilian.	[illegible]
	13.3.19		[illegible] a bay horse suffering from [illegible] [illegible]	
	14.3.19		Evacuate 7 [illegible] D/D horses & one Mange to 4th V.E.S. Corpl Peacock [illegible] [illegible] for demobilisation. [illegible] inspection of Section.	
	15.3.19		Pte [illegible] R.A.S.C. attached [illegible] admitted to No [illegible] F.A. suffering from Influenza.	
	16.3.19		Station [illegible] Sunday afternoon [illegible]	

D. D. & L., London, E.C.
(10340) Wt W5300/P713 750,000 3/18 E 2688 Forms/C2118/16.

Instructions regarding War Diaries and Intelligence Summaries are contained in F. S. Regs., Part II. and the Staff Manual respectively. Title pages will be prepared in manuscript.

WAR DIARY
or
INTELLIGENCE SUMMARY.
(Erase heading not required.)

Army Form C. 2118.

Place	Date	Hour	Summary of Events and Information No 2 Mobile Vet Sectn March 1919	Remarks and references to Appendices
Essig	19.3.19		Evacuate 100 Class D horses to Cologne abbatoir [illegible]	
			[illegible]	
			[illegible]	
			[illegible]	
	20.3.19		Evacuate 6 horses to 9th V.E.S	
			Visit Field Cashier Cologne & draw money to pay Section	
	21.3.19		Evacuate 3 animals including 1 Mange to 9th V.E.S	
			[illegible] from Cologne	
			Pay out Section	
	22.3.19		Capt Stevens returns from leave	
	24.3.19		Visit 51st Welsh & 51st SWB at [illegible] & inspect horses	
	25.3.19		Evacuate 4 Class D animals & 1 Mange to 9th V.E.S	
			Driver [illegible] from No 1 [illegible] to take the place of Dr Lake	
			who was evacuated sick to Base.	
	26.3.19		Receive 35 Class D animals for despatch to Cologne Abbatoir	
	27.3.19		Despatch 100 animals to Cologne Abbatoir in charge of NCO & 14 men	
			DADVS visits & inspects Section	

D. D. & L., London, E.C.
(10340) Wt W5300/P713 750,000 3/18 E 2688 Forms/C2118/16.

Army Form C. 2118.

Instructions regarding War Diaries and Intelligence Summaries are contained in F. S. Regs., Part II. and the Staff Manual respectively. Title pages will be prepared in manuscript.

WAR DIARY
or
INTELLIGENCE SUMMARY.
(Erase heading not required.)

Place	Date	Hour	Summary of Events and Information — No 2 Mob Vet Section — March 1919	Remarks and references to Appendices
Essig	29.3.19		Men return from Cologne.	
	30.3.19		Receive 37 D/2 animals. DADVS visits Section in afternoon & picks out 20 to be retained & dispatched [illegible] with 2 animals.	
			Receive [illegible] animals from 23rd & 26th Field Co RE	
	30.3.19		Notified that I shall be demobilised [illegible] & that Capt [illegible] RAVC will take over command of the Section.	[illegible]
	31.3.19		Send 23 Class D animals to Cologne [illegible].	
			Hand over [illegible] D Class 2 animals to 1st Batt Mach. Gun Corps to take to Duren.	

[illegible]
Capt RAVC
OC No 2 MVS

(10340) Wt W5300/P713 750,000 3/18 D. D. & L., London, E.C. E 2688 Forms/C2118/16.

NAL 46

CONFIDENTIAL

WAR DIARY

OF

No. 2. M.V.S.

FROM 1 - 4 - 19 TO - 30 - 4 - 19.

12

Army Form C. 2118.

WAR DIARY
or
INTELLIGENCE SUMMARY.
(Erase heading not required.)

Instructions regarding War Diaries and Intelligence Summaries are contained in F. S. Regs., Part II. and the Staff Manual respectively. Title pages will be prepared in manuscript.

No. 2 Mob. Vet. Sect. — April 1919.

Place	Date	Hour	Summary of Events and Information	Remarks and references to Appendices
Essig	2.4	19	Visit 3rd Inf Bde. Transport at Munstereifel (?).	
			Pay out Section. Men return from taking D Horses to Cologne Abattoir	
	3.4	19	Capt. Howard RAVC arrives from 13th VES to take over Section	
			Section has afternoon off to attend 39th Bde. RFA race meeting	
	4.4	19	Evacuate 7 animals to 9th VES	
			Go with Capt. Howard to inspect proposed billets for Section in new area.	
	5.4	19	Serg. Bateman & Pte. Bottomley (?) leave Section to be demobilised	
	5.4	19	Prepare for moving Section early tomorrow morning.	
			Evacuate [illegible] horses to 9th VES & bring back (by order of DDVS) [illegible] animals for [illegible]	
Dickopshof Farm near SECHTEM.	7.4	19	Move Section to Dickopshof Farm near Sechtem, starting at 9 hours arriving 11.30 hours. DADVS visits Section evening	
			Good billets for men & good accommodation for animals	
	8.4	19	Set places for cookhouse, forage barn, stores, forge [illegible] fixed up	
	9.4	19	Capt. Howard takes over command of Section.	
	10.4	19	3 men go to Collecting Post at [illegible] to collect sick animals	
			This Post is visited on Mondays & Thursdays [illegible]	

D. D. & L., London, E.C.
(10340) Wt W5300/P713 750,000 3/18 E 2638 Forms/C2118/16.

Army Form C. 2118.

WAR DIARY
or
INTELLIGENCE SUMMARY.
(Erase heading not required.)

Instructions regarding War Diaries and Intelligence Summaries are contained in F. S. Regs., Part II. and the Staff Manual respectively. Title pages will be prepared in manuscript.

Place	Date	Hour	Summary of Events and Information — No 2 Mob Vet Sect — April 1919	Remarks and references to Appendices
Dickopshof Farm.	9.4.19		from 10 – 11 hours.	
			Capt Howard is given veterinary charge of Divisional Engineers [illegible]	
			visit Divisional Engineers [illegible]. Capt Howard [illegible] DADVS visits Section	
	10.4.19		Evacuate 7 animals to No 7 Vet Hosp. Cologne.	
	11.4.19		Pte [illegible] Taylor go with party from Corps [illegible]	
			on the Rhine. Pte Pearce granted leave to England [illegible]	
			Capt Howard granted leave to England & leaves [illegible]	
			[illegible] the 14th inst	
	13.4.19		Operate on two horses [illegible] for [illegible]	
	14.4.19		Visit Divisional Engineers [illegible]	
	15.4.19		Col Barnard ~~[illegible]~~ visits & inspects Section with DADVS [illegible]	
			[illegible] a small piece of ground	
			Dr Grady [illegible] from No 1 [illegible] relief of Dr [illegible] who [illegible] to	
	18.4.19		[illegible] for demobilisation. Good Friday – men have afternoon off	
	19.4.19		Notified that S.S. Allen & Bunce [illegible] for demobilisation [illegible]	
			Sergt Thompson [illegible] for duty	
	20.4.19		S.S. Allen & Bunce [illegible] Thompson leave Section [illegible]	

D. D. & L., London E.C.
(10340) Wt W5300/P713 750,000 3/18 E 2688 Forms/C2118/16.

Army Form C. 2118.

Instructions regarding War Diaries and Intelligence Summaries are contained in F. S. Regs., Part II. and the Staff Manual respectively. Title pages will be prepared in manuscript.

WAR DIARY
or
INTELLIGENCE SUMMARY.
(*Erase heading not required.*)

Place	Date	Hour	Summary of Events and Information	Remarks and references to Appendices
	25-5-19		Capt Barr demobilised	
	29-5-19		Capt P Howard returns from leave & commences command of Section	
	30-5-19		Inspect Section generally with DADVS	

10-5-19

Percy Howard Capt RAVC
OC. 2 MVS.

D. D. & L., London E.C.
(10340) Wt W5300/P713 750,000 3/18 E 2688 Forms/C2118/16.

WAR DIARY

No. 2 M.V.S.

MAY 1ST TO 31ST

Kmy

Army Form C. 2118.

Instructions regarding War Diaries and Intelligence Summaries are contained in F. S. Regs., Part II. and the Staff Manual respectively. Title pages will be prepared in manuscript.

WAR DIARY
or
~~INTELLIGENCE SUMMARY.~~

(Erase heading not required.)

Place	Date	Hour	Summary of Events and Information	Remarks and references to Appendices
Kildenich	1·5·19		Two men go to Collecting Post Dunstekoven + receive two sick horses	
	2·5·19		Pte Pearson returns from leave. Two men go to D. Hdqts to assist with erecting hurdles. D.A.D.V.S. visits Section	
	3·5·19		Ten men attend lecture on Venereal disease at Wesseling. D.A.D.V.S examines horses	
	4·5·19		Pte Keyworth returns to duty from D. Hdqts. Visit 75·76·409 F. Cos R.E. + 6th Welsh Regt. D.A.D.V.S. visits Section. H.D. horse dies at 7·20 P.M	
	5·5·19		Two men go to Collecting Post Dunstekoven + receive two sick horses. Post mortem examination on dead horse + find cause of death intestinal calculus	
	7·5·19		Exchanged two riders with No 8 Vet Hosp. Cpl. Walker promoted A/unpaid L/Sgt. A.D.V.S. visits + inspects Section	
	8·5·19		Evacuated 6 horses + 2 mules. Two men go to Collecting Post, Dunstekoven + receive 2 Horses + 3 mules. Paid Section	
	9·5·19		Visit 6th Welsh Regt + 75·76·409 F. Cos RE	
	12·5·19		Two men go to Collecting Post Dunstekoven + receive 3 horses + 3 mules. Inspected Section Rifles	

D. D. & L., London E.C.
(10340) Wt W5300/P713 750,000 3/18 E 2688 Forms/C2118/16.

Instructions regarding War Diaries and Intelligence Summaries are contained in F. S. Regs., Part II. and the Staff Manual respectively. Title pages will be prepared in manuscript.

WAR DIARY
or
~~INTELLIGENCE SUMMARY.~~
(Erase heading not required.)

Army Form C. 2118.

Place	Date	Hour	Summary of Events and Information	Remarks and references to Appendices
Kildenich	13.5.19		DADVS visits Section & inspects horses for evacuation	
	14.5.19.		Evacuate horses to Animal Collecting Camp Cologne 12 'Z' Cases & 5 Butcher cases	
			Visit 76 & 409 F. Cos. R.E. & 6 Welch Reg.	
	15.5.19		Two men go to Coll'g Post, Dunstikoven & receive two horses. Shoeing Smith Ketching ~~[illegible]~~ reports for temporary duty from No 12 Vet Hosp.	
	16.5.19		Visit 6th Welsh Regt. Col Abut & DADVS inspect Section	
	17.5.19.		Visit 76 & 409 F Cos & Hdqts RE. Dvr Janney RASC returned to his unit	
			1 Horse sent to Cologne Abattoir for destruction - 1 Horse returned to unit.	
	19.5.19		SE.29084 Pte Pearson T. J. sent to Army of the Rhine Concentration Camp, Duren for disposal. Draw money from Field Cashier & pay Section. Six horses sent to No 8 Vet Hosp. Two men go to Collecting ~~Camp~~ Post Dunstikoven. Dvr Grady & Pte Carter report for duty from No 1 Co R.A.S.C.	
	20.5.19.		Take over duties of DADVS temporarily, visit his Office & Units.	
	22.5.19.		Visit 6th Welch, Hdqts, 76 & 409 Field Cos RE & inspect horses & Sdlrs' wallets. Two men go to C. Post Dunstikoven & receive one mule. Visit DADVS on his return	

D. D. & L., London E.C.
(10340) Wt W5300/P713 750,000 3/18 E 2688 Forms/C2118/16.

Army Form C. 2118.

WAR DIARY
or
~~INTELLIGENCE SUMMARY.~~
(Erase heading not required.)

Instructions regarding War Diaries and Intelligence Summaries are contained in F. S. Regs., Part II. and the Staff Manual respectively. Title pages will be prepared in manuscript.

Place	Date	Hour	Summary of Events and Information	Remarks and references to Appendices
Kildenich	24.5.19.		Visit 6th Welsh Reg. DADVS visits Section & inspects horses	
	26.5.19.		Two men go to Collecting Post, Dunstikoven. DADVS visits Section	
	27.5.19		Visit 6th Welsh Reg. 2 horses & 1 mule evacuated to 8th Vet Hospital	
	29.5.19		Two men go to Collecting Post Dunstikoven, 2 Horses removed	
	31.6.19		Visit Bonn & Inspect site of Proposed Advanced Collecting Post to be used in the event of resumption of hostilities	

[illegible] Capt R.A.V.C.
O.C. No 2 MVS

5-6-19.

D. D. & L., London, E.C.
(10340) Wt W5300/P713 750,000 3/18 E 2688 Forms/C2118/16.

War Diary.

No 2 Mobile Veterinary Section.

June. 1919.

Km

Army Form C. 2118.

WAR DIARY
or
~~INTELLIGENCE SUMMARY.~~

(Erase heading not required.)

Instructions regarding War Diaries and Intelligence Summaries are contained in F. S. Regs., Part II. and the Staff Manual respectively. Title pages will be prepared in manuscript.

Place	Date	Hour	Summary of Events and Information	Remarks and references to Appendices
KELDENICH	1-6-19		Visit 409 Field Coy R.E. 3 men report for duty from 11th Leicester Regt.	No. 2 MOBILE VETERINARY SECTION No. .... Date ....
	2.6.19		2 men go to Collecting Post Dunstekoven. Visit Field Cashier – Pay Section.	
	4.6.19		Visit R.E. Units. 1 horse sent to Butcher Wesseling for destruction. Inspect Rifles & [illegible]	
	5.6.19		Two men go to Dunstekoven Collecting Post & receive 2 mules.	
	6.6.19		A.D.V.S. & D.A.D.V.S. visit & inspect Section. 5 men go on Rhine Trip.	
	7.6.19		Driver Brice R.A.S.C. att. sent to Concentration Camp Cologne for Dispersal. Cpls Walker & Harding	
	"		promoted P/A/Sgts as from 1-6-19. 6 men report for duty from No 8 Vety Hospital.	
	8.6.19		Visit 5th Welsh Regt. D.A.D.V.S. visits Section.	
	9.6.19		Pte Clayton L. proceeds to England for 14 days leave 10/6/19 to 24/6/19. Sgt Harding J.	
	"		leaves Section for duty with 21. M.V.S. Visit Hdqts R.E. Two men go to Collecting Post	
	"		Dunstekoven & receive 3 horses & 1 mule.	
	10.6.19		1 horse to Abattoir, Cologne for slaughter. 1 Section Rider to Butcher Wesseling.	
	"		3 horses & 3 mules to No 8 Vety Hospital. S/Sm Kitching permanently posted to the Unit.	

D. B. & L., London E.C.
(10340) Wt W5300/P713 750,000 3/18 E 2688 Forms/C2118/16.

Army Form C. 2118.

Instructions regarding War Diaries and Intelligence Summaries are contained in F. S. Regs., Part II. and the Staff Manual respectively. Title pages will be prepared in manuscript.

WAR DIARY
or
~~INTELLIGENCE SUMMARY.~~

(Erase heading not required.)

Place	Date	Hour	Summary of Events and Information	Remarks and references to Appendices
KELDENICH.	11.6.19.		Full marching order inspection of Section by D.A.D.V.S.	
	12.6.19.		Two men go to Collecting Post, Dunstikoven. 3 horses & 3 mules [illegible]	
	14.6.19.		D.A.D.V.S. visits Section.	
	15.6.19.		Church Parade and Inspection of men by O.C.	
	16.6.19.		Attend lecture on Pay & Mess Book System of Payment along with the D.A.D.V.S.	
			Two men go to Collecting Post Dunstikoven. – Pay Section.	
	17.6.19.		Visit 6th Welsh Regt, Hdqts 76 & 409 Field Coys. R.E.	
	19.6.19.		Two men go to Collecting Post. Dunstikoven.	
	20.6.19.		Pte Ruffles re-posted to 6 : M.V.S. – W/A/Cpl Stevens & Pte Evans [illegible] P/A/[illegible] to complete establishment.	
	21.6.19.		A.D.V.S. & D.A.D.V.S. visit & inspect Section.	
	23.6.19.		Visit Hd. Qts D.E. 75, 76 & 409 Field Coys. R.E. & 6th Welsh Regt	
	24.6.19.		A.D.V.S. visits Section & inspects 4 infantrymen on probation	
	25.6.19.		Pte Clayton. L. returns from 14 days leave – 10.6.19 to 24.6.19.	
	26.6.19.		Pte German. H. granted leave (14 days) to U.K. – 27.6.19. to 11.7.19. – 2 men go to Collecting Post. DUNSTIKOVEN.	

D. D. & L., London E.C.
(10340) Wt W5500/P713 750,000 3/18 E 2688 Forms/C2118/16.

Army Form C. 2118.

WAR DIARY
or
INTELLIGENCE SUMMARY.

(Erase heading not required.)

Instructions regarding War Diaries and Intelligence Summaries are contained in F. S. Regs., Part II. and the Staff Manual respectively. Title pages will be prepared in manuscript.

Place	Date	Hour	Summary of Events and Information	Remarks and references to Appendices
KELDENICH	27.6.19		6 men go on Rhine Trip	No. 2 MOBILE VETERINARY SECTION No. ... Date ...
"	28.6.19		Visit R.E. Units, also 6th Welsh Regt.	
"	30.6.19		2 men go to Collecting Post Dunstikoven. Visit Field Cashier and Pay Section	

P. Amy Athwairs [signature]
CAPTAIN, A.V.C.
O.C. 2 MOBILE VETERINARY SECTION

D. D. & L., London, E.C.
(10340) Wt W5300/P713 750,000 3/18 E 2688 Forms/C2118/16.

WAR · DIARY.

No 2 MOBILE · VETERINARY · SECTION.

JULY · 1919.

Kmm

Instructions regarding War Diaries and Intelligence Summaries are contained in F. S. Regs., Part II. and the Staff Manual respectively. Title pages will be prepared in manuscript.

WAR DIARY
or
~~INTELLIGENCE SUMMARY.~~
(Erase heading not required.)

Army Form C. 2118.

Place	Date	Hour	Summary of Events and Information	Remarks and references to Appendices
KELDENICH	JULY 1.		D.A.D.V.S. visits Section and inspects Horses	
"	3.		D.A.D.V.S. takes over command of Section from Capt P. Howard. Three men go to	
"			Collecting Post DUMSTIKOVEN.	
"	4.		Capt P. Howard leaves for United Kingdom. General holiday for Peace Celebration	
"	5.		D.A.D.V.S. visits Section. 2 horses & 1 mule evacuated to No 8 V.H.	
"	7.		Three men go to Collecting Post. DUMSTIKOVEN	
"	8.		D.V.S. & A.D.V.S. visit and inspect Section	
"	9.		Sergt Walker & S/Smith Kitching leave to United Kingdom 10/7/19 to 24/7/19.	
"	10.		Two men go to Collecting Post. DUMSTIKOVEN. One horse evacuated to No 8 V.H. for sale, &	
"			two horses to Abattoir COLOGNE for destruction	
"	13.		Pte Crosby completes months veterinary course, & returns to 51st Bttn. Welsh Regt	
"	14		Two men go to Collecting Post. DUMSTIKOVEN. & receive one mule.	
"			D.A.D.V.S. visits Field Cashier, & pays Section. No 43488 Pte German returns from leave	
"	15.		S.E. 24860 Pte Taylor J. returns from leave	
"	16		Pte German sent to attend Court Martial at 11th Leicestershire Regt to give evidence	
"	17.		Two men go to Collecting Post DUMSTIKOVEN. 7 animals evacuated & 4 animals admitted	

D. D. & L., London, E.C.
(10340) Wt W5300/P713 750,000 3/18 E 2688 Forms/C2118/16.

Instructions regarding War Diaries and Intelligence Summaries are contained in F. S. Regs., Part II. and the Staff Manual respectively. Title pages will be prepared in manuscript.

WAR DIARY
or
~~INTELLIGENCE SUMMARY.~~
(Erase heading not required.)

Army Form C. 2118.

Place	Date	Hour	Summary of Events and Information	Remarks and references to Appendices
KELDENICH	JULY 18		General Marden visits section. 6 men sent to A.D.M.S. for examination for medical category	
"	19		No S.E. 25199 Corpl. Evans F.R. proceeds on leave - 20/7/19 to 3/8/19.	
"	20		No S.E. 25169 Pte Gregory W proceeds on leave - 21/7/19 to 4/8/19. 1 mule admitted	
"	21.		2 men go to Collecting Post. DUNSTIKOVEN 1 horse & 1 mule evacuated to Abattoir Cologne	
"	22.		S.E. 25168 Pte Keyworth. A. proceeds on leave - 24/7/19 to 6/8/19. 1 mule evacuated	
"	23		T4/234210 Dvr Urquid R. R.A.S.C. proceeds on leave - 24/7/19 to 7/8/19	
"	24.		2 men go to Collecting Post. DUNSTIKOVEN	
"	25.		53590 Pte Carter. H. proceeds on leave - 26/7/19 to 9/8/19	
"	26.		S.E. 17972 Sergt Walker F.G. & S.E. 20354 S/S Ritching W. return from leave	
"	27		85665 L/Cpl King. W.K. 51st Welsh Regt reports for one months veterinary course	
"	28		2 men go to Collecting Post. DUNSTIKOVEN. 2 horses evacuated to abattoir Cologne	
"	"		D.A.D.V.S pays men of section	
"	29		Pte Gorman goes to attend F.G.C.M as witness at Euskirchen Barracks	
"	"		Capt Shearman F.J. R.A.V.C. takes over command of Section	
"	31.		2 men go to Collecting Post DUNSTIKOVEN.	
"				
"				

F. J. Shearman Capt R.A.V.C.

D. D. & L., London E.C.
(10340) Wt W5300/P713 750,000 3/18 E 2688 Forms/C2118/16.

WAR DIARY.

No 2 MOBILE VETERINARY SECTION.

AUGUST. 1919.

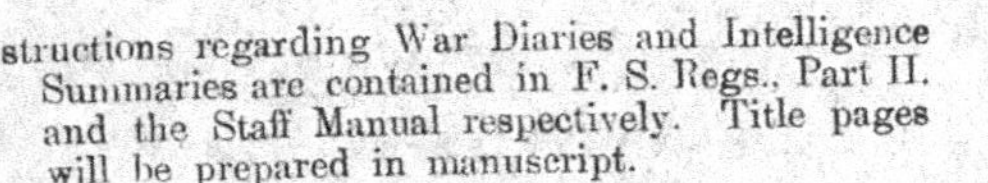
Instructions regarding War Diaries and Intelligence Summaries are contained in F. S. Regs., Part II. and the Staff Manual respectively. Title pages will be prepared in manuscript.

WAR DIARY
or
INTELLIGENCE SUMMARY.
(Erase heading not required.)

Army Form C. 2118.

Place	Date	Hour	Summary of Events and Information	Remarks and references to Appendices
KELDENICH	AUGUST 2		Visit units of 1st Infantry Brigade. No 28119 Pte Stanley granted leave 4/8/19 to 17/8/19	
"	3		D.A.D.V.S visits Section.	
"	4		Two men go to Collecting Post DUNSTIKOVEN. Visit field leashes. Bocheim	
"			30395 Pte Kumro granted leave. 5/8/19 to 19/8/19	
"	5		17810 Pte Wright inoculated. 17972 Sgt Walker refused inoculation	
"	6		T/406114 Dvr GRADY. P. R.A.S.C attached, proceeds to Concentration Camp, COLOGNE for demobilisation. 25169 Pte Gregory returns from leave. 25179 Cpl Evans returns from leave.	
"	7.		Two men go to Collecting Post DUNSTIKOVEN. Capt PORRETT J.E R.A.V.C joins section. Pte Keyworth 25168. returns from leave	
"	8.		Capts Sleeman & Capt Porrett visit 1st Inf Bde & Divisional Headquarters & mallein animals. 1 Stray animal admitted from No 3 Coy Train evacuated 3 mules & 1 horse to Abattoir. Pay Section - Pay & Mess Book	
"	9		25916 Pte D Johnson reports for duty from No 8 Veterinary Hospital. Capt Sleeman & Capt Porrett visit 2nd Infantry Brigade and mallein animals. T4/237210 DR DUQUID R returns from leave.	

D. D. & L., London E.C.
(10340) Wt W5300/P713 750,000 3/18 E 2688 Forms/C2118/16.

2

Army Form C. 2118.

Instructions regarding War Diaries and Intelligence Summaries are contained in F. S. Regs., Part II. and the Staff Manual respectively. Title pages will be prepared in manuscript.

WAR DIARY
or
INTELLIGENCE SUMMARY.
(Erase heading not required.)

Place	Date	Hour	Summary of Events and Information	Remarks and references to Appendices
KELDENICH	AUG 11		Two men go to Collecting Post. DUNSTIKOVEN, & collect 1 animal. T/453266	
			Driver CARTER returns from leave	
	13.		Section animals malleined. D.A.D.V.S visits section.	
	14.		85665 L/Cpl KING. W.K. 51st Welsh Regt, 43778 Pte G. Court, 43782 Pte J. DARWIN	
			43788 Pte H. GERMAN, 11th Btn Leicestershire Regt, left to rejoin their units	
			Two men go to Collecting Post. DUNSTIKOVEN.	
	15.		Requisitioned Stores returned to Burgermeister. WESSELING.	
			Pay section, close Pay & Mess Book	
	16		T.T. 02614 SGT THOMSON. R. promoted to P/A/S/Sgt.	
	18.		22 animals evacuated	
	19.		T.T. 02614 SGT THOMSON. R. re-posted to No 9. V.E.S. T/453266 Dr CARTER	
			returned to No 1 Coy Train. Equipment sent to BONN GOODS STATION	
			Paid men of Section	
	21.		Capt Pownett goes to MIEL as V.O. i/c No 2 Horse train	
			68851 Pte LEE. H. 52nd Btn Cheshire Regt transferred to D/104 Bty R.F.A	
	22		Section leaves KELDENICH AND entrains at SECHTEM. 25199 Cpl Evans & 25116 Pte Calgeey	
			entrain with equipment AT BONN.	

D. D. & L., London, E.C. (10340) Wt W5300/P713 750,000 3/18 E 2688 Forms/C2118/16.

3

Army Form C.2118.

Instructions regarding War Diaries and Intelligence Summaries are contained in F. S. Regs., Part II. and the Staff Manual respectively. Title pages will be prepared in manuscript.

WAR DIARY
or
INTELLIGENCE SUMMARY.
(*Erase heading not required.*)

Place	Date	Hour	Summary of Events and Information	Remarks and references to Appendices
CALAIS	Aug 24		Section embark at CALAIS and disembark at DOVER, entrain DOVER	
KINMEL PARK	25		Section arrive at KINMEL PARK CAMP.	
	26		30395 PTE MUNRO. J. returns from leave, after reporting at KELDENICH	
	29		Capt Shearman. F J takes over duties of D.A.D.V.S. during the absence on leave of Major Goodridge	
	30		1st Infantry Bde hand in to Section Veterinary Chests + Wallets	
	31		Pay and Mess book completed. 25199 CPL EVANS F.R. + 25166 PTE CARGEEG. H rejoin unit on completion of duty as guard on equipment train	

1.9.19.

F. J. Shearman CAPTAIN, A.V.C.
O.C. 2 MOBILE VETERINARY SECTION

D. D. & L., London, E.C.
(10340) Wt W5300/P713 750,000 5/15 E 3688 Forms/C2118/16.

SEP 1919
WAR OFFICE

www.ingramcontent.com/pod-product-compliance
Lightning Source LLC
Chambersburg PA
CBHW080924230426
43668CB00014B/2192

* 9 7 8 1 4 7 4 5 0 2 5 1 1 *